ENID STARKIE

ENID STARKIE

Joanna Richardson

Cop.a

MACMILLAN PUBLISHING CO., INC.

New York

Contents

Illustrations

Introduction

One morning, in my first term at Oxford, I arrived for a prose class at Somerville. I had lost my way, I was fifty minutes late, and I was dismissed for a week. That was my first encounter with Enid Starkie.

She was diminutive and dressed in electric blue, to match her eyes; she was original, responsive, gay. When, later, she observed that the accents in my French prose were inconsistent, I admitted that I felt safer if I put one on each way. 'You must learn, Miss Richardson,' she said, 'which horse to back.' While we laboured to turn Thackeray into plausible French prose, she settled down by the fire to read *The Times*. Her horizons lay beyond that tiny college room—House 3. Unlike some of one's other tutors, she kept in touch with the world.

I went to her lectures on the French Romantics. She used to come into the hall rather late. She was withdrawn and preoccupied, almost shy. She always wore red or blue, she looked particularly small in academic dress, and she always seemed to be swamped by her black silk doctoral gown. She wore theatrical rings on the middle fingers of each hand. Most of her audience had come to hear Enid Starkie as much as the lecture.

She clambered rather awkwardly up the steps to the stage at the Taylor Institute at about eleven o'clock on Wednesday mornings. She spread out her notes with an air of resignation, almost of apology. She was said to be one of the fastest speakers in Oxford, and, even when she lectured, she was hurried. Her voice was deep, unmistakably Irish—especially when she grew animated. Some said she spoke French like a native who had lived abroad for years. In fact she spoke it fluently—she was never less than fluent—and she spoke it with a heavy Irish accent. She murdered any poetry she quoted, but she made one concerned with those who wrote it. Her lectures were not elegant, they were not profound, but they had a human quality. She infused them with her personality. She warmed to her subject, strolled up and down with her hands in her pockets, and regaled us with accounts of the *bataille d'Hernani*, or told us how Gérard de Nerval had exercised a lobster round the gardens of the Palais-Royal (unlike a dog, he said, it didn't bark). Then she turned to literary theory. She had the gift—not universal in academic circles—of making the abstruse intelligible.

I went to her flat in St Giles' for tutorials on *Les Feuilles d'automne*, and I recorded gaily that 'she curled up in her chair and damned Victor Hugo'. Her ideas were often unexpected, always stimulating, and she presented the Paris of 1830 with the *entrain* of Musard. She did not impose her erudition, but—again, unlike other tutors—she made me feel that I could be intelligent. She showed me the excitement of learning. She enormously increased my affection for the French nineteenth century. She taught me more than any other tutor at Oxford.

She had glamour for me, as I know she had for many other people. She owed it to her academic distinction, to her red-and-gold *mise-en-scène*, to a certain air of mystery about her, and, of course, to the many-faceted Starkie legend. She very soon earned my affection. 'I want to talk to *you*', she once explained to me at a party. 'You're not just a pupil, you're a friend.' It was enough to disarm any undergraduate of eighteen. Most of one's women tutors were dry, sarcastic and impersonal, and they matched their proverbial grey stockings. They were absorbed by books and, it seemed, indifferent to life. Enid was outgoing, impulsive, full of *joie de vivre*; I always felt that she was on my side. She did not condescend to me; alone among the dons, she seemed contemporary—and this quality she always kept. She was old enough to be my mother, but I did not think of her age.

By the last years of her life, I belonged to the inner circle of her friends. I had come to specialize in the literature of nineteenth-century France, and the telephone line between London and Oxford often buzzed as we discussed our literary finds. She still explored the period with undiminished pleasure. She remained a fount of knowledge about its novelists and poets, their famous and their unfamiliar works. Once, as a challenge, I mentioned a work of fiction, written under a pseudonym, which touched on Mallarmé and Verlaine. It was unfindable in the British Museum. I had not read it—but Enid had. '*Le Soleil des morts*? I've always thought it a rather indifferent Symbolist novel.'

On my visits to Oxford we dined together, and talked into the small hours of the morning. Sometimes we browsed round antique shops. She had a flair for finding bargains, making discoveries. She liked an endearing piece of nonsense: a miniature brass jaunting-car for her study mantelpiece, or a musical box concealed in a tiny barrel-organ. She enjoyed the rich and strange: she once acquired a multi-coloured, sequin-studded totem-pole. She also loved the elegant and the conventional: a Queen Anne bureau, a Regency bookcase, or a pair of Empire console tables.

Her behaviour, like her aesthetic sense, could be original or orthodox. On some occasions she behaved like an *enfant terrible*. When she asked me to guest night at Somerville, she instructed me on protocol as if I were being presented at Court.

By this time I had come—or so I thought—to understand her. I could break the tension she often felt, give her the encouragement which she unremittingly demanded. She remained life-enhancing. She lived intensely, and made one live more intensely, too. Late one evening, after dinner, we explored the half-finished Wolfson Building at Somerville. The staircases had no banisters; the doors (where there were doors) had no handles. But Enid, torch in hand, was already assessing the hall as a place for a party to celebrate the publication of *Flaubert*. She revelled in parties. She was funny, warm and shrewd, perpetually alert. She enjoyed the minutiae and the splendid moments of existence, she had a gift for making colours brighter. In these ways she was never disappointing.

In February 1970, two months before her death, she and I were discussing the books she hoped to write; and I urged her, yet again, to complete her autobiography. She made it clear that, if someone else ever wrote her life, she wanted me to do so.

Introduction

It has been hard to write this book. It is always hard to write, freely, about someone recently dead. But Enid's papers revealed a person whom I had not known or suspected. They destroyed an illusion which had lasted since I first knew her, and they presented a wholly different truth. Enid had been silent about her private life. She was silent to me, as she had been to her executors and, I believe, to many other friends of long standing. But, since she kept the evidence for more than thirty years, she clearly intended it to be published. The papers that she kept explain much that seemed inexplicable about her. One cannot write her life and ignore them.

I must record my grateful thanks to her brother, Professor Walter Starkie, and to her sister, Mrs Nancy Cooper, for telling me about their Dublin childhood. I owe my largest debt to her executors, Dame Janet Vaughan and Mrs Mary Proudfoot. They have given me constant help and advice during my research, and they have more than once read my typescript; but I am indebted to them, most of all, for their unfailing encouragement and kindness. Dr Robert Shackleton, Bodley's Librarian and Enid Starkie's literary executor, has given me valuable counsel and assistance, and he has read my final typescript; I warmly appreciate his interest in this biography. I am especially grateful to the Principal and Fellows of St Anne's College. They enabled me to live in Oxford and work on the Starkie Papers, and without their help I should have had an even more difficult task. I record my warmest thanks to the Principal and Fellows of Somerville College. For two years they have given me generous hospitality, answered my queries, shared their recollections of Enid Starkie, and allowed me to appreciate the world in which she spent most of her adult life.

Mr Hamish Hamilton kindly gave me unrestricted access to his correspondence with Enid Starkie, which enabled me to place her in her literary setting; Miss Rosemary Manning, the literary executrix of Alyse Gregory, gave me Enid Starkie's letters to Alyse Gregory, a rich and intimate correspondence which covered twenty-seven years. Both these collections have been added to the Starkie Papers in the Bodleian Library. Miss Marianne Eyles and

Miss Frances Fowler sent me, from America, their substantial correspondence with Enid Starkie; they replied to my many questions about her. Dr Eleanor Herrin and Dr Frank Ridehalgh kindly let me consult all the relevant medical papers, so that I have been able to chart her remarkable medical history.

Mr W. H. Auden has generously allowed me to quote his letters about the election to the Chair of Poetry in 1956; and Mr Robert Graves has given me permission to quote his correspondence about the election of 1968. I have freely used the letters of Sir William Rothenstein by courtesy of his executors, Sir John Rothenstein and Mr Michael Rothenstein. Mme Catherine Gide has approved, in principle, of my quoting from the letters of her father, André Gide. It has, alas, proved impossible to trace M. Édouard Dermit, the heir of Jean Cocteau.

I gladly record my gratitude to the following for letters, reminiscences and generous help: Miss Peter Ady; Monsieur P.-E. Artur; Miss L. A. Baggs; Mr David Ball; Mr Giles Barber; Mr and Mrs Frank Barnett; Mr Samuel Beckett; Sir Isaiah Berlin; Professor Louis Bonnerot; the late Sir Maurice Bowra; Professor LeRoy C. Breunig; Mrs Monica Brooksbank; Mrs Rica Brown; Dr Alice Carleton; Sir Michael Cary; Lord David Cecil; M. François Chapon; Mr Richard Cobb; Professor Nevill Coghill; Miss Thyra Creyke-Clark; Mrs C. Davidson; Miss Rosemary Davidson; Mr and Mrs D. M. Davin; Miss Elizabeth Ellem; Miss Vera Farnell; Professor John Fennell; Professor Roy Fuller; Mr Patrick George; Mrs Richard Goodwin; Miss Elizabeth Goulding; Mr Graham Greene; Miss M. E. Griffiths; Mrs Hamilton-Meikle; Mr W. D. Handcock; Professor Agnes Headlam-Morley; Mr T. F. Higham; Mr Brian Hill; Dr Christopher Hill; Mr Derek Hudson; Mr C. A. Johnson; Professor Douglas Johnson; Mrs Eithne Kaiser; Mr Bryan Kelly; Mr Cecil King; Miss Anne Kirkman; Mrs Ida Leach-Levi; Miss Rosamond Lehmann; the late Mr Iain Macdonald; Sir Henry Mack; Mr Felix Markham; Professor H. T. Mason; Sir John Masterman; Miss Gwendolen Mawdsley; Mrs Hilda Mellor; Mrs Susan Miller; Dr and Mrs W. G. Moore; Mrs S. A. Morgan; Dr A. N. L. Munby; Professor R. Niklaus; Mrs

Introduction

A. J. Outon; Mr Michael Pakenham; Mrs L. M. Patterson; Mrs Rosemary Peto; Mme N. de Praingy; Dr Alan Raitt; Miss M. Rankin; Professor T. B. W. Reid; Rev. Dr W. G. Roe; Dr A. L. Rowse; Mrs Norma Russell; Professor Peter Russell; Miss Constance Savery; Professor Mitchell Shackleton; Mr Robert Speaight; Mrs Philip Spencer; Mr and Mrs Francis Steegmuller; the late Mrs Herman Strauss; Mr and Mrs D. W. Sutherland; Dame Lucy Sutherland; Monsieur R. Tallard; Miss Dorothy Wadham; Mr Francis Warner; Dame Veronica Wedgwood; Mrs Wedgwood-Benn; Mrs Cecil Woodham-Smith.

I should like to thank the staff of the Bodleian Library, Oxford, for their patient help while I was working on the Starkie Papers; I must also thank the staff of the British Museum Reading Room and the library of the Victoria and Albert Museum.

It is, of course, a pleasure to thank my British publisher, John Grey Murray, for his personal help with this book.

Oxford—London
1970–1973   JOANNA RICHARDSON

PART ONE

<><><><>

A Lady's Child
1897–1916

On Wednesday, 18 August 1897, shortly before noon, Lord Ardilaun, representing the Lord Lieutenant of County Dublin, went on board the royal yacht *Victoria and Albert* in Kingstown Harbour. There he welcomed two illustrious visitors. The Duke of York, in naval uniform, appeared on deck with the Duchess, who was wearing 'a dress in which green Irish poplin predominated, and a toque of cream lace and green poplin and pink roses'. The weather was brilliant, the sun (said *The Times*) 'shone on the dancing water, the vessels in the harbour were dressed rainbow fashion'. The warships at anchor off the coast fired a royal salute. Half an hour later, 'between the scarlet lines of soldiers which kept the route, the great military procession started . . . The excitement was at its climax as, to the music of the National Anthem, the Royal carriage turned from Nassau Street into College Green.'[1] That August day in the year of the Diamond Jubilee seemed to symbolize the permanence and the majesty of English rule in Ireland.

On that day of splendour and celebration, of dignity and warmth and gaiety, all of which she would come to love so well, Enid Mary Starkie was appropriately born.

A genealogical tree of the Starkies, drawn up by Enid's mother, traces the family back for six generations to Matthew Starkey of Dromolin.[2] Nothing is recorded of him, except that he had a son, William, the father of Walter Starkey of Burgatia, who was born in 1685, the year of the accession of James II. Walter married a Miss O'Sullivan of Bandon, and their son, Robert, took to wife a Miss O'Donovan of The Island. His son and namesake Robert— the first generation, apparently, to use the surname Starkie— married a wife from Kilkerran, and their elder child, William

Robert, born in 1824, married Frances Power of Grace Dieu, Waterford. The fifth of their eight children, William Joseph Myles, was the father of the subject of this book.

There is no trace of English ancestry in this venerable family tree; and Enid herself, despite her British passport, was to assert her Irishness—and, of course, her Anglophobia—all her life. Yet the Harleian MSS. record that Ralph or Randal Starkie, 'a youngerson of *Starkie of Stretton*, co. Chester, married, in the fortieth year of King Edward III [1366], Agnes, the daughter and heiress of Hugh de Pennington, of Pennington, co. Lancaster'.[3] Enid's father claimed a connection with the English Starkies. In 1919 he was elected President of the Dublin Branch of the British Empire Shakespeare Society; he told a friend 'that I expected someone wd. suggest a "Wm. Starkie" as author of the plays: I advised him to look up the records in Cheshire where my people come from.'[4] Soon afterwards he returned to the point: 'I said . . . I myself had an ambition during my Presidency, to look up the records of my family, wh[ich] resided in Elizabethan times, and still resides on the outskirts of Warwickshire, and I thought I might find an ancestor W.S. who might be the author.'[5]

Wherever the Starkies originated, their character remained constant. In 1967 a correspondent, Geraldine Starkey, wrote to Enid: 'All down the centuries from Viking days the Starkys have been indomitable as to the sword, and then for culture! . . . The name comes from Sterky—stork—which was the crest on the shield of Harald Hadrada's standard-bearer. "For love of future fame" being the superscription!'[6] In 1937 when Enid's brother, Walter, visited Malta, he was 'amazed to find that our ancestor, Sir Oliver Starkey, was the only English knight in the famous Siege. I saw his tomb: he was turcofolier and secretary to the Grand Master La Vallette and is buried by him. The Governor of Malta told me he was the most warlike of all the Knights. He died in 1588.'[7] Pugnacity was not the only characteristic which Enid inherited from the Starkies; they had strong religious convictions and even, it seems, a trace of French blood. Walter Starkie mentioned a Dr Starkey, chaplain to Henry VIII.[8] In 1968 a Starkie in

Chester told Enid: 'I have collected quite a lot of information about the family in Lancashire—the Preston area is particularly rich in STARKIES and there is there, a STARKIE Street and a "STARKIE ARMS" pub: as there is also at Clitheroe.'[9] The correspondent added: 'We have had passed down in our family a story of a French nobleman, one of our ancestors, fleeing from France during the Revolution and settling in East Anglia where he took up brewing.'[10] The *Boston Guardian* ignored the French nobleman, but it published the story of 'Monsieur Starkie and his family, who sought forgetfulness and peace in Lincolnshire, accepting service under the Lord Willoughby de Eresby at Grimsthorpe Castle, where he occupied the post of brewer and fisherman.'[11]

Enid's father was the fifth son of William Robert Starkie, J.P., of Gregane Manor, Roscarbery, Co. Cork.[12] He was born on 10 December 1860, at Rosse's Point, Sligo, where his father was Resident Magistrate. After a short time at Clongowes Wood College, he entered Shrewsbury School in 1877. He became one of the Shrewsbury crew (he later listed his recreations: 'at one time rowing, Alpine climbing, cycling, lawn tennis and golf'). He was also Head of School before he left, in 1880, with a foundation scholarship to Trinity College, Cambridge. Three years later, he took his First in the Classical Tripos. Then—for the Starkies were never entirely conventional—he abandoned the chance of a Fellowship and set off to wander in Italy and Greece.

He was finally driven home by the need to earn his living, and he chose to lead an academic career in Ireland. Obliged to begin again as a freshman at Trinity College, Dublin, he won the first classical scholarship, the Berkeley gold medal for Greek, a classical studentship, and gold medals in his final examination. He was later awarded the Madden Prize, which allowed him to travel in Palestine and Persia. In 1890, having obtained the highest recorded marks in classics, he became a Fellow and Tutor of Trinity College. In 1897 he published his edition of the *Vespæ*: the first of the Aristophanic works which established his distinction in the field. That year he resigned his Fellowship to become President of Queen's College, Galway.

In 1899 he was appointed Resident Commissioner of National Education for Ireland. It was thought that his ability and energy would enable him to make the much needed reforms in elementary education. He showed all the energy required. 'With a vigour and freedom from conventionality unusual in holders of official positions, Dr Starkie exposed unsparingly what he believed to be the defects and vices of the existing educational system . . . His opponents had no little reason to dread the vigour of his onslaught.'[13] In 1898 Dublin gave him an honorary degree, and in 1909 he received another from the Royal University of Ireland. In 1914 he became a member of the Irish Privy Council. It was rumoured that he had refused a knighthood.[14]

In 1893 he had married May, the daughter of Cornelius Walsh, a Dublin solicitor who came from the west of Ireland. She was seventeen. She was eleven years younger than himself: indeed he had met her at Alexandra College, in Dublin, where he had once taught classics, and she had been a pupil in his class.[15] In *A Lady's Child* Enid was to describe her mother's family: the wild Uncle Gerard, the elegant and witty Auntie Ida, and, most important to her, Auntie Helen, imaginative, understanding and beautiful. Mrs Starkie herself left a lyrical account of her visit, as a child, to her grandparents at Coolnaleen, in Kerry. Enid must have heard it in her youth. It was part of her background and inheritance.

One summer day in about 1880, May Walsh and her brother John had set out from Dublin. They were put in charge of a guard on the train, and met at their journey's end 'by Grandpapa and Maurice, the coachman'. They drove off to Coolnaleen, and at last

the covered car stopped at the side near the coachhouse and we had to cross Grandmama's 'flower-knot', with its numerous little beds of musk violets, pinks, each with a little border of box. The house was covered with ivy, . . . and at the entrance was a stone slab with an ancient inscription, spread out like a mat. In the doorway stood Grandmama, handsome, fat, with the loveliest dark eyes, a beautiful smiling mouth, thick in the middle and going off into fine points at each side; a black net cap with bunches of little ribbons . . .

Inside, the house was always giving one surprises as there were rooms in the most unexpected places up little stairs and down little stairs, as if it was added to whenever another room was necessary for the new babies. The drawing-room looked into a wood where quantities of fairy thimbles grew . . .

At the back of the house was the yard, and here was a running stream of glistening water flowing over cobble-stones and joining a rivulet down the centre. At the right side was a large dairy, with its delicious smell. In it were large tubs of cream, hand-skimmed by little wooden plates or shallow bowls. There were dozens of flat wooden pails with the milk set out ready for skimming. The churn was a barrel turned by an iron handle. There were huge quantities of salt and yards of butter muslin. The butter intended for the home was made into shapes of shamrock and roses. The special kitchen for the dairy had enormous boilers always kept going by one of the six dairymaids. The maids were under the direction of the butter woman, Debby. She had a wonderful face, a rather long nose and a very long chin. Always with a spotless white cap tied under her chin, her skirt pinned up over a petticoat of black, yellow and red stripes. The dairymaids were all barefoot, some of them quite young . . .

Every day, at the end of dinner, a decanter of whiskey, a lemon, lump sugar, and boiling water were all placed before Grandpapa. He made himself a tumbler of punch and presented Grandmama with a wineglassful out of his tumbler, and the boy and girl each got a lump of sugar soaked with punch. This was a ceremonial act which ended the day's work.

Grandmama had many children but they were all scattered. One son was in Canada, another in the United States, a third was a doctor in the Royal Navy, and the youngest was in Rome to be a priest. Two daughters were married and the youngest was a nun . . .

One day Grandmama got a letter, with a ship on the envelope and under it OHMS. It was from Uncle John: he was coming home on leave. . . . At last the day came. Maurice brought him home with several trunks full of all sorts of interesting things. The most beautiful collection of butterflies, just like flowers, brown, blue, yellow, red. There was also a wonderful solid leather shield and a spear used by the Turks, a hammock made of coarse twisted grass, a long ivory stick, the handle a snake's head . . .

Another letter came for Grandmama, and this time it was from Rome.

Uncle W. had been made a priest and he was coming home. . . All the people came flocking to get Uncle W.'s blessing, for there is a special grace attached to the first blessings of a young priest.[16]

Mrs Starkie added:

My grandfather Walsh I remember as a big handsome old man with beautifully cut features . . . He was twice married, the second time to a Fitzmaurice. My father and his brother and [a] daughter were of the first marriage; the daughter became a nun, the brother died young and my father was sent for the good of his health to Australia, where he made a good deal of money, over £6000, came home, studied for the law and became a solicitor. He was a very clever man, passionately fond of music, taught himself the violin and had a nice tenor voice, used to sing Moore's Melodies and songs . . . He had a great love for old jewellery and antiques and loved going to auctions and roaming about the antique shops . . . He took great interest in teaching John and me to sing Moore's Melodies and learn little poems by heart . . .

The Starkie side has the tension of the 2 religions, the men always married Catholic women; but Fanny and Edyth both became Protestants. The religious side was v. strong on the part of both Walter and William in Pater's family. Pater had serious intention of becoming a Jesuit.[17]

This inheritance does much to explain the person that Enid was: Anglo-Irish, pugnacious, romantic, troubled by religious tension, loving music, art, and, above all, learning.

Her elder brother, Walter, was born in 1894; she was born in 1897. She was followed by Muriel, Ida (known in the family as Chou-Chou), Nancy, and Humphrey Robert, who died in infancy. As the *Irish Times* observed, the family 'helped to colour Irish life for more than half a century'.[18]

⋄ 2 ⋄

Enid's childhood was that of a lady's child.[1] She later used the phrase as the title for the first volume of her autobiography.

A Lady's Child

Dublin, at the turn of the century, was a Victorian capital—but, like all provincial cities, it was dated by metropolitan standards, and as it moved into the twentieth century, the Edwardian era, it kept its rigid Victorian way of life. Dublin society revolved round the Castle: the seat and symbol of British rule. It was not only a closed society, but a hierarchy more precisely defined than that in London. It was a hierarchy determined by class and occupation, and complicated by differences of religion—though not yet by differences of politics. Dublin society was content to be part of the British Empire, to remain under the remote but paternal care of Westminster.

But Dublin society was small, and those who composed it were jealous of their status, and constantly aware of appearances. Social barriers were strictly maintained (Dr Starkie confessed his 'lifelong hatred of the lower classes');[2] social standards were rigorously imposed. Enid's childhood world seemed a world in which correct behaviour was more necessary than the understanding of human beings. Childhood, she felt, was a malady that had to be suffered. Small girls existed to be pretty, well-dressed and polite; they made official visits to the drawing-room, but they felt no close relationship to their parents. Enid led the usual life of an upper-middle-class Edwardian child; but she 'often longed for the animal warmth of simple maternal love'.

Enid's mother was formal; her father was imperially remote. He remained a distant dignitary surrounded by despatch-boxes, an awe-inspiring scholar closeted in his study with his Greek texts.

I never used to feel that my father was very much interested in the depths of human beings, in all their complexes and inner turmoils [Enid told a friend in middle age]. I think he was more interested in the quality of their mind, in their ideas . . . He had a very shrewd understanding of how men would show up in the various works and struggles of life. But he wouldn't be able to understand the human problem in the way you would. I don't think he'd have the compassion and understanding you'd have of failure. In fact I don't think that my father understood failure at all.[3]

Enid found romance and imaginative understanding in her

mother's sister, Auntie Helen; she enjoyed the simple affection of Lizzie O'Beirne, the cook, whom she later drew so fondly in her autobiography. But she was a passionate child who needed much more love than orthodox Edwardian parents gave her. In her childhood she became unsure of her value to other people, anxious because she could not conform to accepted patterns. In adolescence, she ceased to worry about her nonconformity; but she could not find emotional security. To the end of her life she longed for the love which she had missed in childhood: she longed, like a child, for uncritical love and total admiration. A colleague who met her in Paris, in her final years, still had the impression 'that she had perhaps lacked and missed the glow of affection—which to my mind is the one thing in life we can't do without.'[4]

As a small girl, Enid was especially devoted to her brother. Walter, three years older than she was, had the glamour of age, he more nearly touched the adult world; his childhood friends, his boyish interests, and, in time, his tales of life at Shrewsbury, brought a new, refreshing element into the nursery and the school-room. Enid and Walter were drawn together not only by their closeness in age, but already, perhaps, by their keen minds and their rebellious natures. Their affection for one another was always to be profound. They came to share not only past experience but present understanding. After Enid's death, Walter was to write:

Enid and I had never forgotten the ancient days in the family when we were closely akin. We were apart from the rest of the family owing to our personalities. We had, both of us, an incredibly developed sense of memory—so vivid that we often carried on a kind of short-hand communication with one another, recalling scenes and events from the past by a word or a phrase . . . All our lives, whenever we met, we could in the twinkling of an eye bring back whole vistas of memory. This was one of our great joys together, and it gave us the feeling of living many lives.[5]

In time, Enid's younger sisters, Muriel and Chou-Chou, came to be companions in the classroom, in childish escapades, in the musical performances which they arranged to please their mother's guests. For her youngest sister, Nancy, who was her junior by thirteen years, Enid felt an affection which was almost maternal. Nancy still remembers how, at Christmas, Enid did not merely decorate a Christmas tree, but transformed a whole room to delight her.

Enid was brought up by a nurse, and then by a series of governesses. The most important was the French governess, Léonie Cora, who earned a chapter in *A Lady's Child*. Enid also discussed her when, in time, she discussed the French influence on her life.

She arrived when I was just seven. She was small and plump, with a continental figure—as they say in Ireland—and she had that ample bosom which, if we are to believe certain advertisements in French papers, can only be obtained by the constant use of *pilules orientales*. She had an original character, she was quick to be moved, and she had the art of extracting the quintessence of drama out of the most everyday event. '*Dieu que la vie est quotidienne!*' So the poet Jules Laforgue has sighed. But, for Léonie Cora, everything had glamour. A good musician, she had—she said—been a pupil of Pugno, the famous pianist. But her real passion was opera, and, in her youth, she had dreamed of joining the Opéra-Comique. She had hardly sprung out of bed in the morning before she was singing lustily, in front of the wide open window. She sang songs from opera, of which she had a large repertoire. For me, this music became a sort of barometer which told me the mood she was in for the day. When she got up and sang the Toreador song from *Carmen*, the weather would be stormy . . . When, however, I heard the *Méditation de Thaïs*, I snuggled back happily under my bedclothes. My brother and sisters and I could relax; it was going to be fine.[6]

Léonie Cora was not merely frustrated and temperamental: she was sometimes almost unbalanced in her behaviour. Yet her conduct remained unknown outside the nursery. She inflicted her moods on all the children, but especially on Enid. She saw her as a rebellious child who had to be tamed, and her methods were so rigorous—and, at times, so sadistic—that at nine years old Enid attempted suicide.

I no longer remember what Mademoiselle said or did to me—probably nothing worse than usual, but it was sufficient, in my nervous state . . . I was standing near the stairs and without thinking any further I flung myself over the banisters into the hall below.

I do not recall what happened then . . . I know that I spent some days in bed and that I lived them in a sort of dream. Then I went back to the schoolroom and life went on as before . . .

Mademoiselle and the family jumped to the conclusion that I had been sliding down the banisters and had fallen into the hall. By the time I had recovered I was thoroughly ashamed of what I had done and I allowed them to believe that version of the episode.

Léonie Cora was largely responsible for Enid's unhappiness as a child; her disturbing influence was to last throughout Enid's life. But Léonie Cora also inspired her with her profound love of France.

I have to go back very far into my childhood to recall a time when France was not the Eldorado I dreamed of . . . My French governess never stopped talking of France, and she talked with all the nostalgia of the exile. She conjured up the swelling wheat-fields of La Beauce, the hills of the South of France, sprinkled with the velvet grey of olive trees, she conjured up the palm-trees of the Côte d'Azur, the orange-trees, the vines. All these landscapes were still unknown to me, but her descriptions whetted my imagination . . .

She talked to us nostalgically, too, about French cooking: *poulets à la Marengo, soles bonne femme, babas au rhum*, and wines with romantic names. From time to time she made us omelettes, which she cooked over the fire in our room. I still remember the Shrove Tuesday pancakes which she tossed into the air and caught again, deftly, in the pan. There were pancakes flavoured with vanilla, with orange-flower, even rum . . .[7]

They were pancakes as light as bog-cotton.

Even when I was a child [Enid wrote, in later life], everything French seemed to me to be impregnated with Romanticism. I already loved the French passion for the sublime, the French passion for panache . . .

But not all romanticism is pleasant, and [Léonie Cora] used to make me eat powdered eggshell to give me good bones, and threatened to take me to the butcher so that he should give me a glass of ox blood which she claimed was the best thing for anaemia.[8]

The great moment of the schoolroom year was the arrival of the catalogues from the Paris shops. The very names on the catalogues were enough to make her dream: Le Printemps, Le Louvre, and Le Grand Magasin de Blanc.

Our dresses, our pinafores and all our children's underclothes came from Paris. I can still see the arrival of the enormous parcels wrapped in thick tarred paper with lead seals. When the railway employé brought them, it was like the coming of the caravans from Samarkand. That day we had no lessons, and we spent the morning looking at the pretty things and arranging them in cupboards . . . On the day of my First Communion, I remember that I wore the full dress and white veil and all the finery of a First Communicant in France.

Since we were taught entirely in French, at the age of nine I knew French literature better than the literature of my own country. My children's books were not English books, but the volumes of the *Bibliothèque Rose*, bound in red, with gilt edges, which were ordered from Hachette in Paris. I had all the works of the Comtesse de Ségur . . . Some years ago [this in 1943], I rediscovered *Les Mémoires d'un Âne* in the house of some friends, and I re-read it with emotion.

The Comtesse de Ségur had only increased my curiosity about France and my longing to know it. What a wonderful country France must be, I thought to myself, where the donkeys are so intelligent, all endowed with principles and consciences! What a country, where children of my age enjoy such freedom that they cook with real provisions, over a real fire! In *Les Mémoires d'un Âne*, the children had cooked an omelette, and cutlets with fried potatoes, and prepared a *crême au café*, and then they had eaten it all and washed it down with a bottle of wine! I had never drunk wine, but to me it represented the nectar of the gods.

It seemed to me that France must be the children's paradise, that they were more spoilt and better understood there than anywhere else. Later on, when France became my adopted country, I did not change my opinion.

When Léonie Cora left us to get married, my father made me take private French lessons before he sent me to school. I had an old professor by the name of Guilgault. Yes, I believe he was called Hippolyte

Guilgault. I remember his fine silky beard, peppered with grey, a beard scented with benzoin, a magnificent beard, a Sultan's beard, the first beard I ever knew. I also remember his study, which was furnished in the Henri IV-Troisième République style, all in solid oak. The windows of this room could never have been opened since it was occupied, and it smelt strongly of snuff and *papier d'Arménie*. Indoors, Monsieur Guilgault wore a little black velvet *grec* with a red tassel, and he had a muffler round his neck. He cursed the dangers of draughts, as if he was talking about the dangers of sticking pins into wax images. I had never seen the word for draught, *courant d'air*, in writing, and, by analogy with the word *dromadaire*, I imagined that it must be some exotic animal.

All the French people whom I met during my childhood had led a dramatic life; they were never like anyone else. Monsieur Guilgault had fought as a volunteer, at the age of sixteen, in the war of 1870, and—so he said—he would have been decorated if it had not been for the defeat at Sedan. After every lesson, he used to re-enact his military exploits for my benefit. I forget the exact number of his victims—I have a feeling that it tended to vary.[9]

In *A Lady's Child*, Enid recalled the different houses in which she spent her childhood: Undercliffe, at Killiney; Somerset, near Blackrock; and Melfort, in Dublin. She recalled the tennis parties, the amateur dramatics, the musical 'At homes' which her mother delighted to give. George Russell (AE) had been a guest, and W. B. Yeats and his brother Jack, the painter. Oliver Gogarty arrived, 'a twentieth-century Horace Walpole', and one regular Sunday visitor was James Stephens, who sat on a pouff, and 'looked for all the world like one of his own leprechauns sitting on a toadstool'. Sarah Purser came, and told Enid romantic stories of an art student's life in Paris. She had been a contemporary of Marie Bashkirtseff, and a friend of Enid's aunt, Edyth Starkie, when she had studied art at Julien's. Edyth Starkie, 'full of Cork gaiety', was an accomplished painter and sculptor; she married the artist Arthur Rackham.

Enid grew up in Dublin in the age of Lady Gregory, at a time when claret and good conversation were everyday amenities. Yet when, in time, she published her account of her childhood,

Stephen Gwynn found small trace in it of the Irish literary movement, which was then at its height. 'Neither Yeats nor Synge nor the Abbey Theatre seems', he wrote, 'to have affected the consciousness of these highly cultivated Dubliners . . . Literature to some extent in Ireland took the side of nationalism and was therefore suspect; Miss Starkie and her family were more concerned with the literature and art that came to Ireland across the sea than with what was home grown.'[10] Edwardian Dublin society had their spiritual home in an Ireland that was never quite real. They finally disappeared because they had failed to cast any roots in Irish soil.

◦ 3 ◦

Soon after the Starkie family moved from Blackrock to Dublin, the three elder daughters were sent to Alexandra School, near Stephen's Green. It had been founded in 1873 to prepare girls for their higher education at Alexandra College. When Trinity College accepted women as undergraduates, Alexandra College ceased to fulfil its original function; it became merely a senior school which took girls at fifteen or sixteen and 'finished' them, or prepared them for university.[1]

Mrs Starkie had been a pupil at Alexandra School, and some of her teachers were still there when her daughters arrived. In the intervening years, said Enid, they had modernized neither their teaching nor their ideas. Dr Mulvaney, the headmistress,

. . . was a woman of brains and force of character, . . . like what I imagine Miss Beale and Miss Buss must have been. She was always dressed in stiff black clothes, the style of which never changed, and her straight grey hair was drawn into a tight little knot at the back of her head. She wore steel-rimmed glasses. She was of colossal size, but claimed that she had been as slim as a poplar in her youth. 'You should have seen me ride bare-back', she used to exclaim. But I thought, as a child, that nothing smaller than an elephant could have carried her. In spite of her great bulk, she had a distressing habit of moving completely silently down the corridors, and of appearing unheard and unannounced when some unfortunate child was misbehaving. She was a woman of inflexible personality, and many were oppressed by her and frightened of her . . .[2]

Enid was accustomed to her governesses; she was used to learning at home. She found school life a strain, and she was constantly afraid of failure.

In 1913 she won a Pfeiffer Entrance Scholarship to Alexandra College. The massive gothic building in Earlsfort Terrace was a monument to the pioneers of higher education for women. It had been founded in 1866, and since 1881 the girls had sat for diplomas and degrees at the Royal University of Ireland. The Principal, Dr Henrietta White, had hoped to see the college accepted as part of Dublin University; but Alexandra was not to achieve university status. However, for the girls themselves there was an important change from the uniforms and bells of school existence to the relative freedom of college life. They wore their own clothes, and they were considered as students rather than pupils. 'College seemed a very civilized place', Enid remembered. 'We were treated as adults and I blossomed under the treatment.'[3] She blossomed, and she was friendly. She already had a reputation for brilliance, for hard work and ambition. Clearly she wanted to make herself a name. But someone who knew her in her college days thought that she never looked happy: she 'seemed to live at a pitch all the time'. She was always tense, and different from the rest.

She described her days at the college in her autobiography. Another record remains: a collection of her French essays. They show her idiomatic knowledge of the language; and already, perhaps—in the essay on Lamartine—one may detect her fondness for the nineteenth century. The French teacher at Alexandra College was, so Enid said, responsible for her specialization in modern languages.[4]

It was about now, when she was fifteen, that she encountered one of the great influences in her life.

A Lady's Child

One day, as I was coming home along the quays, I stopped at a bookshop where they sold second-hand books. I was rummaging in the boxes when a little book in a paper cover caught my attention, I don't know why, for the title, *Les Nourritures terrestres*, meant nothing to me, and the author was unknown to me. Perhaps it was the white cover with the pretty title in red which charmed my youthful eyes? Perhaps it was that the book was small and I could easily thumb it through with one hand while I held my satchel with the other? Perhaps it was simply fate? I read a few lines at random and it was a *coup de foudre*—a sudden revelation. In Gide, I found the explanation of my adolescent malaise, the justification of my desires of rebellion. It seemed as if the sentences had been written for me.

Nathanael, I should like to give you a joy that no-one else had given you. I know not how to give it to you, and yet I possess it. I should like to speak to you more intimately than anyone else has done. I should like to come at that hour of night when you have opened many books and shut them again—seeking in each of them more than it had yet revealed to you. I should like to come at that hour when you are still waiting: when your fervour is about to turn to sadness, because it does not feel it is understood. I write for you alone; I write for you only in these hours.

These lines seemed to crystallise the state of my soul as I could not have done, they seemed to say what I wanted to hear. I wanted to keep the little book for myself alone and to extract all the essence from it. I had no pocket money; but I saved the pennies I was given to buy a bar of chocolate at mid-day, and after a few weeks I had the small sum I needed to buy the book. To me *Les Nourritures terrestres* were sweeter food than chocolate: they were salvation. This book freed me from the most agonising wish of all my childhood, the wish to be like everybody else. Mademoiselle had never stopped saying: 'Enid always wants to be different from the rest!' That phrase had tolled for me like a funeral bell. Gide freed me from my desperate efforts to be like my school-friends. He incited me to look into myself, to find my real self, and, once I had found it, to keep intact that central core of integrity, to protect it against everything that might corrupt it: against the assaults of false ambition, of self-conceit, and, above all, of self-indulgence. Some readers have claimed to find in Gide an influence which is unhealthy, vicious and demoralising . . . For me, however, Gide has always been a source of strength . . .

It was Gide who put the red cap of revolution on an Irish adolescent. I took the *envoi* of the book for myself.

Nathanael, cast my book away! Do not be satisfied with it. Do not believe that the truth can be discovered by someone else . . . If I sought your food you would not have the appetite to eat it; if I made your bed, you would not be drowsy enough to sleep in it.

Cast my book away; and remind yourself that it is only one of the thousand possible attitudes to life. Seek your own. What another could have done as well as you, do not do it. What another could have written as well as you, do not write it. Attach yourself only to what you feel is in yourself alone, and make yourself, impatiently or patiently, into the most irreplaceable human being.

After my discovery of Gide, my passion for France and French literature increased. It seemed to me that in them alone might I find the solution to all my problems.[5]

When Enid discovered Gide, there were already two powerful influences in her life. The first was religion.

I know that at one time of my development my Catholic religion greatly helped me and gave me balance and some soil from which to grow. As a child, a small child, I very greatly missed love in my life, something beautiful and kind. I thought that grown up people were hard and cruel—perhaps I was right in that belief. Then when I was eight I began to have religious instruction and then I began to realise the conception of God as love. Perhaps I was lucky in having a very saintly nun to instruct me. I know that with religious instruction I began to develop emotionally, to blossom emotionally and to be less hard. I know that I then felt very strongly that I was opening out towards the world, towards all sorts of beauty and experience. It was as if before that I was in a tight little shell.[6]

At the age of ten, she took her First Communion. The preparation had given her intense religious feeling: a feeling so intense that she determined to be a nun. Since there was always a streak of fanaticism in her nature, she decided not merely to be a nun, but to belong to a cloistered order. In her religious mania, she tried to mortify her flesh. She beat herself with a hairbrush for want of a scourge.

It was not surprising that Enid felt such fervour; she had inherited strong religious feeling from both sides of her family. But
she did not merely inherit piety: she needed its emotional release,
she needed its support in her solitude. She eventually became a
daily communicant, and went to Mass before she went to school.
'Some people—and I was one of these as a girl—need frequent
communion, the real presence constantly with them. With the
total possession by God it is as if all doors were barred and fortified
against temptation. It is as if a hand were on our shoulder, as if a
friendly hand were clasping ours.' So she wrote in *A Lady's Child*;
and she added: 'For some years after my First Communion religion
filled my thoughts entirely, and later it blended and fused with my
love of music, forming one single deep stream of emotion.'

Music was the second motive force in her life. Soon after her
First Communion, she was taken by her mother to hear a piano
recital at the Royal Dublin Society. Madame Carreño played
Beethoven's *Appassionata* Sonata. Enid responded to music as
swiftly and as ardently as she had responded to religion. The sonata
exalted her as only prayer had done. 'That night, I knew that
music was what I wanted, that a pianist was what I wanted to be.'

It was an age for music in Dublin. Among her mother's acquaintances were the violinist Achille Simonetti, the pianist and composer Michele Esposito, and the cellist Clyde Twelvetrees. They
formed an instrumental trio and played every year at the Royal
Irish Academy of Music, where they taught their respective instru-
ments. The three elder Starkie girls attended the Academy, and
Enid had piano lessons there from Annie Lord: the finest pianist,
she said, whom the Royal Irish Academy had produced. The girls
also began to compete at the Feis Ceoil, the annual music festival
in Dublin, 'but I only achieved second medal—two years in succession,' lamented Enid, 'though each time I missed the first medal
by only one mark. Fanny Davies, Clara Schumann's last pupil,
was examining both these years, and I can still remember her kind
and encouraging words to me.'

During her last year at Alexandra College, Enid's passion for
music increased. Music was the outlet for all her turbulent feelings,

for the adolescent emotions which she did not understand. She heard a recorded performance of Beethoven's Ninth Symphony, and suddenly she became aware of the deep connection between mysticism and music. At her mother's musical parties she heard Annie Lord play Debussy and Ravel. She spent at the piano all the time she could steal from her books. She took lessons in interpretation from Esposito. During the opening weeks of her last year at Alexandra, she thought of little but the Vandeleur Scholarship at the Academy. She was going to compete for it, and the music which had been prescribed was, strangely enough, part of the *Appassionata* Sonata. Since the day she had heard Madame Carreño, it had been her ambition to play it.

Her dreams of a musical career were destroyed by the Principal of Alexandra College, who told her that she must give up the examination. She could not compete for the Vandeleur Scholarship as well as the Entrance Scholarship to Somerville College, Oxford, the following March.

In *A Lady's Child*, Enid records how she struggled with her emotions. She suddenly understood how much her father expected of her, how much her academic success would mean to him. She wanted his approval and his understanding and she felt that she could not disappoint him. 'I admired him very much,' she explained to a friend, years later, 'he seemed to me so much finer than most other people in my life, and I thought that what he was was so much better than the ideal of a Lady's Child which was what I was expected to be. I wanted to be what he would have liked.' She did in fact compete for the Vandeleur Scholarship. She did not win it, but she won a prize. The following March she left Ireland for the first time in her life, and took the examination at Somerville. She was awarded an open scholarship in modern languages.

Enid did not cease to dream of a musical career; but just after her nineteenth birthday, passionate and immature, she left the shelter of Dublin and embarked, half-heartedly, on her Oxford life.

PART TWO

❖❖❖❖❖

Scholar of Somerville

1916–1920

Somerville Hall (as it was called until 1894) and Lady Margaret Hall had been opened in October 1879: one with twelve students and the other with nine. They had had financial support, but they received no benefaction on a large scale for more than forty years. The attitude towards women in Oxford had remained strictly conservative. It was true that in the early seventies society had begun to change. Fellows of colleges were allowed to marry, and some of them began to take an interest in women's education. But the reactionaries remained. Dr Pusey had described the establishment of the women's halls as 'one of the greatest misfortunes that has happened even in our own time in Oxford'; and a correspondent in *The Times*, in 1884, had anticipated the disappearance of true learning, of cricket and rowing, and the loss of the virility of the University. However, that year a statute authorized the use of Honour Moderations, and the Final Schools of Mathematics, Natural Science and Modern History, for the examination of women. In 1886 St Hugh's Hall was founded, and the same year Miss Beale of Cheltenham took the first practical steps towards the foundation of St Hilda's. The Society of Home Students was duly established—the nucleus of a fifth women's college.[1]

The women's determination remained; but intellectual recognition was slow. In these early days, the two senior halls concerned themselves only with residence; and, since the University would not accept women as members, their academic welfare was watched over by the Association for the Higher Education of Women at Oxford. Application for admission to lectures was made through the Association's office (strategically placed in the Clarendon Building); and it was the Association's duty to provide and, if necessary, pay chaperons for lectures when they were required.[2] Such was the need for decorum in these early days that a Somerville student, asked to a tennis party, had to be conveyed to it in a cab; she could not walk through Oxford with a racquet.[3] Even as late as 1920 the College rules decreed that 'students may not accept invitations to the rooms of men members of the University, or enter such rooms except under special circumstances and with the sanction of the Principal. Students may not invite men to their own rooms, nor receive them there.'[4]

Women were tolerated in Oxford, but they were discounted until, in 1907, Lord Curzon was elected Chancellor of the University. He urged that they should be admitted to Oxford degrees. Two years later, after prolonged discussion, the Hebdomadal Council agreed in principle with his memorandum. The War reminded the authorities of women's large capacities for work. In 1918, when women were granted a limited franchise, it was clear that higher education could no longer be officially denied them. Miss Penrose, the Principal of Somerville, was a woman of austere personality and dominant mind. Her determination was largely responsible for the fact that, after the War, Oxford took advantage of recent legislation and gave degrees to women, while Cambridge refused them.

On 11 May 1920, in Enid's final term at Oxford, a statute was passed admitting women to membership of the University, and to all its degrees, except those of divinity, On 14 October Oxford saw the first degree-giving in which women had taken part. Before the ritual began, the five Principals of the women's societies became M.A.s by order of Convocation, and the Sheldonian Theatre rang with deserved applause as they put on their gowns and took their seats behind the Vice-Chancellor—a ceremony which the Principal of Somerville had practised for nearly an hour the previous day.[5]

Among the graduates, that first day, was Dorothy Sayers. Several years later, she made Somerville the setting for *Gaudy Night*. When, in her novel, Lord Peter Wimsey finally proposed to Harriet Vane, he asked: '*Placetne, magistra?*', and Harriet Vane, M.A., accepted him with the word '*Placet*'. Miss Penrose had made it possible.

Somerville, in Enid's student days, was ruled by Miss (later Dame Emily) Penrose. She came of a distinguished line, with relations in the Arnold and Huxley families, and she had been the first woman to obtain a First in Greats. She had been Principal since 1907, and she was to remain in office until 1926: tall, fine-featured, Olympian, 'secure in the legend of her purpose, her omnipotence and her inhumanity'.[6] Yet perhaps this portrait, by Vera Brittain, remains incomplete. Constance Savery, one of Enid's contemporaries, remembers:

Miss Penrose had a slight fixed smile without which she was never to be seen. College said that she wore it in bed to be ready for the next morning. She was not easy to know: her great administrative gifts . . . left her little opportunity for the lecturing or teaching that would have brought her into closer relationship with the students. Only now and then did we catch glimpses of the human being under the professional mask. We all called her 'The Pen'—but we did not know that she herself used the nickname until a returned letter was posted on the College notice-board addressed simply 'Pen, Somerville College'. And if I had not met her maid Alice worriedly chasing an intrusive cat down the august staircase, I should never have known that the Pen, in company with many other notabilities, suffered from cat phobia.[7]

When Enid made her notes on Oxford, she scribbled simply: 'Miss Penrose. Her eccentricities. Her loss of memory at the end.'[8] She also noted: 'Miss Pope. The greatest person met at Somerville.'[9] Since Mildred Pope was Enid's tutor, since she earned such praise, one may pause a moment to record her. She had been Tutor in Modern Languages since 1894. Constance Savery found that she

possessed the magic power of putting the shyest person at ease immediately. She was so genuinely friendly and sympathetic, such a genial lover of humanity, even clumsy calf humanity. At the same time, she was so common-sensical, so free from sentimentality, so pleasantly brisk and wholesome. I remember her always in neat close-fitting dark clothes with a look of friendly intelligence beaming from behind her glasses.[10]

Dorothy Sayers, one of her pupils, gave her permanent life in *Gaudy Night*.

Miss Lydgate's manner was exactly what it had always been. To the innocent and candid eyes of that great scholar, no moral problem seemed ever to present itself . . . So many young people had passed through her hands, and she had found so much good in all of them; it was impossible to think that they could be deliberately wicked, like Richard III or Iago. Unhappy, yes; misguided, yes; exposed to difficult and complicated temptations which Miss Lydgate herself had been mercifully spared, yes. If she heard of a theft, a divorce, even worse things, she would knit puzzled brows and think how utterly wretched the offenders must have been before they could do so dreadful a thing.[11]

On the death of Miss Pope, Enid wrote in very similar terms:

During the 65 years of her association with Somerville, few have been so much admired for distinguished scholarship and beloved for warmhearted humanity . . . A burning desire to redress wrongs struggled in her for supremacy with an unquenchable belief in the native disinterestedness and good-will of everyone . . . She was incapable of believing that there existed idle or unsatisfactory pupils, but only unhappy or unfortunate ones. She had the humble and disinterested love of learning of a mediaeval monk, whom she resembled in temperament and appearance.[12]

Vera Farnell, the Librarian and French lecturer at Somerville, was also to have figured in Enid's memoirs; but no substantial notes remain, and again one must turn to Constance Savery. 'Tall, exceedingly slim and willowy, [she had] a glorious head of hair and a pale face out of which looked two great dark melancholy eyes set in deep hollows. No-one could have guessed that she was no ghost-like being, but the wittiest of all the dons.'[13] Helen Darbishire, the senior English lecturer, 'lived in a remote, gracious Wordsworthian and Miltonic world amid beautiful surroundings, from which she emerged with something of an effort.'[14] Indeed she did: a pupil once encountered her at a tutorial, wearing a red velvet gown with a fur ruff.[15] Hilda Lorimer, the classics tutor, was somewhat more conventional: she was 'a trim person of medium height and a habit of constantly removing and replacing her eyeglasses while she talked.'[16]

The most arresting don was clearly the tutor in modern history, Maude Clarke. 'You would not forget the impression she made on you,' so Llewellyn Woodward was to write, 'the life and colour of her eyes, the poise of her head. She had a quiet voice, a quiet and noble style.'[17] Maude Clarke had been born in Belfast in 1892. Her father, the Rector of Trinity Church, had later accepted the living of Carnmoney, on the outskirts of the city, and there she had grown up at Coole Glebe, the rectory house. She had gone—like Enid—to Alexandra School in Dublin; she had taken first class honours in history at Queen's University, Belfast. In 1919 she was appointed to Somerville. Despite her academic distinction, she was almost more remarkable for her personality. Her fineness of nature was apparent; and yet she seemed withdrawn and strangely unknown. 'She did not appear inhuman,' Vera Brittain would explain, 'but though her keen incisive mind could be moved to sympathy by intellectual struggles, the emotional conflicts of those whose work she directed seemed to leave her singularly unmoved. To many of her former students, the memory of Maude Clarke . . . remains an enigma which time is unlikely to solve.'[18] Helen Waddell, who was taught by her, perhaps most nearly solved it. 'I think physical passion was left out in her. It was for a long time a nightmare to her . . . But, physical passion left out, she was infinitely richer in loving than most of the world.'[19] Her influence was profound on those who knew her, and it was felt in Somerville years after she had died.

The Oxford to which Enid came in October 1916 was the Oxford of the First World War. Somerville had been commandeered for use as a military hospital; some of its students were in exile in the St Mary Hall quadrangle of Oriel, but most of them lived out in groups in lodgings. Oxford seemed a half-dead war-time city of elderly dons, women students, and wounded men on crutches. Some of the women students felt unbearably marooned, guilty at leading an academic life, and they constantly wondered whether they should devote themselves to war service. The atmosphere was unreal and unsettled. Yet, for the women, Oxford had advantages which had been unknown in earlier years. Because of the War, many women were taught by dons from the men's colleges who otherwise would have had no time for them.[20]

The atmosphere of Somerville in the First World War, and some of the more remarkable students, have been recalled by another of Enid's contemporaries, Hilda Mellor.

I had come from a large Manchester school where we were much encouraged and stimulated by our teachers, and I found the atmosphere of Somerville strangely disconcerting. Our morals were supervised most strictly and we were only allowed to take tea or coffee in the men's colleges if we were in a group or with a chaperone. But, where work was concerned, we got very little advice . . .

However, there were highlights, especially as I began to discriminate. There was a wonderful course of lectures by Sir Walter Raleigh, as handsome and distinguished looking as his ancestor. We also attended six lectures on 'How to write' by Mr Masefield and Hilaire Belloc—the former, I remember, in an immaculate white tussore suit and the latter as immense as I had pictured him.

I was at Somerville just in time to meet several famous women beside Enid.[21]

Among them was Winifred Holtby. She had passed her entrance examination in 1916, but patriotism had led her to take up nursing. The work had proved too arduous, and the following year she had come into residence.

On the first day of my first term [Constance Savery records] I went in accordance with custom to report myself to the Principal. Another student . . . was waiting outside Miss Penrose's study door. She was tall and dignified, a Norse goddess—if one can imagine a Norse goddess impeccably clad in the long sweeping garments of 1917, with a little eye-veil on her elegant small hat . . . It was my first sight of Winifred Holtby.[22]

After a year at Oxford, the Norse goddess was again overcome by her sense of duty, and she joined Queen Mary's Army Auxiliary Corps. Constance Savery continues:

When Winifred Holtby followed the example of Vera Brittain and went down to do war work, there was a certain amount of unrest among the students . . . Some of us began to wonder whether we were doing our duty to the country in wartime.

Miss Penrose called a College meeting in the course of which she stated emphatically that after the War the country would need educated women to serve her in all walks of life. We could contribute to the war effort better by remaining at Oxford for the very necessary part we had to play. The remonstrance must have been effective, for no more was heard about going down 'for the duration'. But throughout 1918 and part of 1919 we did various pieces of social service: attendance at a Town play-centre, digging in the Somerville potato-patch, sewing for wounded soldiers and wheeling them out in bath chairs, flax-picking in vacation . . .[23]

Winifred Holtby returned to Oxford in 1919; she took her degree in 1921, established herself as a novelist, and remained an ardent supporter of social reform. She died in 1935, at the age of thirty-seven.

It was a remarkable generation at Somerville, for it also included Margaret Kennedy. 'One afternoon,' writes Hilda Mellor, 'I was most flattered when Margaret asked me to go with her for a walk round the Meadows and I must have been the first to hear what she always referred to as an *idée* for a book. Much later, I realized that this was the germ from which grew *The Constant Nymph*.'[24]

Winifred Holtby planned her first novel, *Anderby Wold*, while she was at Oxford. Vera Brittain recalled Somerville as Drayton College in her own first novel, *The Dark Tide*, Sylvia Thompson was to remember it in *The Hounds of Spring*. Doreen Wallace, in *A Little Learning*, recorded, if not her college, at least North Oxford, where 'the red suburbs glowed clearly like geranium beds'. Hilda Reid, the historical novelist, was a Somervillian. So, as we have seen, was Dorothy Sayers. So was Rose Macaulay. Small wonder that the Press referred to 'the Somerville School of Novelists'.

Some thirty years later, June Barraclough went to Somerville for interviews. Enid, she wrote, 'was the person I remember best, and I'm sure she got me in . . . She asked me what I *really* wanted to do. I suppose, like many people, I said "to write novels" and she immediately said "Well, you've come to the right place." '[25]

❖ 5 ❖

During the winter of 1916–17, Hilda Mellor first set eyes on Enid. 'My first glimpse of Enid Starkie was when I saw her on a cold snow-bound night standing in the middle of Oriel College quad, a small still figure gazing at the full moon.'[1] Dorothy Wadham, who remained a friend of Enid's all her life, also remembers her in her first term:

Enid had a room in St Mary Hall . . . [She] established herself very soon as an eccentric. One night in the very cold winter of 1916–17, when snow was on the ground, I saw her in her dressing-gown in the quad, returning from a bath in the more-or-less modern Rhodes building that faced the High. She was apparently searching in the snow. I called out to ask what she was hanging about for, and she replied: 'I've lost a hairpin.' That was fairly typical of one aspect of her personality.[2]

She was already nonconformist and original, she was already creating her legend. 'An intelligent person never observes regulations', she told an undergraduate fifty years later. 'I myself never observed regulations.'[3] And again, in her notes: 'The chaperon rules. How I got out of them. Climbing into college. My boy friends then . . .' She let off a red gas-filled balloon during a formal dinner, which predictably brought dinner to a standstill. She invited two men into Hall, disguised as women. 'No-one found out, but one of them had very large hands, and I couldn't take my eyes off them. To this day [in 1966], if I see a woman with large hands, I think it must be a man disguised.'[4] 'Stories about Starkie went round College,' Constance Savery continues. 'At a time when bobbed hair was not at all popular with male parents, Starkie bobbed hers . . . Starkie, having committed one crime, plunged headlong into another. She was ploughed in an examination, I think a French Group. Somerville heard with horrified amusement that the examiners had said that brilliance in translation did not compensate for total ignorance of the set books.'[5] In her notes for her memoirs of Oxford, Enid recorded that she was nearly sent down.[6] However, she stayed at Somerville, and she continued to astonish Constance Savery. 'Surprising—to me at any rate—was her entrance into the J.C.R. at after-dinner coffee time, carrying a huge pale purple balloon . . . Starkie was soon the centre of a balloon-snatching game—and not even the dons seemed to think her an idiot.'[7] They showed remarkable tolerance of a young woman of twenty: a woman who behaved with all the wildness of a child.

From her first moment in Oxford, Enid established herself as unforgettable. 'I was only a first-year student and hardly knew her,' Hilda Mellor writes,

but her personality was such that I have never forgotten her—her curly dark hair, her bright eyes and delightful Irish accent.

Apart from her knowledge of the French language which was phenomenal, the love of her life was playing the piano.

She used to sit playing in her room on sunny summer evenings, with the window open, thundering out the fiery music she loved. She had a special fondness for Chopin's Revolutionary: this was always included in her repertoire.

Once a year, I was told, she held a concert for the rest of Somerville. There was a collection—to pay for the rent of the piano for another year!

These trivialities may help to show another side of a woman who was, I think, in her way not far from a genius.[8]

Vera Farnell adds:

I remember her of course as an undergraduate, . . . when I had just been appointed Librarian and Principal's secretary. In those days Enid was to a young and overworked don remarkable chiefly as a talented but obviously 'neurotic' student, the centre of attraction in a group of friends which included Viola Garvin and Dorothy Crook. She looked fragile, and was an unwilling object of concern to the

Bursar, responsible for the health of students. She never seemed to have any money to spare, and it was, I was told, with the object of getting hold of some, that with the encouragement of her friends she hired a room in the Town Hall and gave a Piano Recital.[9]

The concert was given in the Assembly Room; it included *La Cathédrale engloutie* by Debussy and Sonata No. 23, op. 57, by Beethoven: the *Appassionata* Sonata which Enid dearly loved. Miss Farnell remembers:

The Hall was pretty full thanks to the recruiting efforts of her friends. When the 'young artist' appeared in a new frock bought for the occasion, . . . she was clearly extremely nervous, and many in the audience feared throughout that she would break down. She had chosen a programme probably beyond the powers of so young a performer, however talented, and I think I remember something very near to a breakdown. The money brought in by this venture just succeeded in paying for her dress.[10]

Enid was too temperamental to be a professional pianist. As a student of modern languages, she remained impressive. Dorothea Townshend wrote: 'She had an electric personality enhanced by her gamine appearance . . . We all realized she was brilliantly clever.'[11] Dorothy Wadham was informed by one of Enid's tutors that 'the most remarkable thing about her as a scholar was her unusual power, for someone so young, to *correlate* her knowledge—a symptom of maturity.'[12] Gustave Rudler, the Professor of French Literature, found her 'sentimental and romantic', but he remained her faithful supporter throughout his career.

There was a shadow side to the picture. Enid had enjoyed too little human warmth as a child, and at school she had been notably withdrawn. She had led a strict, uneventful, provincial life. At Oxford she was suddenly plunged, vulnerable and immature, into a sophisticated world. It was a world in which she needed guidance, and there seemed to be no-one to guide her. Women dons, in those days, were often unworldly; and, at Somerville, they remained remote. Miss Penrose had created an almost impassable gulf between the Senior and Junior Common Rooms. 'In the difficult University of 1919 to 1921,' Vera Brittain wrote, 'there was certainly need for a greater measure of personal wisdom than most of us encountered.'[13] Enid did not encounter it at this critical moment in her life.

As one of her friends would tell her, she was 'supremely a woman, physically';[14] but sometimes she needed a woman's gentleness and understanding. She tended to attract more dominant women; and she herself was sometimes drawn to them. As a student she became emotionally involved with another woman: so involved that her health became affected, and, for a while, she had to return to her family in Dublin.[15] The crisis occurred, apparently, in 1918, for her father records her at home during the Oxford Michaelmas term. The episode was no doubt in her mind when she wrote: 'It was at Oxford that I met for the first time the full violence of impact with human personality and of clash of temperaments. I learned there of the bitter cruelty of human beings to one another . . . I learned then how much suffering is the price of human friendship and love.' It was a lesson she would learn again. She would more than once be drawn to other women, and the attraction would bring her predictable unhappiness.

She was clearly unsettled when, in the winter of 1918, she found herself at home. On 25 November, her father noted:

I criticized at dinner last evening Enid on her letting down her appearance . . . I began by saying Alexandra College was the nicest women's college in the Kingdom. Enid denied this and asked me why. I said because the girls there kept themselves so well. She asked me what I knew about English girls. I replied I had seen many of them taking their degrees in Trin. Coll., . . . whereat she blushed, and got angry. Indeed she is sometimes awful: I have seen her go without having her boots cleaned, with mud on them![16]

To Enid, now accustomed to Oxford, Dublin must have seemed, suddenly, intolerably limited. 'Enid was at a curious party last night', noted her father, 'from wh. she returned in a car at 1. Curious specimens there in morning suits and spats.'[17] Society remained limited, and the Starkies remained critical. It was an unpromising way of life. On 6 February 1919, Dr Starkie recorded, with some anxiety: 'In Dublin there is hardly anyone now worth knowing. It is sad, but the world is *kaput* here, as everywhere else. I pity the young: this insignificant planet is not so pleasant to live in as I remember it.'

One follows Enid, intense and unhappy, lonely and stubborn, through the pages of her father's diary. In January and February he recorded her at local dances, and playing César Franck at a musical tea and going to a performance of *Lohengrin*. She returned to Oxford for the Trinity Term. On 8 May: 'Letter from Enid . . . Oxford is crowded, they have to sit on the floor at lectures, and write on their knees. The bill is £26 12s., an increase. She is now in lodgings.'

In her third year, in King Edward Street, her behaviour remained as wild as ever. Constance Savery wrote home with innocent excitement:

I don't think I told you much about Hilda Reid's cocoa-party . . . Miss Starkie was there; she is an Irish third-year, rather eccentric and a bit of a genius. She nearly had a row with Lady Reid because Lady R. said something about 'no ordinary rules were observed in Ireland' (such as the wearing of hats or gloves). She also told us that she had a bath every night in quad, and then walked home to Teddy Street where she lives, lightly but elegantly attired in her nightdress and an overcoat! We hardly knew how to believe her. Fancy anyone walking up the High in the face of all the world in a nightdress and an overcoat and nothing else. If the Pen heard, there'd be the most unholiest row that ever was. We're not allowed even to cross Oriel Street without a hat on.[18]

Constance Savery adds:

I had the happiness to be present when the secret exploded.

Some friends and I were sitting on the steps [which led to the Principal's rooms] in the late evening. Along came Starkie in airy attire, bent either on having a bath or paying a social call. She stopped for a brief chat with my friends. It was her undoing. One of the dons, Miss Niven (Mrs Sorley), happened to pass by. Struck by something unusual in

Starkie's appearance, she paused, looked, looked again . . . 'Miss Starkie, is it *possible* . . .?' Starkie began a voluble explanation. She was perfectly decent, it was quite all right, what was the harm? Explanations were useless. 'Miss Starkie, will you kindly come with me to the porter's lodge?' And Starkie was led off, still loudly protesting, there to wait until a messenger had been sent off to fetch the missing clothes.

I never heard the sequel, if sequel there was. Starkie had all the Irish charm and doubtless she used it on the Pen.[19]

She was not as gay as she might seem. She had become aware of her father's failing health and of his financial anxieties. 'The children now want to know why I make an old man of myself', he recorded in his diary. He was disturbed by his growing weakness; he lost himself increasingly in books. On 9 April 1919 he had noted an overdraft of £1200. Some months later he wrote soberly: 'I am thinking of sending the family to Cologne, where life is cheap, and teaching good: but that wd. be hard on me. Still I am afraid it must be done, as it is quite impossible to get a suitable house.'

For a moment it had seemed that the problem might be splendidly solved. In April 1919, John Pentland Mahaffy died, and there was lively discussion about his successor as Provost of Trinity College, Dublin. 'I hate the prospect of intrigue, with regard to the vacancy', Dr Starkie noted. 'I shd. much prefer that M. had continued during my lifetime. Tho' a lover of power, the other side of my nature loves simple, straightforward methods, and the struggle for place has never had charms for me . . . As a social person, I think I shd. fill the place well: and certainly the family wd. be an improvement on anything they have ever had in the Provost's House.'[20]

He became more and more aware of the advantages of the Provostship. Yet he knew that, as a Catholic, he was unlikely to rule the College which had been founded by Queen Elizabeth to foster the Protestant faith. On 5 May he added: 'There is no doubt that Catholics cannot look for preferment in Trin: no case could be stronger than mine—I am popular with them, I am not a priest's man, and I am known, in addition to being a scholar, an administrator, and a fighting man.' On 7 June, he learned with bitterness that the next Provost of Trinity was to be John Henry Bernard, the Archbishop of Dublin.

It was not surprising that his eldest daughter should have had university politics in her blood.

At Oxford, the first postwar summer was enlivened by inter-collegiate debates between men and women. Somerville's pro-gramme included debates with New College, Oriel and Queen's. On 16 June Dr Starkie recorded:

Enid says she has been speaking at mixed debates only from notes, and that Miss [Penrose] said her speech was the speech of the evening . . . Enid says Bolshevism prevails at the Union: a Sinn Fein resolution for Ireland was passed by an overwhelming majority. All the speakers were in favour of doing away with Parliamentary institutions. She says there is a movement to introduce women into the Union: they are thought to be better speakers than the men. Miss Penrose has asked her to be a public speaker: she says she makes a v. good speaker because she has a light touch, such as women generally lack, and she is not too didactic. But Enid thinks it is so easy to be amusing, without good stuff. But Miss P. rightly says women are too serious. I am glad she took my hint: I always felt she and Walter's line was speech.

Enid returned to Dublin on 1 July. There were tennis tourna-ments, garden-parties, a piano lesson from Miss Lord, and a dance with 'champagne in torrents'. On 9 October she left again for Oxford. Silence followed. On 17 October she had still not written home to announce her arrival. Her father noted: 'We telegraphed to Miss Penrose yesterday, and received a reply "daughter arrived safely last Friday". What a girl!' On 22 October: 'Enid has sent a letter . . . She says S. College is v. cold, and draughty.'

The event which marked the Michaelmas Term was the return of the College to its home. After four years, the exile in Oriel was over. The term also saw the birth of a new Somerville debating society, which organized discussions on topical subjects. Constance Savery watched 'Enid's stocky little figure bristling with defiance as she rebuked English phlegm and stolidity in the course of a College debate. "You are a mouldy lot, you English. It's awfully hard to get up a fight. When I go out to tea at home, I always come back with a black eye".'[21] The comment was presumably rhetorical; but no-one could deny that she had fire.

The academic year ran its course. On 18 December she came home to Christmas festivities: among them a fancy-dress ball to which she went dressed as a Roman. Her father's diary for 1920 continues to record both social life and domestic vexations. It suggests the Starkies' conventional ways and Enid's constant, pugnacious independence. On 10 January: 'Enid made a mess in cutting her hair, and is a perfect show, wh. led to the usual row with May, who told her she thought she was mad. For the first time in her life, Enid admitted she had made a mistake; but May as usual rubbed it in too much.' Next day, a Sunday, came a large tea-party. 'James Stephens is an ugly, baldish, dull-looking little man, with plenty of sense of humour. He thinks man is a fool to have handed over beauty to women . . . He said if God had given him a decent body, he wd. have started the cult of the male figure . . . Enid played Debussy's *Engloutie* v. well—but few understood it.'

She was still determined to show her Gidean independence, still resisting parental authority. The diary continued to record her father's vexation. On 16 January she left, once again, for Oxford. On 19 January: 'Enid has not announced her arrival, in spite of what I said. "Hybris" personified.' Soon afterwards there came a letter. 'Enid wants to go to France, to take up a job in an *école normale* after summer, in preparation for a travelling scholarship. She will have to get a first in Greats [*sic*] if she is to get a University post, as she desires.'[22]

The future of the family was taking shape in Oxford and, more sadly, in Dublin. On 2 April Dr Starkie had a disturbing diagnosis from his doctor. He was suffering from diabetes. The doctor urged him to call in a second opinion, but his own view was so serious that Dr Starkie considered he must be dying. 'I slept v.

badly and got up 3 times [16 April] and was generally miserable, thinking of what wd. become of the family when I was gone. The whistle of a thrush (wonderfully clear and close to the window) woke me at 6 a.m.; I thought it was the whistle of a Sinn Feiner about to attack the house.' Next day, a Sunday: 'Our last Musical (I wonder whether it will be my last) came off at 3.30: quite a large gathering . . . Enid played Debussy v. well, esp. *Cath. engloutie*, wh. pleased.'

Enid returned to Oxford for her final term, and he continued to brood. 'I was thinking over the future of the family all night [26 April]. It is curious how indifferent to life I am—as far as I am concerned. I seem not to care whether I live or die: at any rate, death by my disease is painless.' Next day he wrote to the Provost of Trinity, resigning from the council, 'on the ground my health was not v. sound, and my hands full in other fields. So ends my connexion with Trin. of 35 years, and I don't regret it . . . My resentment ag. them is too great. I have never forgiven their rejecting me on the ground of my religion.'

However his resignation would not take effect until October; and in the meanwhile he still had moments of pleasure and amusement. On 14 June he noted: 'White King told me his son at Christ Church took Enid and some others up the river, on a picnic. One of the men overturned a punt and gave a ducking to a girl!'

The Christ Church undergraduate was the future Press magnate, Cecil King. Enid was always to feel affection for him. In 1936 she told him:

You are one of the people I see with most pleasure . . . When I see you it all comes back what I used to feel about you when you were an undergraduate and I was little more than a silly schoolgirl at college; I do not think that I have ever known any man more beautiful than you were at nineteen—and I have known many men—the daffodil I used to call you in my own mind. I always remember with gratitude having known you then.[23]

In 1946 he gave her a set of silver-gilt spoons to mark her election to the Readership in French Literature. 'I suppose,' he said, later, 'the person I knew longest was Enid Starkie. I'm Irish and she was very Irish, she could be very, very amusing. I suppose she regarded me as a friend.'[24] 'You go back very far into my life,' Enid had told him, 'farther than anyone who is not a member of my family, and with whom I have kept up. I am very fond indeed of you. Your 'vermeil' spoons are amongst my most treasured possessions . . . I hope that everything goes well with you, that you are as happy as you can be. You are certainly very successful, but that does not always fill one's heart.'[25]

On 22 June 1920, Dr Starkie recorded with jubilation: 'Enid wires to say she has got first with distinction. Her future is now secure, thank God.'

Dr Starkie's diary is a strangely unemotional document. He rarely expresses the affection he feels for his family, the pride he must have taken in their achievements. But Enid's First delighted him. On 24 June he wrote happily: 'Enid's "distinction" is in the colloquial use of French. There was only one other in the 1st class, Kate Clark of Somerville, of whom I had never heard. Only one man got the same distinction in French. I sent a notice to the *Irish T[imes]*.' Legend said that Enid's papers were so excellent that, at her oral examination, the whole examining board stood up and shook her hand.

Enid left Oxford with her distinction of intellect recognized. She had established herself as a personality. She had also become acutely aware of her emotional problems, and she had lost the faith of her childhood. Years later, in her autobiography, she recalled how she had fallen from the practice of Catholicism into atheism. A critic observed how 'the women's Oxford of her day completed the spiritual shipwreck Ireland had begun'.

Meanwhile, on 26 June, the family set off for their summer holiday at Cushendun, in the glens of Antrim. 'Car packed with luggage,' Dr Starkie noted, 'and Muriel, Nancy, Lizzie, Mademoiselle and myself. We did 28 miles an hour.' Cushendun proved to be cold and gloomy; the house was sparsely furnished, and the rain was torrential. On 29 June: 'Slept v. badly, and, as there was no oil in the lamp, I cd not read. My thoughts were not pleasant—

death, ruin for my family, etc. but with the light, as usual, optimism returned . . . The day closed inclemently with an indigo
sky. We have a fire.'

On 2 July a letter arrived from Enid, who was staying in
Denbigh. 'She writes . . . that she . . . was ill at the Exam.,
and did not expect a first. Her letter was, as usual, v. arid.' Next
day came a telegram 'to say she wd. arrive by 10.30 train . . . She
was 1st. of all who took French', Dr Starkie added. 'She has taken
a school at Haslemere for a year at £100, pending getting a travelling scholarship of wh. she is pretty certain.'[26]

It was a strange and fitful month, the coldest July on record. On
5 July he forgot his ill-health, and 'bathed at 8, in a wonderful
calm sea—no one else on shore, but Enid went down later.' Next
day it was so cold that he 'sat in furs all the evening'. 'Wet—and
cold', he added on 7 July. 'Did not bathe, but Enid did . . . Enid
told May yesterday that she was second on the list of travelling
scholarships, the first being given to a science man, and it is
arranged she shd. go to the Sorbonne, as a pupil of Le Franc—not
to attend lectures or to teach. She will require £50 extra, and
wants the Intermediate Examinership. She is a curious girl not to
have told us these things before: Miss Pope has arranged the whole
thing.' It was his final comment on a daughter of whom he felt
proud, a daughter whom he did not understand.

There was no time, now, to understand. He had recognized the
gravity of his condition, and for months he had expected death.
It came to him at Cushendun, on 21 July. He was fifty-nine.

⟡6⟡

Enid was later to recall the final days at Cushendun in her autobiography, *A Lady's Child*. She recalled them again in her unpublished novel, when the heroine sat by her father's deathbed,
just as Enid had sat by that of her own father. 'All she had ever
known of intellectual life it was he who had shown it to her . . .

The room was warm and still and, in the silence, she felt as if she could almost hear the moments gliding past, dropping, one by one, heavily and slowly over the edge of the world.'[1] 'I've never really got over my father's death', she told Alyse Gregory in 1942. 'I can still feel it with the same intensity as I did so many years ago, when I stop to think of it. Many things still remind me of my father when I see them.'[2] In 1950, discussing Proust and the trains of thought which some simple object might stir within him, she wrote: 'For many the death of a loved one is recalled by the sudden whiff of white roses in a garden, or of drops of hot wax from candles, in a church, because these things had been present when he lay ready for burial.'[3] It was, again, a memory of Cushendun. And years after her father had died, when a pupil of hers was mourning her own father, Enid sent her a letter which seemed to contain reflections of her past.

Nothing makes things any better at first. I never think it is any use to say that those who are dead have been mercifully spared pain. We do not think of them in their moment of weakness, but at the time when they were most themselves, in their greatest strength. Their illness had only seemed a phase to get through. We miss intolerably the person they were. Nothing can alter that. Indeed it would not be right not to feel sorrow. That would be the saddest of all. Our sorrow and pain is the measure of what they were for us. And you will find—as many have found—that it is from the greatness of the sorrow that comfort eventually comes. If we have grieved greatly then those we love remain longest with us and in us. To have been spared the grieving would mean also that one was denied later the comfort. One would not wish to grieve less.[4]

Dr Starkie's diary reveals a scholar, a civilized man who showed a quiet enjoyment of food and wine, of music, and outdoor pleasures: these last, perhaps, a legacy from his athletic past. Enid had inherited her father's love of life, the toughness he had shown in his youth. 'I was an oarsman and mountain-climber', so he had written, 'and still sat for days like a log over the fire. Enid inherited the first taste, and M[uriel] the second.'[5] Enid had also inherited her father's devotion to scholarship—though he was a pure intellectual, and she was an intellectual moved by emotion. She had wanted, before he died, to take up an academic career; now she felt it a duty to sacrifice all else to her work, and to succeed as he would have wished.

In a draft ending for her Paris book, she set down some disjointed sentences:

I had promised my father to make a success or try to . . .
My father had wanted chair. I would give that sacred value . . .
I hoped I might be someone my father would meet without being ashamed, that I'd have the integrity of him.
Someone said to me once (about being someone my father would have been proud of). That was the nicest thing I believe ever said to me. I would like to be able to believe it was true.

Perhaps he would not, in fact, have wished her to sacrifice her personal happiness for an intellectual ideal. But she felt a need to sacrifice, and to do him honour.

Enid would one day write that she needed to be understood in her dreams; and perhaps she created a dream of her father. She tended to idealize relationships when her deep emotions were involved. Dr Starkie had had the makings of an ideal father, but he had not achieved the ideal. Only in the last years of his life had he emerged a little from his remoteness, and then he and his daughter had talked together: talked of their literary interests and of his ambitions for her. 'Madame Roland was 5 ft high—Enid's height, whom she much resembled in character: force, insight, learning— but she was not so cynical.' So he had written in his diary, and he had added: 'I fancy Enid has a better head.' He had recognized his daughter's abilities, he had appreciated her lively mind; but one suspects that he had not seen the vulnerable nature that lay beneath them. He had been vexed by her persistent, angry independence; he had not recognized that she was an unhappy adolescent. Gide had encouraged her to assert her individual nature ('what I wanted most passionately', she wrote, 'was to be allowed to be myself, to be free'); but in fact she depended on her father, needed to depend much more on his understanding, and he had not recognized her need. This personal failure was the saddest failure in Enid's youth.

'I left it until it was too late to tell my father what he meant to me.' So she told a friend in middle age; and in *A Lady's Child* she regrets that she did not know him better. But the most striking quality in his diary is the lack of warmth, the responsiveness which Enid largely possessed. They were qualities which she usually sought in other people. Perhaps he had these qualities, but he could not express them in writing. Perhaps she admired him for his intellectual distinction, and endowed this withdrawn and little-known man with the qualities she needed. Probably, after his death, she created an image in her mind, and came to love her creation more than the reality. As Sir Maurice Bowra said, she longed for some altar on which she might sacrifice her love.[6]

As it was, she felt a lasting need for emotional security. She wanted a dominant figure to replace the father she had lost; she also wanted the maternal warmth which she had not known as a child. The death of her father led her to seek the reassurance of some older friend; it led her, more than ever, to seek the gentleness of another woman.

She found immediate protection in the friendship of Sibyl Eastwood: a doctor whose career had taught her understanding and compassion. Sibyl Eastwood—whom she had met at Oxford—was considerably older than herself; and her married status and her age allowed her to show maternal sympathy and, at times, maternal asperity. She was to be a confidante, a medical adviser, a friend who would help to furnish a flat or invite herself on holiday, an essential, reliable, undemanding background figure to whom Enid would turn for years, and not in vain. Sibyl Eastwood was to show her constant devotion, and to earn the dedication of *A Lady's Child*: 'For S., who only knew the end of the Lady's Child, but who sped her on her way with so much sympathy and kindness.'

Child, child, I am so sorry [she wrote when Dr Starkie died].
Some people's fathers mean so little to them. But you loved yours, I know. You must be feeling as if you had come to the very end of the world, and were looking over the edge into a terrible sort of blankness. And with all the personal loss it must mean such a break-up of home

things too. Enid dear, it seems a trivial thing to say in the face of death, perhaps? But I *am* glad you got your 'first'. You only wanted it to please him, and it symbolised for him that you were doing the kind of things he valued in the best kind of way.[7]

Even before her father's death, Enid had taken a post as assistant mistress at Lingholt School, Hindhead. Since he had died, the financial situation of the family had worsened. He had had no private means, and there was no widow's pension attached to his office. All he had left was a life insurance premium.[8] Enid was determined not to be dependent on her family. She had also undertaken to provide for her youngest sister, Nancy. She had done so out of love for the child, and love for her father; but it was hard to reconcile her academic hopes with her immediate future in a school. She felt that her personal life was ended, and her future bleak.

Enid, dear [Sybil Eastwood wrote, from Scotland], it is good of you to let me in, to let me feel that I'm of any use to you, . . . if only to be someone to whom you can say the things you can't say out loud. . .

And although it makes holes in my heart to realise that you are suffering, . . . I am cheered by the fact that I believe in you. You have really great gifts, not of the brain only, but gifts of character, the spirit. You aren't going to go down. Your courage and tenacity are going to move things . . .

It's a very important part of life to know your own limitations—as well as your own powers. There are some achievements, good and bad, that lie beyond the capacity. Now it is absolutely outside you to become the average humdrum narrow-minded schoolmarm. The bricks aren't in you to fashion it . . .

As for your personal life being ended, it may or may not be. Probably one's real life doesn't begin until one believes the personal life ended . . .

I'll come down and see you as soon as I get south, the first week in October, and I shall always be in London then . . . Don't bother to apologise for what you say about religion. Mine, such as it is, grew out of opinions not unlike yours.[9]

Enid was suffering, now, not only from her father's death, but from her inability to accept Catholicism. Intellectually she rejected it, but emotionally she continued to need it. She felt uncertain, too, about her powers.

Yes, I do believe in you [Dr Eastwood reassured her], and that for reasons I don't mean precisely to define. To do so would be to define in words every nuance of intuitive impression you have made upon me . . .

There is no one quality perhaps that makes more for achievement in life than that of seeing to the heart of things, or (to put it another way) of preferring truth to avoidance of pain . . . [That quality] issues very variously—as intellectual honesty in philosophers and scientists, as an instrument of creative power in great artists. It's the chief weapon of all real criticism. It is essential to genuine understanding of other people. And it's rare. O my God, how rare it is! Having it, you have perhaps hardly realised the rarity.[10]

Late in September, Enid arrived at Lingholt School. Gwendolen Mawdsley, one of her pupils, remembers her as 'a little person with bobbed dark hair'.

Her father had just died and out of doors she was always in a black beret and a black tweedy coat which I thought looked coarse and cheap . . .

It was a small private school, only 36 girls. Few took public exams as few were likely to aim at a profession . . .

I remember clearly Miss Starkie's voice and her Irish accent and her enthusiasm for her subject. No public exams were in mind so she was free to teach us in any way she liked . . . The maths mistress in the same way did as she pleased. She would sometimes tell us to put away our books and listen for a change to a discourse on anthropology. . . . In short the school aimed at a general alertness.[11]

Enid was not impressed by the general alertness. She unburdened herself to her confidante yet again.

We'll have a real talk when I get south [came the answer, from Scotland]. Something must be done, not in too desperate a hurry, but done it's d——d well got to be. I utterly refuse to have you teaching arithmetic to some idiot children on a moor, in a houseful of terrified white rabbits with a cat at their head. It's nonsense. If you'll allow me to help, . . . we'll try to work out a scheme by which you can earn a share of your sister's education and also give your own soul a suitable environment to expand in. So don't despair, down there in the cold, with your absurd spinsters . . .[12]

But Enid's depressions were Celtic, and she would always find it difficult to conquer them alone. At times she floundered in self-pity, and did not even try to control it. She sent her laments to Sibyl Eastwood, and to many other friends from Oxford; and, early in the new year, her former German tutor, Miss Beard, now headmistress of Putney High School, sent her an astringent reprimand: 'Dear Enid: I hear of your complaints from half the dons at Somerville when I go there, and from any of your friends whom I know. For your father's sake and your own sake, you've *got* to pull yourself together . . . And don't be always thinking about yourself.'[13]

PART THREE

⬧⬧⬧⬧⬧

Sorbonne Student

1921–1924

Some time later in the year, 1921, Enid gave up teaching at
Lingholt to return to academic life. She had been awarded a
Gilchrist Studentship, and she decided to work for a doctorate at
the Sorbonne. In the final pages of *A Lady's Child* she described
how she had broken with her family and set off, alone, from
Dublin for Paris. It was the first time she had gone abroad.
When she had paid for a third-class ticket to Paris via Newhaven
and Dieppe—the cheapest route—she had, she said, £10 in her
pocket.

I arrived in Paris on a late evening in November [she recalled in
1959]. As I came out of the Gare Saint-Lazare, I met, for the first time,
that curious smell—not wholly sweet—which I later grew to recognize
as characteristic of Paris, and which always arouses in me acute nostalgia. It was raining, and I felt very young, frightened and lost . . .
  I had one address in Paris, that of the former French governess of
some cousins of mine, and I hoped that I would be able to live with her,
for a time at all events, until I had found my feet . . .
  I took a taxi, it was extravagant in my financial state, but I did not
know where anything was. I drove to Mlle Savi's apartment, in the rue
Bargue, a mean street near the Abattoirs de Vaugirard.
  I was shocked when I caught sight of Mlle Savi. In Dublin she had
been elegantly dressed in creations of the latest fashion. But now she
was drearily clad in black, and looked like the *patronne* of a poor restau-
rant. She had obviously ceased to care about her appearance. She lived
with her old mother, whom she called Maman, in an over-crowded and
stuffy flat. In the sitting-room there was what the French call a 'cosy',
a curious arrangement of divan, whatnot, bookcase and cupboard. The
place seemed to be full of *pensionnaires*, and I understood immediately,
with a sinking heart, that there was no place there for me, that every
bed in the apartment had to bring in its quota of fees.
  I slept that night in—or should it be on?—the cosy, and next morning

I had my first experience of café-au-lait in a bowl, with dry *pain de ménage* which I was expected to dip into it.

My first task was to find somewhere to live, and [something] to do, as my £10 was already broken into and would not last long.

I had never booked a room anywhere in my life, and had no idea of what to look for—I only knew that it had to be cheap . . .

I tried various cheap, low and dirty hotels, often bug-ridden . . . I stayed in one called Ideal Hotel, an expression of Anglophilia, but it was far from ideal, being of very doubtful cleanliness and morality. I remember the horrified expression on the face of an old professor when I told him, later, I had lived there.[1]

It was a time of inflation, when many lived in oppressive poverty. Every foreign worker seemed a potential rival to a Frenchman, and, for a foreign student, life was hard.

Students were not organized then as they are now [Enid remembered in 1959], and there were no *bourses* or subsidised meals. Paris was overflowing with refugees from Russia and Eastern Europe. The middle twenties was the period of the middle-class influx from Russia, which followed the aristocratic exodus. These first refugees had had jewels to sell, but the middle-class possessed nothing but the clothes they arrived in, and often they had endured great hardships to get to France. I remember one of my closest friends, Natasha Stretovitch, the daughter of a mere officer, had escaped from Russia, through the Crimea, had worked as a boy in a Turkish factory, and had finally reached Paris.

I lived entirely with Russians and Serbs, for they were the only students who had as low a standard of living as I had. No English or American girls were as poor or as unprotected as I was. As for French middle-class girls, they just did not go to the University, except from the protection of their own homes.[2]

She later said that she had lived more humbly than George Orwell in *Down and Out in London and Paris*. 'Orwell wasn't as poor as I was. I was glad I was poor. Poverty helps one to see another layer of life.'[3]

Dorothy Wadham, her Somerville friend, met her in Paris during her stay. Enid, she writes, was 'very hard up, but I don't think many of the students were otherwise. But being hard up was not enough. It was dramatized into being "starving" both then and later, but if you ask me what I think was the key to Enid's often fruitless search for satisfaction, I would say it was this need for *drama*.'4 Enid kept not only her Irish need for drama, but her unremitting need of sympathy and attention. Her memories of Paris may have been coloured as a consequence.

And here some persistent facts assert themselves. She might have earned her living in England. She had won a First at Oxford; she did not need a Paris doctorate to qualify for an academic career. In 1921, as a Gilchrist Student of Somerville, she doubtless had some financial allowance; perhaps she need not have gone to Paris with only £10. It was almost as if—and here one recalls her old religious fervour—it was almost as if she wanted to show the completeness of her sacrifice to her father. She seemed almost to choose humiliation as an offering. She seemed deliberately to seek the most exacting life, as if she were attempting to prove herself. One feels, too, that she longed to destroy the Lady's Child that she had been. She wanted to smash the shackles of her past, to be (as Gide had sanctioned) her individual self. She wrote, in her Paris notes, that she had 'run away from old standards'. Perhaps the Jansenist and the fanatic in Enid demanded self-abnegation.

Whatever the complex reasons for her life in Paris, there is no doubt that she knew poverty. She went to Paris only four years after the Russian Revolution; White Russian exiles fought for work, drifting from attic to attic, living in a Bohemian world as hard as anything in Murger's day. She was thrown among them, and she felt strangely at home. The Russians, like the Irish, had 'that feeling of the depth of things, unexpressed often, only suggested. It was as if I was meeting something I had always known.'5 The riff-raff of Western Europe, they lived from day to day, without security. They lived in a communist spirit, but they lived with generosity, knowing the value of all that they gave. Enid was often hungry, she had no possessions, and yet she was happy But she was alarmed by the drinking among the refugees. 'I was afraid of all the drink. Afraid of my own weakness. That it would make me fail.' And again: 'I was a bit of a prig then. I was so afraid of being overcome by my weaker nature. I was very hard on myself. I never went to entertainments, spent no money on drinks.'

She was twenty-four when she went to Paris, but she remained almost an adolescent, she was innocent and timorous. She was still the sheltered Dublin child. They laughed at her, but she was not yet ready for love. 'Show her fear of getting engulfed in love', she wrote in the notes for her Paris novel.

No time for it yet.
An instinctive knowledge of my own weakness.
Would be taken up by pity. A woman's pity.
But I must use my talents first, not be engulfed yet . . .
The defeat of the Serbian girl. The defeat of Alexei. The smell of defeat and failure . . .
I saw so much failure and defeat.

Among the defeated was Boris, the consumptive artist who painted her portrait.

Have the living in the attic.
The artist dying. Far from Russia. The goddesses he sees in the sky. He looked like a weak Christ himself.
I wanted you to love me. It is all I ever wanted.
Suddenly she realised.
But I did love you, do love you, she said . . .
There was so much compassion.
The *raté*, the typical Paris figure, the *raté* more than anything else.

'His death in her arms', she wrote, elsewhere. 'His love for her, for art, bad art. The sun shining in through the attic window as he dies.' And again: 'The dying of Boris, his courage. The few at last moment . . . The beauty of the day when Boris died. The sun over roofs. Could she only have given it all to him . . . The picture, so much love went into it.' The picture remains: no work of art, but an impression of Enid, dressed in charity clothes, gazing through the spectator with penetrating blue eyes.

She was always followed by the memory of those years. They made her permanently austere, and she carried her austerity beyond the normal limit. 'I live very frugally [this to a friend in 1949] . . .

Except for public occasions, I live as poorly as I did when I was a penniless student in Paris. I have no expensive tastes and only smoke two cigarettes a day and don't drink except when I have friends. When I go to Paris I go back to my student life.'[6] The thought of her student poverty, the poverty of her friends in Paris, remained with her. 'Put in about Russian dancer. His starving all the week, his big meal on Saturdays. The beauty of his movements. His weakness when he came off the stage.' His portrait hung in her study in St Giles', in her library in Walton Street.

In the notes which she left on her years in Paris, Enid wrote simply: 'Night porter in hotel.' Perhaps this was the *hôtel de passe* which she mentioned elsewhere; and no doubt she was recalling her experience as a night porter when she described sleeping under the stairs (Sibyl Eastwood referred to her sleeping in a cupboard). The hotel was in one of the poorer quarters. Inside, there were reddish stains on the walls where bugs had been crushed. The passages were so dark that one could not read the numbers on the doors.

> Under the stairs is where the maid slept.
> Under the stairs the bells. The *poire automatique* for door.
> Often she didn't wake.
> Banging on door. '*Nom de Dieu. Est-ce qu'on est mort?*'
> Feeling round for *poire*.
> The client came in, got his number.
> She tried to recognise voice or shadow on the glass door.
> Occasionally someone went out. '*Cordon, s'il vous plaît!*' Where is he going to one wondered . . .

If the notes for her novel are indeed a record of her life, Enid also worked as a cleaner; and once, in an office, she found a thousand-franc note. She resisted the temptation to keep it. She could only take these casual jobs, because there were so many refugees and students in search of work, and because she needed time to read at the Bibliothèque Nationale.

Her clothes came from Student Relief:

Ill-fitting clothes, far too big for me, for I was very small and thin . . .

I often suffered from real malnutrition, near starvation . . . Frequently I had no meal, except when I was invited out—I would certainly never have dreamt of buying myself a meal on the day when I was invited to one. I got into the habit of trying to space my invitations to cover as many days as possible.[7]

For a time, she lived in an attic in the rue Jacob. It was here, perhaps, eating a hunk of bread, that she suddenly caught sight of herself in the mirror, and saw the ravenous look on her face. She flung herself on the bed and wept in despair. 'I ate in soup-kitchens', she wrote, 'intended for the destitute—I was as destitute as anyone else—amongst tramps and vagabonds, next to *chômeurs*—the out-of-work. I washed up in restaurants, I was a *plongeuse*, for the sake of a meal.'[8]

An American couple engaged her as a baby-sitter while they went dancing; when they finally came back, she had missed the last métro, and had to walk home across the sleeping city. In time, in her unpublished novel, the heroine, Sheilah, also walked through Paris in the small hours of the morning.

The Boul' Mich' was almost deserted for it was long past midnight. There were couples of lovers on the seats beneath the trees of the quiet boulevard and in the sleeping darkness of the rue de Médicis. The long stream of market carts was slowly wending its way towards Les Halles, laden with its coloured burden of vegetables: red carrots freshly washed and tied in bundles; green cabbages looking painted and unreal in the artificial light; white cauliflowers like heaped-up snowballs. The drivers were seated up aloft fast asleep, letting their horses guide them . . .[9]

Sheilah and her confidante, a woman doctor, Maude, walked on down the Boul' Mich', and sat on a parapet by the Seine, talking until a vague pink light appeared behind Notre Dame. And here Enid's love of Paris irrupted into the story, lighting it up with sudden feeling. This was Paris as she saw it in her student days.

Her devotion to Paris also overflowed into the notes for an unwritten novel. She set down dozens of details, observed with sharp, compassionate eyes. She recorded the humble quarters of Paris, where mattresses and sheets were hung out of the window to air, and, in the early morning, women delved for rags in the *poubelles.* She noted the *boucheries chevalines* with the golden horse's head over the door, and the little laundries where the ironing was displayed in the windows. She recalled the antique shops, cluttered with their Rouen ware, their Quimper and Delft pottery, their snuff-boxes, crucifixes and glass. She remembered the liquefying Brie, and the red globes of Dutch cheeses in the dairies, the Chambertin and Chablis and Châteauneuf du Pape in the wine-shops. She noted the exotic colours of the flowers in the Jardin du Luxembourg, she recorded the provincial, romantic intimacy of the Place de Furstenberg, where she longed to live. Above all she recorded the simple people of Paris.

In 1943, she wrote lovingly:

Now that the desert of the war separates me from the Continent, I often think of my friends in France.

I think of Monsieur and Madame, the owners of the little bistro where I had my café au lait and my croissant at the counter in the morning, before I went to work. For some months I even had a room in the small hotel next to the café, on the sixth floor, with a superb view over the rooftops of Paris, a film panorama worthy of René Clair. This hotel should have been called *La Porte Étroite* because there was only one small door on each floor; I very much doubt, however, whether Monsieur or Madame had ever been assiduous readers of Gide. They were good people, simple and honest, Monsieur and Madame. Often, when they knew that I was penniless and was staying in because I could not buy food, they used to ask me to take pot luck with them— and they did so in such a tactful way. Madame made a bœuf bourguignon the like of which I had not tasted. There was always a bottle of wine on the table, and a petit verre with the coffee on special days. The table itself was in the little kitchen at the back of the café, and Jules, the washer-up, used to take his meals with us. Jules came from Marseilles and he had the gift for telling tall stories which is common to all Southerners. When he had a free moment, he asked me to 'come and have one' in one of the smartest cafés in the neighbourhood—Dupont's, for example—and I always accepted, his conversation was so entertaining. He was the local Don Juan or Casanova, and he told me about his love-affairs. If one was to believe what he said, they were of the most astonishing kind, like the ones in Balzac's *Contes Drôlatiques*. He always felt obliged to pay court a little to every young girl, whoever she might be, but I evaded . . . the suggestion. 'A pity! You're making a mistake!' he used to say, and he went on at once to another story.[10]

Enid's love for Paris owed something to literature and history, and something to her own romantic nature; it owed much more to emotional intimacy. In Paris she had led the life of the working-class; she had known the harshness of existence. She had also come to understand a life where conventions were unimportant. Nothing could have been further from upper-middle-class Dublin, or, indeed, from Somerville and Oxford. For the first time in her life she was completely independent. For the only time in her career, she felt that she belonged. She belonged not only to a place ('my own quarter, the Quartier Latin') but she belonged to society. 'I've never had difficulty in fitting into any life into which I was thrown', so she explained in her Paris notes. 'But, except in that time in Paris, I've always been a different "breed of animal", and they've always seen through my efforts.'[11]

Yet, even in Paris, Enid knew the problem which would always trouble her. She wanted to hide, to be self-contained, independent and unknown; and, at the same time, she longed, like a child, to be noticed. She had felt these conflicting needs since the days of Léonie Cora; she would feel them all her life, and, as she grew older, she would emphasize increasingly that she was 'a different breed', in order to be the centre of attention. Yet what people came to see was the actress, not the true personality. Enid helped to defeat her own deepest wish: her longing to be known and understood.

The Aloneness even in Paris. It was much later that I became sociable, developed an outside character.

Sadness, doubt. I could not bear to be observed, to be known, yet longing to be understood, understood by one person.

The later personality was a confession of failure.

I accepted the responsibilities, the burdens. But gave up the dreams.

There was perhaps a blunting. There was a hardening outside certainly.

Nothing would ever hurt so much again.[12]

~ 8 ~

Enid did not lack friends to smooth her plebeian life. Sarah Watson had come to France in the First World War with the American Y.W.C.A. After the Armistice she had stayed on in Paris, to become the first Directrice of the Foyer International des Étudiantes. She was to occupy the post for forty years, until her death. Enid was introduced to her by an American helper at a Y.W.C.A. canteen. For a time she lived at the Foyer; when she found cheaper rooms elsewhere, she continued to use its amenities.[1]

Sarah Watson was barely forty, but she mothered Enid, gave her comfort, reassurance and advice. She gave her books of free meal-tickets, and she sometimes took her to the Saturday rehearsals of the Concerts Colonne. At Christmas there were student parties at the Foyer, and carol-singing. Enid was still sadly immature, still seeking compensation for her past. She needed this maternal care, she needed the institution as a home.

Sarah Watson was not the only friend to encourage her. Albert Vaudremer had been a doctor at Cannes, and spent his holidays in Paris, working at the Institut Pasteur. During the First World War he had gone with an army hospital to Salonika. On board the ship that took him there he had met Hilda Lorimer, the classics tutor at Somerville: she was to do six months' service with the Scottish Women's Hospital. They became fast friends, and Miss Lorimer came to know the Vaudremer family. She asked them to look after Enid during her stay in Paris. At the Villa Montmorency, in the Avenue des Sycomores at Auteuil, Enid was received as a daughter.

Once a week—and often more—I used to dine at Auteuil with some friends who lived in a little house near the race-course . . . My place was always laid there, I had my napkin in a silver ring, and a glass which they had put at my disposal.

Papa was not only an eminent scholar, but an elegant and witty man of the world. For me he represented all the delicacy and wit of the French. He had the faculty which nearly every Frenchman possesses—especially the men of his generation who pride themselves on good manners—the faculty for giving every woman the illusion that she is beautiful and desirable. At that time I was poor and badly dressed, ill fed and disheartened; but Papa always made me feel that I could please . . .

I particularly remember Maman in her garden, watering her flowers or feeding her turkeys—or her pigeons, which fluttered round her shoulders. In her little garden at Auteuil she had a bit of everything, and gave herself the illusion that she was still a countrywoman. She had sown a small plot of wheat which gave her seed for her birds, and so she imagined that she was still very close to the earth.

When I finished my work, I always went straight to Auteuil, and I rested on a chaise-longue in the garden till dinner-time. I heard Maman singing old French tunes as she watered her plants, and Virginie, the maid, used to follow her, grumbling in an amicable way. I did not hear what she said, but it sounded like a droning accompaniment to the song. Virginie had seen the children born, and she allowed herself to talk to them freely. Nothing was done in the house until Virginie had been consulted. She even gave her opinion about marriages. With her rustic good sense, her complete devotion and her rough manners, she reminded me of the maids in Molière. She spoke to me brusquely, with the affection she showed the family, and she reprimanded me when—according to the custom of my own country—I went out alone at night, with friends from the Sorbonne. 'It isn't wise, my dear! Men are always men. You're innocent if you trust them!'

At last we used to hear the click of the garden gate, and Papa appeared with his briefcase under his arm. 'Ah!' he used to cry, when he saw me. '*Ma chère petite collègue!*' I burst with pride, although I was just a poor little student of literature.

Then we dined in the dining-room, where the windows were wide open on to the garden. The intoxicating smell of syringa floated towards us on the evening breeze.

What *soles au vin blanc*, what velvet *bisques*, I ate in that house! How many *chateaubriands pommes pailles*, how many *bombes glacées*! And on our great days there was a bottle of wine, with a seal, and we drank it out of small glasses, beside the big ones which were put out for the *vin ordinaire* . . .

At table, they used to talk brilliantly about everything, science, literature, politics and art, and the conversation used to continue in the garden over the coffee and the liqueurs. Then I took the last métro home, but I never left empty-handed; I always took a small parcel, a turkey egg, a pâté—the speciality of the house—or a pot of jam.[2]

Against this background Enid worked for her doctorate. Soon after her arrival in Paris, she had signed on at the Sorbonne. It was intended that she should be a pupil of Abel Lefranc, professor at the Collège de France, but he proved to be unsympathetic. If Lefranc seemed conceited, Victor Basch, the Professor of Æsthetics, deterred her by his ruthless sarcasm, and she knew she could never work for him. Then she went to Gustave Reynier, Professor of Poetry at the Sorbonne. He suggested a subject for a thesis, but she felt it was insignificant. Finally she thought of writing a thesis on Verhaeren. 'That was a really big subject, it would take me in many wide fields. I'd learn something . . . I was so ignorant. I had had little schooling and at Oxford I hadn't really worked. My First had been undeserved . . . I began with a good heart on Verhaeren.'[3]

It was a demanding enterprise. Émile Verhaeren was the most significant Belgian poet associated with the Symbolist Movement. He had died as recently as 1916; his widow lived at Saint-Cloud, and there were still many people who had known him. He was near enough in time to be a subject for debate; he was far enough away for posterity to assess his achievement.

Enid attended Paul Hazard's fashionable lectures in the Amphithéâtre Richelieu at the Sorbonne; she observed the extreme simplicity, the honesty of the medievalist Joseph Bédier.

I think that Bédier would have been a novelist if he hadn't preferred scholarly research to the creation of character . . . I remember his telling me that all his great discoveries were sudden flashes of intuition and that then he proceeded laboriously to build up the proofs of his inspiration. But I believe that his intuition was as sure as it was because he had so much knowledge, . . . knowledge which he kept in a state of movement . . . Some scholars want their facts to create something from them.[4]

Enid admired Bédier. She recorded her gratitude to Edmond Estève; his encouragement alone had enabled her to finish her thesis. But the professor who earned her affection was Fortunat Strowski. He had specialized in Saint François de Sales and Pascal, he had written on La Fontaine, and he was editing the essays of Montaigne.

He lived in an old apartment in a little street in the sixth arrondissement, without any modern comforts. Hall, dining-room and study: the books encroached upon them all, accumulated on everything, like the sands of the desert swallowing up a city in ancient times. His study was lined with books up to the ceiling, and on the floor the brochures and the typescripts of theses advanced towards the table where he worked, like the tide rising up a rock which will be submerged. One room in the apartment remained free of books: this was Madame's drawing-room, furnished in the Louis Quinze-Second Empire style. Armchairs, upholstered in red satin with broad black stripes, stood like thrones in this austere sanctuary, and here, on the first Friday of every month, her 'day', Madame received the wives and daughters of her husband's colleagues.

The professor himself used to receive his pupils on Sunday mornings. Madame would open the door to us, in her dressing-gown. Her hair was still starred with curlers, and they framed her forehead like the vipers framed the head of the Medusa. Monsieur was in his study, in his dressing-gown and slippers, taking his morning café au lait and buttered *pistolets* . . .

We cleared the chairs of books and settled down, as comfortably as possible, where we could. We talked about our work, and asked advice. Monsieur went on eating his breakfast, undeterred. Then he read us poetry or recited passages from modern plays. Like nearly all the Frenchmen I have known, he thought he had a vocation for the theatre, and he never missed a dress rehearsal. Then, if he was in form, he would offer us a glass of Dubonnet or Byrrh. At last Madame, made-up and elegant, curly-haired like a poodle, opened the door. 'My dear,' she would say, 'if you want your bath before *déjeuner*, have it now. And hurry up! It's nearly twelve o'clock.'

We slipped out quickly, and on the stairs we used to pass the little *pâtissier* bringing the Sunday pudding—a fruit tart or a large *baba au rhum*.[5]

On the Left Bank there were still reminders of the late nineteenth century. Enid met René Ghil, who had been a friend of Verlaine and Mallarmé. He invited her to the rue Lauriston, introduced her to André Breton, and to a woman who proudly displayed a book bound in negro skin. Enid also came to know Léo Larguier, the author of *Saint-Germain-des-Prés, mon Village*. A romantic figure, with flowing hair and a broad-brimmed hat, he was always at Les Deux Magots, and he rarely left the Latin Quarter. He had a fifth-floor apartment in the rue Saint-Benoît, cluttered with knick-knacks.[6] He might have been invented by Anatole France.

Enid left a number of vignettes of Parisian figures.

I saw Raoul Ponchon on the quais. Between 70–80. The last of the Bohemians. Red cheeks, black *lavallière*. Short black pipe. His pockets filled with books. . . . De Billy, the friend of Proust. The lovely things in his house. Dinners there. The cooking. The manservant. The marvellous food. Afterwards priceless treasures. His contempt for Claudel. The taxi. Counting out pennies. Yet spent thousands on books. Ferdinand Hérold with his dark beard like a Sultan or a patriarch. Vielé-Griffin at his desk like an American senator. None of the Symbolist poet left, white-haired, red-faced, solid and square. Mme Verhaeren. House in St Cloud like a Belgian provincial house.[7]

Mme Verhaeren lived in the rue Émile Verhaeren. She was old and paralysed. She showed Enid much kindness.[8]

Her only object now in life is to keep her husband's memory green [so Enid wrote in 1926, on the tenth anniversary of Verhaeren's death] . . . She lives in the same little house at Saint-Cloud, on the fringe of the woods, where Verhaeren always spent the winter months. The poet's study is just as it was, . . . on the writing table are still the same papers and letters, now yellow with the passing of the years.

If it had not been for his wife, it is very doubtful whether Verhaeren would ever have written his greatest poems . . . And it is no small thing to have kept twenty-four years, one's husband's love as passionate and as deep as in the early days . . .

Verhaeren had been a fervent Catholic in his youth, and even when, intellectually, belief had left him, the depths of his nature remained impregnated with Catholic mysticism. One may become naturalized in another country, but one does not shed one's racial characteristics. Verhaeren's reason refused to believe, but in his heart there remained this craving for religious faith . . .[9]

Religion was a subject which Enid frequently discussed with Charles du Bos. Of all the people whom she met during her Paris years, he had, perhaps, the most lasting significance for her. He had been born in Paris in 1882, and he was partly of American ancestry. A man of letters and a critic, he also exercised his influence through his friendships. They had their effect on literary history. In 1927 he was converted to Catholicism. Enid found peace of mind when she talked to him, the peace of belief. He was fifteen years older than she was, and his delicate face reminded her of her father's. His conversation seemed to ennoble even the commonplace. He bore his chronic ill-health with courage, and kept a sharp sense of humour. When he was melancholy she was carried away with emotion. 'I walked in the golden woods at Versailles with Ch. du Bos. He talked of things so movingly.' They used to talk together about Gide.

She also met Mauriac. 'His hoarse voice. The acuteness of his mind . . . A tortured soul. Maurois. Suave, good-mannered, brilliant. Yet even then I felt a weakness . . . Shakespeare and Company, looking in . . . Only much later met Sylvia Beech and Adrienne. Very intelligent, Adrienne.'[10] Enid 'saw Hemingway and Joyce and co. every day in the cafés. I never spoke to them, but I think Joyce would have like to meet me—an Irish girl, from Dublin, and a lapsed Catholic. I was living among East Europeans most of the time. Not many girls would have done what I did.'[11]

The statement was true. But Enid's life in Paris was happy as well as hard. She noted: 'Parties in Meudon forest. The gaiety of youth. All the berets. The singing. Walking back in dark.' On May evenings she used to walk back with great bunches of lilies-of-the-valley, which she had picked in the forest. In later life she never saw the flowers without remembering her student days. And again, she wrote: 'The queuing up for theatres and concerts. The cheap students' tickets.' It was one of the richest periods in

French theatrical history, and, from her seat in the gods, she
watched Jouvet and Valentine Tessier, Copeau, Dullin, Lugné
Poë, and the Pitoeffs.[12]

Her love of music remained unabated. Her friend Alice Storms
recorded how,

> one evening, in the heart of the Latin Quarter, there arose some
> music pregnant with unshed tears and with unsung joys . . . Chopin,
> Debussy, Bach and Beethoven followed one another, bearing with them
> the overflow of the soul of the unseen pianist . . .
> The fear of breaking the spell bound me to my window, in spite of
> a kind of uneasiness—for I had a distinct impression that I was overhear-
> ing confidences . . . And so I was almost relieved when suddenly a
> noisy throng burst into the music room, and drove out the mystery
> with a flood of light and laughter . . .
> Next day I learned that the nocturnal pianist was Enid Starkie.[13]

In 1923 Enid fell ill through malnutrition. Student Relief arranged
to send her to a sanatorium in Haute Savoie. 'I thought I was dying,
wasting away through consumption, and I thought it romantic to
die so young—I felt like Marie Bashkirtseff, Mimi from *La
Bohème*, and la Dame aux Camélias . . .'[14] So she said, later. But,
at the time, she lost her determined self-sufficiency. She felt that
she could not endure the attrition of hardship any longer. In
desperation, she decided to give up her rigorous life, and to accept
conventional existence. Characteristically, she went from one
extreme to the other. She could hardly have made a more conventional choice. She applied—a Lady's Child—for the post of
French mistress at Roedean.

> I was called for an interview. I was ill and shabby and my only pair
> of shoes needed repairing. The school did not send me the money for
> my fare and I had to borrow it. I didn't borrow enough. I arrived at
> Newhaven with no money left. I took a taxi and expected someone to
> pay it when I arrived at the school. Perhaps my standards had deterior-
> ated but I did that quite naturally, as that is what any of us in Paris, in
> my circle, would have done. It is only nowadays that I realize the

monstrosity of my behaviour . . . I felt very poor and weak, and far from *courageuse* beside those huge, well-fed girls in jibbahs. I didn't get the job. I was told that I looked too delicate—but that was only the sugar-coating of the pill! The Senior Mistress took me aside before I left—I know she was intending to be kind—and told me never again to go in for a job, with such lack of organization. I returned to Paris in a great state of gloom and depression, with a bitter feeling of failure, that I had not even been able to get a post as French mistress in a girls' school . . .

However, shortly after I got back to Paris, I was asked by an American agency, for which I worked sometimes, to teach some American children while their mother was in Paris obtaining a divorce . . .

She was, if not exactly a millionaire, a near millionaire, and certainly the richest person I have ever known. She came from New York with a chauffeur, a lady's maid, a secretary, three children of 10, 8 and 5, and their nursery governess. She took a whole floor in a rich hotel, near the Étoile, where one could not take odd rooms, or go in for odd meals, the Hôtel Beauséjour. The children had, besides, a French girl who came to speak French to them in the afternoons and take them round Paris. I was appointed 'to instil culture into them'—as the mother said—but which really meant giving them ordinary lessons. I was the only one who really worked.

Everything for them came from the United States, in large cases—all their lesson books, their paper and pencils.

The children had their own sitting-room, in which we did the lessons —but the chauffeur and the maids also had theirs, and the mother.

We had lessons from 9 o'clock until 1 o'clock with a break at 11 o'clock of a quarter of an hour when I had to take them to the Bois de Boulogne. I dreaded that, as there were so many crossings. The policeman on duty got to know me and my cavalcade. There were two other children, from another family, that a nurse tacked on to mine, and I had to take charge of five extremely naughty, undisciplined and spoilt American children, with mechanical scooters, on which they could do a good pace, all in different directions . . .

As we set off each child was given 'a piece of fruit'—a most expensive apple, with a design stencilled on it, I remember, it had been allowed to ripen in this way; or an enormous orange, or peach. But there was no 'piece of fruit' for the person who was 'instilling culture' into them!

The boys of 8 and 5 were rather sweet, though very wild and naughty, but the girl, Laura-Elizabeth, was one of the most abominable children I've ever known. She had 75 dresses of which she was very proud and she was nasty in always pointing out the deficiencies in my wardrobe.

She was very worldly-wise for her ten years, and knew to a franc the price, or value, of most of the jewels she saw on the women in the Bois. She said to me once about a pearl necklace: 'That necklace isn't real. But it doesn't matter if a necklace isn't real pearls, if the clasp is real!' And the joke is that, of course, she was right . . .

The mother was a foolish, frivolous but smart woman, who spent most of her time at dressmakers', or at night-clubs, from which she often returned in the mornings when I was teaching the children. She was often not at all sober. Laura-Elizabeth knew this perfectly well, and used deliberately to ask me questions about what I thought had happened to her. The mother always created a disturbance, interfering with the lessons and asking the children wrong questions, and trying to find out whether I was earning the handsome salary she was giving me. I used to read fairy stories to the boy of five, and he loved them and used to repeat them very well. He used to sit in my lap while I read them, while the others were doing something else at the table. She said she didn't pay me to read fairy stories.

After only a few months, alas, she obtained her divorce, and took her caravanserai back to the United States, and I returned to my life of poverty.[15]

Enid lived in various rooms and *logements*, in working-class tenements, all over the Latin Quarter; but, as the rooms were unheated, she worked in libraries, as long as they were open, and even in the Métro, 'as one could go round and round all day with the one ticket. I also got to know the stations where the light was best, where one was least interrupted, and where one could find a corner of peace.'[16]

By March 1924 she was living at 1, rue de Passy, in the sixteenth arrondissement, and she had returned to Verhaeren. She had gone to Paris to discover learning, and, perhaps, to discover herself. She still dreamed of a career as a concert pianist. Now, suddenly, her life took another turning. It was no longer enough for her to be independent of her family. On her father's death she had undertaken to provide for her youngest sister. Now she was reminded of her responsibility. She must continue to work on her thesis. She must also begin to earn her living, for she had bad news from home.

PART FOUR

Assistant Lecturer, Exeter

1925–1928

Enid's family, as she once observed, were like an amalgam of sweets in a schoolboy's pocket. They were closely stuck together, and distinctly individual. When Dr Starkie died, his children were already beginning to go their different ways. Walter had embarked on his academic, musical, Bohemian career; Enid had chosen her academic life. And since their work would usually keep them out of Ireland, they would see little of their mother, or of Chou-Chou, who married a senior officer in the *garda*, the Irish police. Muriel was to become the wife of an English army officer. Nancy was in time to marry, and then to join the Women's Royal Air Force, a career which often kept her abroad. But Nancy was a child of eleven when Enid went to Paris; in 1924 she was a schoolgirl, and Enid needed to help with her education, and to give financial assistance to her mother.

Once again she took a post in an English boarding school. In January 1925 she joined the staff at Langford Grove, near Maldon, in Essex. The school had been started two years earlier by Elizabeth Curtis, a former housemistress at a girls' school in Norfolk. Langford Grove, recalls one of the staff, 'was a very fine Georgian house, alas now demolished . . . It was really rather an unusual school for about 60 boarders, run with quite advanced aims in education, certainly not concentrating on examinations, though results were quite good.'[1] This was not surprising, for Gwen Raverat taught art, and history was the province of Norma Lewis, one day to be Mrs Russell and Librarian at Somerville.

Langford Grove was a soothing change from Paris, and Enid was happy. But she clearly lacked scope in a school. She left at the end of the summer term. That autumn she became assistant lecturer at the University College of the South-West, at Exeter.

At Exeter she found herself in an institution still fighting for university status. In 1925 Walter Moberley became Principal, but within fifteen months he was called to Manchester, and in October 1926 the long, distinguished reign of John Murray began.[2] But to Enid, who had known Somerville and the Sorbonne, Exeter was intellectually arid. Her junior assistant, M. Tallard, writes:

> The staff of the French department consisted of Professor W. Schopp, German-born, who took French Philology, Enid Starkie, Mabel Wilson and myself, the three of us teaching both the language and the literature.
>
> Enid specialized in nineteenth-century prose and poetry, she was then writing her thesis . . . She was brilliant and certainly the most intellectually gifted of all of us. She was a first-class pianist and I am grateful to her for having introduced me to the music of my compatriot Debussy.
>
> She was physically very attractive with fascinating but somewhat uncanny blue eyes.
>
> But although two members of the university college staff—much older than she was—were extremely fond of her and took her out quite a lot, she was not popular with most students or staff. When I say that her blue eyes had an uncanny quality, it is for lack of a better word. There was something cold, opaque, ironical in her eyes, a sort of barrier that one could not get across.
>
> And although the word 'sneer' would be an overstatement, I think her superior intellect and the way she looked at men and women from the high peaks of her intelligence had a deterrent effect on many that approached her.[3]

Enid taught honours French, pass German and elementary Italian. The professor of French was, she wrote,

> a slave-driver, who liked to get the department up early, and lectures for us started at eight o'clock; one of his illusions was that the department was one jolly family and he expected his assistants to come and have cold supper with him and his wife on Sundays and to help in the garden or at the washing-up. I never was much good in a garden.[4]

Photographs show Enid in her moments of leisure: sitting on a Devon beach, or in an exceedingly primitive aeroplane, or posing happily with a tennis party. The photographs were no doubt taken in her early days at Exeter; for she often wrote to Dorothy Wadham, and sent her instalments of a novel in which she was using her own life as the main theme. Dorothy Wadham found it 'full of self-pity and quite incredibly badly written', and discouraged her from sending it to a publisher.[5] It was the story of her unhappy love-affair at Exeter, and it was eventually called *All Remedies Refusing*.

Throughout her time in Paris, Enid had been afraid of love, determined not to let it deflect her from her career. 'I wanted to keep myself innocent. I wasn't ready yet . . . There were too many things yet to do, to find out.' Her academic ambitions were strong; the dominant thought of her father remained. Her Catholic upbringing still had its influence. But she was also afraid of her passionate nature. 'Life to me was like a tight-rope walk', she wrote in her Paris notes. 'I tried to control life and to control myself . . .' And again: 'Armand said to me: "Nothing matters to the artist except the cultivation of his gift. Keep yourself free until you know what that is to be." But I've never been able to protect myself except by flight.'[6]

It was, it seems, at Exeter that she lost her idealism. The experience was so disturbing that, some twenty years later, she would still remember it in detail. It was so important to her that perhaps it should be told. It appears to have changed her attitude to love and to the significance of sexual relationships.

In my first love-affair [so she wrote to Rosamond Lehmann, in about 1945], it was not the man I loved who had me but another who made me feel that I had given him such a hope and had incurred an obligation towards him . . . The man I loved—and who loved me too in his own weak and tortuous way—left me late that night by the river where we used to meet. Never in all my life, before or since, have I felt such anguish and despair as I felt that night. I can never feel it again in the same way. I felt I could not go home alone carrying this with me. And the impulse towards suicide which I had felt once before as a child came back to me again. The same pattern, to throw myself down from a height. I got onto the parapet of the bridge to throw myself into the swirling waters of the weir. I knew that nothing could save me if I fell in there. Then I thought of him and felt I could not do it. I thought of how the hue and cry would be raised for me next day when I would be missed. He was a married man, no-one knew of our relationship and he was always timid and frightened of what others would think and do. When people were looking for me what would he do? Would he come forward and say he was the last person to see me? If he did not come forward with news of me and tell them to drag the river, then I knew he would have remorse and guilt for the rest of his life. I knew he could never stand all the questioning, that he could never bear all that weight of guilt. I felt that I could not do that to him. There was no-one near, I thought no-one would come at that hour and I lay on a seat and got relief in wild and hysterical weeping. Then a man I knew came along over the bridge. Any woman always interested him and he came over to the seat where I lay. He was a friend of mine, a good ten years older than I, and he had always been very good to me, especially when I'd been unhappy as I'd been so often during this affair. He took me in his arms and comforted me and I accepted his comfort. I was distraught and wanted only someone to protect me against fear. He was a man of the world, a sensualist—a good-hearted sensualist—and he had wanted me as a lover for a long time, had tried everything to get me. But I was in love with someone else and didn't want him. I did not know what he was saying to me this night, I didn't listen, I only knew that I was glad to have someone with me and not to be alone with anguish and fear. But he thought I was yielding at last, that he had at last persuaded me and suddenly I realized what he expected. I tried to explain to him but he was thinking then of one thing only. 'You can't leave me now,' he said, 'it isn't fair! No-one should!' There was urgency in his voice and I thought it was pain. I was so ignorant and inexperienced that I imagined I might harm him physically by withdrawal then. I remembered what my French friends had said of English girls who led men on and then withdrew at the last moment. I thought I had incurred obligations towards him. I knew nothing at all. Nothing of that scene has faded from my mind though it is many years ago now. It is burnt into me . . . For I know how mistaken I was. For him it was merely an episode, one amongst many. I've never told this story to anyone before. I made a novel of it once because I could not bear to carry the weight of it any more. Maybe you will think it a small thing, but to me it was the most terrible thing in my life.[7]

Enid was to work on the novel, sporadically, for years. Some fifteen years after the event, she told another friend that it was

a true account of my first love-affair. It all happened when I was very young, when I first went to Exeter, and I've transposed the whole thing from an academic milieu to a musical one . . . I think that Sheilah's manner of giving way to Geoffrey explains a lot of her character . . . When that happened to me I thought it was a very terrible thing and I can still not think of it without pain.[8]

More than twenty years after the episode, she was still haunted by it. In June 1950, at the age of fifty-two, at the height of her career, she returned to Exeter to give a lecture. She retraced the setting of her novel, walked through the familiar streets and along by the canal and the river. And, so she told Alyse Gregory,

I felt all the poignancy again that I felt when I was young. These feelings never really fade. I stood under the same tree where I waited for him to come, a tree from which all approaches could be seen; I hid in the same old archways. It seemed to me that all the years were gone and I was again twenty-two as I was then [she had been at least twenty-eight], when I knew so little about life and suffered so much.[9]

◇ 10 ◇

It was, presumably, in her vacations from Exeter that Enid returned to Paris. Long afterwards she told Rosamond Lehmann:

That was one of the darkest periods of my life. The whole affair in England had seared me and had broken something in me. I was having difficulties with my work, with the Sorbonne professors, and thought I was never going to get my doctorate, never going to escape. It was then I toyed for a bit with the idea of marrying a working man whom I knew, to escape all complications, to be just a working wife. He was a good little fellow, but somehow I felt I could not do it, I thought also it wouldn't be fair on him, that he was too good to get a wasted intellectual.[1]

In Paris she had come to know a waiter at Le Vert Galant. ' "*Si*

79

on se mettait ensemble", he said to me.' This was perhaps the working man in question. Marriage to him—for a moment, at least—
seemed sensible. 'The advantages', she wrote. 'The problemless
life. It was sacrificing nothing . . . He was good like French
country bread. When I saw him last 1939 September. His chunky
figure in blue uniform . . .' By then he was married, with two
daughters. In the notes for Enid's Paris novel, he was called Pierre.
His real name, I think, was Jules Bernard. Enid later mentioned
Jules Bernard in conversation with me; and elsewhere in her notes
she wrote: 'I toyed with [the] idea of marriage to Jules because I
wanted scope and I thought that the marriage of the working
class was the only one left with real meaning for a woman.'[2] Such
a marriage would have made few social demands; it would have
left her free to be herself. But she finally rejected the prospect.

At this time [she told Rosamond Lehmann] I saw quite a bit of a man
I'd known earlier, a *raté* if ever there was one. Maybe it was that his
pessimism matched mine, maybe it was that he didn't leave me alone
and that I was too weak to resist him. What I do know is that inside I
had more courage and hope and determination than appeared outwardly, and that in spite of everything I was determined not to be
beaten. But he didn't see that and I suppose saw in me a *compagnon de
misère.* Anyway he wanted me and pursued me. He called me *la belle
dame sans merci,* with the accent on *sans merci* . . . And here again I
made one of my bad mistakes. I've always thought that this episode
would make a bitter story like one of Maupassant's . . . Weariness,
disgust and sadness came over me and I wondered whether anything
would ever give me a feeling of value and importance, so that I could
feel comfortable with myself and treat myself with care and respect . . .[3]

She later hinted that she had touched the depths, the *bas-fonds,*
of Paris life. Possibly she invented or exaggerated; possibly she
told the simple truth. Perhaps, already, she identified herself with
Baudelaire, in his tortuous search for morality; perhaps, even now,
she identified herself with Rimbaud, and believed in the system-
atic destruction of conventions. 'I suppose I have no real moral
standards', she was to write. 'I'd find it hard to give anyone a set of
moral standards.'[4]

Yet, after the episode with the *raté*, Enid came as near as she would ever come to conventional life.

It was after this [she told Rosamond Lehmann] that I fell in love with the man to whom I became engaged for a short time. He was preparing the examination of the Affaires Étrangères and I taught him English, or rather helped him to perfect his English for the oral part of the examination. But soon I didn't teach him very much. I thought his English so enchanting that I could not bear to correct him—in any case by that time I wasn't taking any fee from him. He would never talk anything but English and he used to make love in English so that often I could do nothing but laugh. 'Darrlang!' he used to say, and 'this little heart why beats it so fast?' He was one of the few people in my life who has made me feel valuable and precious, valuable and precious to someone else, so that I could just accept attention and care and not worry about what I need give . . . I loved him very deeply—or rather I was deeply in love with him.[5]

In the notes for her Paris novel, Enid recalled Roger. He was rich and elegant, he belonged to *la jeunesse dorée*, he had Italianate beauty, and 'a certain poetry of love in him'. He took her from her library, from her menial tasks, into a romantic world. 'It never occurred to me to think about marriage', she explained, again to Rosamond Lehmann. The statement seems a little surprising.

Then he got through his examinations and was to be sent to Cairo. He wanted to marry me so that I could go to Cairo with him. I allowed myself to be persuaded at last. Then I went to see his family with him and I knew that it wouldn't be possible. I think that I'd have made a bad wife for a diplomat—especially a foreign diplomat. His family would have done everything to break the marriage. He was the only son, adored by both parents. They would have cut off allowances to bring him to his senses. They could not have borne the idea of their son marrying a penniless foreigner. I was only in the category of the *courageuses*. If he had been a big man I don't think that it would have mattered, or if he had loved me enough, but I didn't think he loved me enough to stand all the hardships and difficulties. If he'd been big enough to get strength from opposition it might have worked also. Later, when love and passion had faded, I felt that he would think that he had wasted and broken his life. I felt that he would think the price too high a one. I saw that he was timid and afraid before his family . . . So I broke off the engagement. He was amazed and could not believe that it was possible that anyone could refuse him, that I could. I was still in love with him then and thought that I couldn't bear it. I had such longing for him. Then later he came back from Cairo for a period. By this time I'd got my doctorate and was at Oxford. He came to Oxford to see me, I went to London to see him and I saw him in Paris when I went over there for vacations. But there was no kindness left between us. He had lost trust in me, saw me as something which was antagonistic to him, that he could not mould. He was cruel now and tried to hurt me in every way . . . I thought there was nothing to do but put an end to the relationship and I've never seen him again. During the Battle of France in 1940 I thought of him with anguish . . . He was a cavalry officer and I believe would have been amongst the first to have been called up.[5]

Enid's reasons for breaking off her engagement do not sound convincing. Perhaps, even as a young woman, she felt herself unsuited to marriage. Perhaps, even then, she could not have devoted herself to her husband's career. She was already too self-absorbed, too intent on her own. She said to me, years later, that she 'felt no sense of shame at not being married', that she had never thought of herself as being married. Agnes Headlam-Morley writes: 'So far as I know she was not particularly attached to children.'[6] It is hard to know the truth. Enid told me, repeatedly, that her only regret was that she had not had a child. In 1945, she explained to Alyse Gregory: 'I've always been afraid to embark on building up a family of my own because I know well that I'd allow it to bind me . . . But at the same time I see that most people are happier in a family . . .'[7]

She could discuss the emotional problems of others with shrewdness and sanity, but she could never understand or solve her own. For most of her life she lived in unease. She was drawn to men and to women. She wanted independence, and yet she always longed for some secure, profound relationship. She must have known that she was unlikely to find it outside marriage. She must have known that no love-affairs, however long or passionate, would compensate, or satisfy her need. In middle age, a poignant personal comment escaped her: 'You cannot give happiness—your own kind of happiness—to anyone else—it can only grow from fusion.'[8] She had learned that truth with suffering.

◆ I I ◆

In 1927 Enid was concerned not only with her lamentable novel, but with the publication of her thesis: *Les Sources du Lyrisme dans la poésie d'Émile Verhaeren*. She herself was later to remark on its naïveté; and yet perhaps one is most impressed by the very innocence which she deplored, by the earnest feeling, the personal commitment. Enid found in Verhaeren certain moods and aspirations which matched her own. Verhaeren's childhood love of the sea recalled her own love of Killiney, and of Dublin Bay:

Everyone who is born near the sea feels far from home [when they leave it], they wilt and die, like a tree transplanted from its native soil . . .

Oh, all those childhood things! How they hold us in their thousand tentacles, however far away we may be! We go abroad; we try to break completely with the past . . . That past is never conquered . . . Verhaeren lived abroad for many years, but he could never break with his childhood beside the sea and the Scheldt.[1]

Verhaeren had been drawn to the sea, as Enid would always be; Verhaeren, like Enid, had known religious doubt. 'All his diatribes against religion and Catholicism spring from the struggle between his intellect and his heart.'[2] It was the conflict which she herself had known since her student days.

The thesis was finished and published, and dedicated to her father's memory; but the *soutenance* remained, and the thought of the public *soutenance* at the Sorbonne was naturally alarming. 'You will deal with the situation splendidly when the time comes,' Dr Eastwood reassured her. '. . . I am seriously considering whether I can come over for the week-end and hear you do it.'[3]

The official account of the *soutenance* remains in the archives of the Sorbonne, among the reports for 1927. Professor Reynier presided over the jury, and the other members were Edmond Estève and Enid's old professor, Fortunat Strowski.[4] Enid remembered:

I went in the day beforehand, to see the *appariteur*, the usher, and he showed me the dressing-room I'd use, with its long mirror and powder waiting for me. '*Mettez un joli chapeau,*' he said to me, '*cela fait toujours bon effet!*' . . .

When I went in next day, there was a great crowd there—in fact the hall was full. The *soutenances* of theses are a highly considered form of entertainment, and they are announced and reported in the press. I was described, in a paper, as '*petite, menue, les mains tremblantes*'.

The *appariteur* banged on the ground with his staff, announcing: '*Mesdames, Messieurs, la Faculté!*' The audience and candidate rose up, while the jury settled itself on the platform, with the candidate below them at a little table, with his thesis and notes, and the carafe of water, the tumbler and the bowl of sugar. He has twenty minutes to open, and to answer all the objections which may be made to his thesis, and then he is left to the tender mercies of the Jury, who mostly want to show off before an appreciative audience.

After a couple of hours of this sacrifice in the arena, the examiners march out, preceded by the *appariteur,* to deliberate. In the meantime the friends of the candidate surround him, encourage him, or criticize his performance, but all he wants is to be left in peace.

He knows that he has already got his doctorate—otherwise he would not have been permitted to print it, . . . but what he does not know is what 'mention' he will get, and there are four possibles. *Mention Bien, Mention Très Bien, Mention Honorable*, and, finally, the best, *Mention Très Honorable.*

After what seems an interminable period of deliberation, one hears the sound of the *appariteur's* staff banging on the ground, as he says, '*Mesdames, Messieurs, la Faculté!*' and the professors file in again to their platform. Then the President of the Jury announces the result.[5]

Enid won the doctorate of the University of Paris with the highest distinction. A newspaper reported: '*Les juges charmés accordèrent la Mention Très Honorable aux petites mains toujours tremblantes.*'[6]

It was clear that Exeter could no longer keep her. Her thoughts had already returned to Oxford, and on 2 May 1928 Dr Eastwood wrote: 'I really feel you will get the Oxford job, and very lovely it will be for everybody.'[7] Sibyl Eastwood's conviction was justified. Soon afterwards, Enid was appointed the first Sarah Smithson Lecturer in French Literature at Somerville. The Lecturership had recently been founded to promote the study of modern languages. The salary was £400 a year, and she was appointed for three years.

◇–◇–◇–◇

PART FIVE

Sarah Smithson Lecturer, Somerville
1928–1934

In one notable way, the college had changed since her student days. In 1926 Dame Emily Penrose had been succeeded as Principal by Margery Fry.[1] The necessary Metternich who had fought for women's acceptance had been succeeded by a gentler statesman: a Principal who did not need to show militant devotion to a cause. Margery Fry had been a student at Somerville, and she had been its Librarian; but she had had more than academic experience, she thought life more important than learning, and she had inherited her family's interest in penal and social reform. The sister of Roger Fry, she had moved in the Bloomsbury circle, and Radcliffe House, off Woodstock Road, which soon became the official house of the Principal, duly reflected Bloomsbury tastes. Roger Fry was responsible for some of the interior decoration (he later painted his sister's portrait for Hall), and Margery Fry once enquired of a former student why she did not gild her mantelpiece. Enid left cryptic notes on Miss Fry: 'Her weakness and strength. The evening with Chinese pictures. Her fear of not seeming unconventional.'[2] But Margery Fry was more progressive than Enid understood; she had vitality and fire, and she was not apprehensive about her image.

Enid herself, as a young don, was determined, from the first, to be independent. Soon after her appointment at Somerville she found a flat at 6, St Aldate's, almost next to Christ Church. 'What have you actually got in the way of furniture?' Sibyl Eastwood asked on 5 October. 'Would you like me to give you one or two electric lamp things? If so do you like them best in wood or brass? . . . Enid mine, this letter brings you lots of love, and my very good wishes for your first term as an Oxford don.'[3] On 18 October Dr Eastwood wrote again, expressing what would seem excessive sympathy. 'How I hope the lecture *went*! Anyway, it's over now,

and you have all the others undevastated by the horrible firstness
of this one. I have been feeling so sorry for you.' She added, on a
more practical note: 'I've found you a few blue plates after all, so
will you reckon dinner plates, soup plates, and salad plates, all
rather cracked, arriving soon?'[4]

Enid's flat in St Aldate's had low windows, and it was dark. She
enlivened it by painting the fireplace red and gold.[5] Whether or
not Miss Fry had exercised her aesthetic influence, Enid was already proclaiming her love of colour—though not, perhaps, with
the conviction which she showed in later years. 'For my part I liked
your orange curtains,' her usual correspondent reassured her. 'The
loveliest room I know in London is curtained and done in some
shade between orange and flame.' And Sibyl Eastwood added: 'Lots
of people always feel sick before public speaking—even at 90!'[6]

And so Enid Starkie embarked on her career as an Oxford don.
A critic in *The Quest*, reviewing her *Verhaeren*, announced that
'the students of Somerville College are fortunate in their newly
appointed Lecturer.'[7] *La Revue bibliographique* considered that
'Monsieur Starkie's criticism does not probe to the very depths of
Verhaeren's inspiration . . . It is, however, a work which is a
classic of its kind.'[8] Humbert Wolfe, in the *Observer*, thought that
Enid had claimed too much for her poet.[9]

Despite the reservations of critics, Enid's *Verhaeren* was crowned
by the Académie-Française, and awarded the Prix Narcisse
Michaud. On 25 May 1929, at the Golden Jubilee Dinner of
Somerville, the Principal announced that 'Miss Starkie was the
first foreigner to be "crowned" by the University of Paris'. The
statement was inaccurate, but the pride was real.[10]

Enid had an Oxford mind which had clearly been trained at
Somerville. When I asked her, once, why the Somervillian differed
from the rest, she answered in a word: 'Independence'. Her mind
was swift, penetrating and responsive. Her memory was encyclo-
paedic. She saw a subject in detail, and in perspective. But she was
more concerned with people than with ideas. She was more
fascinated by Baudelaire and Rimbaud themselves than she was by

their poetic achievements, more concerned with Flaubert the man than she could ever be with the history of the French novel. Literature, to Enid, was of secondary importance; one doubts if she ever read it for pleasure. Literature was above all, to her, a work of art created by human beings; and these complex creatures enthralled her. She was concerned with their appearance and their mannerisms, their way of life, their incomes, their food and clothes; she was absorbed by their spiritual development, their sexual problems, their emotional and their everyday lives. 'I know, from Flaubert's correspondence, about the suicide of his brother's son-in-law. He had lost a little daughter from measles I believe, and had never been the same since . . .' So she wrote to me not long before she died. It was a typical observation: made, as it were, by one of Flaubert's family. Enid was devoted to Flaubert; she detested his niece, Caroline Commanville, for her mean, self-seeking behaviour ('How I hate that woman!' she said to me. 'Let me know if you find out anything nasty about her'). Enid commiserated with Sainte-Beuve in his humiliating physical disability. She eagerly discussed the sexual complexities of Verlaine. She had a human approach to literature. 'The very first time I met her,' writes a pupil, 'at an interview for a place at Somerville, she asked me to my utter mystification: "If you had the choice, which would you rather be: Andromaque or Hermione? Why?" Fresh from school, I had expected to be asked to identify Racine quotations maybe, but not that. In no way was Enid Starkie ever predictable.'[11] Enid did not want to be a conventional teacher; and, indeed, she could not have been one.

When, in 1928, she returned to Oxford, she was still inspired by her promise to her father. But her promise, and the need to earn her living, drove her into a life that was not her own. Some twenty years after her time in Paris, when she was an established Oxford don, she reflected:

I have often been sickened at the demands made on me just to 'teach' to fill up a [pupil]. I'm not a good teacher and I know it . . .

I think I have always been interested in people as much as literature and ideas. And I have liked my pupils, been interested in them. I've not

wanted to teach them myself. I've wanted to release what was themselves, for themselves and because it interested me to find out. And I
have always tried to save my 'troublesome' pupils, particularly when I
thought their trouble came from the effort to be themselves . . .

It would be easier to be a good teacher if one knew what one wanted
people to do.[12]

And, in another draft for the end of her Paris book, Enid explained:

I would have liked Collège de France. [They have] work but research
before them. I have a horror of influencing, of imposing my personality
on anyone, of leading . . .

All I ask is to free the ground so that the plant may grow, no props,
no pushing, warping . . .

I am thankful I have not to teach the young to form character.

I don't think I have done much good. I hope I have done no harm.
A good doctor prefers to let nature work. I hope I have protected the
delicate minds in my charge until they are sure.[13]

Enid did not impose as a teacher, it was not in her character to
do so; but she revealed, and she fired any spark that might be there.

My dear Enid [wrote one of her pupils, on going down],

With these three words I seem to have shed for ever the commoner's
gown. Do you mind? I do, a little, because it was a very pleasant feeling
to be your pupil. Sometimes when people . . . remarked on my good
fortune in having you for a tutor, I used to wonder whether I knew—as
one of your colleagues put it—how to 'get an awful lot out of a mind
like that'. I even resented, at times, your Gidean fear of influencing your
pupils, because it so often gave one the tantalizing sensation of having an
inexhaustible source of interesting knowledge and ideas *just* out of
reach. But perhaps that very inaccessibility made it into something
more valuable . . . One invariably felt happy and sort of wound up
after a tutorial with you . . . You never held forth at great length, like
most other 'full-of-knowledge' tutors, you rarely interrupted the reading of an essay, . . . your criticism was never scathing or even con-
descending, but it wasn't calculated to encourage smugness either; but,
. . . by your amazing ability of making one forget what would be the
awesome greatness of your intellect while one is actually with you, and
enjoy and benefit from the remembrance of it afterwards—you taught
us to think for ourselves.[14]

Enid's pupils caught her fire. She herself repeatedly deplored the conflict between her writing and her teaching, between literary pleasure and academic duty. And yet one wonders how serious the conflict could have been. She frequently lamented the pressure of her work, and yet she always took on more, and she appeared to enjoy it. She constantly complained about the time she spent on administration, and yet she was eager to undertake faculty and college work, and she administered very well. She perpetually insisted that she did not fit in Oxford, and yet she remained there for more than forty years. One is tempted to wonder if her grievances owed more to her Irish nature than to genuine dissatisfaction.

However, she remained in conflict with herself and with her life, and, inescapably, with the Oxford system.

I think that I'm just as much of a rebel as you are [she told Alyse Gregory in middle age] . . . Where I differ from you is that you want to turn everyone else into a rebel. It's queer, I belong to the teaching profession and yet I've never felt any desire to teach anyone anything, though if they want the truth from me, as I see it, I try to give it to them. I seek the truth myself, or what I consider is the truth, and I would never teach something I didn't believe. But I've a horror of being formed and moulded by someone else and then I suppose too that I'm too uncertain of what positive truth is. I suppose that makes me loath to disturb the beliefs of others . . . I wouldn't dream of preaching 'free love' to my pupils though I believe in it myself. I should think it wrong to persuade my pupils to embark on a line of conduct that they might afterwards regret and that might not afterwards seem to them to have brought them such freedom. If they talk to me—and many of them do—I tell them what I think for myself, but I also put the other side before them and I also try—you would I know disapprove of this— to dissuade them from dashing too easily into sexual experience, at the first feeling of desire. I think that love taken too easily and lightly can blunt sensitivity and susceptibilities. I think it dangerous—and perhaps even cruel, perhaps arrogant—to force others to adopt one's own idea of emancipation. I see of course that all freedoms have been gained by showing others that they were in chains. My difficulty is that I am moved more by the individual problem than I am by the general and mass problem. As a college tutor, I've supported everyone in rebellion but urged no-one towards it. Perhaps this is a very contemptible attitude. But I am always moved with compassion when I think of all that the pursuit of truth entails of suffering, all that an anti-social attitude entails of persecution. Everyone is not suited to be martyr. What have I got to give them in place of what they are giving up? Stark truth is not a diet for everyone. I admire the seekers for truth, but I have often loved and felt great sympathy for the very simple and trusting, for the weak, for the self-indulgent, for those who were not strong enough for freedom . . . I think also that I'm interested in discovering what it is that makes life worth living for others, what gives it price in their eyes, what is their *moyen d'ivresse*, as Baudelaire would say, rather than in giving them mine.[15]

Such beliefs perhaps set Enid apart from her colleagues. They made her a lonely rebel. In her tension, her rebelliousness, her determined originality lay her contribution to Oxford life.

Emotionally she remained frustrated. She had now abandoned her dream of a career in music, and she felt atrophied without this means of expression. 'We are forced', she wrote, 'to limit ourselves to the attainable . . . Many far too many aspects of life which should have been expressed are in the lumber room amongst dusty memories. Sometimes even they are glowing coals under grey ashes.'[16] 'To me,' adds Agnes Headlam-Morley, 'it was always a sad mystery that she gave up playing altogether when she realized she had not the nerve for public performance.' And again: 'I rather think that it was the one really deep disappointment of her life and that for that very reason she never spoke of it.'[17]

Her deep disappointment was, I think, her inability to find a close and permanent relationship. At Oxford she felt the burden of being an intellectual woman. 'I think that her abilities, the capacity she had for shaping her destiny, were at odds with her femininity.' So writes Gordon Roe, who was one of her pupils in later years. 'She wanted to be accepted and loved, and as a wife and mother she would have been able to combine the rôle with the rôle of a scholar. But I cannot imagine her married.'[18] Enid could not imagine herself as a married woman. All her life she delighted in masculine company: she was keenly aware of a man's good looks, and she would light up for the least presentable of men. She seemed to have little time for women, even the most intelligent; the ordinary housewife clearly bored her. But Enid was secret and unpredictable, and she was sadly complex. In her notes on Paris, she wrote:

Armand said to me 'your tragedy is that you think like a man, indeed in many ways feel like a man, have need of development like a man, and yet are supremely a woman physically. If you were a Lesbian it would be easier, or if you were just a woman with desire to please, further a man's career. Or if you were frigid and intellectual. You have been made of bits and scraps, nothing properly put together.'[19]

That, I believe, was her tragedy.

⋄ 13 ⋄

Enid's first years as an Oxford don are thinly documented. January 1930 brings two letters from Natasha Stretovitch, in Cairo. Enid had known her as a student in Paris. Natacha asked to be kept *au fait* with her life, 'and with your novel, which interests me very much'. Exeter lay in the past, but Enid had not forgotten her wretched book.

In the summer of 1930, she lent her flat in St Aldate's to her colleague at Somerville, the historian Lucy Sutherland, and set off, as usual, across the Channel. She went first to the Abbaye de Pontigny. Long afterwards, the *décades* at Pontigny were to be respectfully remembered.[1] Louis Martin-Chauffier recorded how, every August, for sixteen years, most of the intellectuals of Europe had come at least once to spend ten days talking, debating, and fertilizing ideas, in this former Cistercian abbey. The attic and cellar had become the library and refectory. Pontigny had nothing Cistercian about it any more, except the splendid church, but a certain monastic spirit still prevailed there. Among the French visitors were Charles du Bos and Gide. Among the foreign visitors were Benedetto Croce, Lytton Strachey, T. S. Eliot, and

Heinrich Mann. The conversations rivalled those of the historic *salons*. 'After lunch and coffee, everyone assembled in the ground-floor drawing-room and soared to the heights of literature or philosophy.'[2] Not everyone could be admitted to the *décades*. The rites of introduction obeyed an unwritten law. One of the elect would inform you that, if you wished to join the faithful, you would be accepted in the sanctuary. Enid had no doubt been invited by Charles du Bos.

She left Pontigny to spend a few days working in Paris on Baudelaire. Monday, 24 August, found her installed, for twelve francs a day, over the Marine Bar in Cassis. Here she paused to write Lucy Sutherland an account of her travels.

Dear Lucy,

. . . I stayed on at Pontigny until the end . . . The gathering was rather like an Oxford Common Room gathering; though most of the people I personally did not find interesting they were all clever and specialists. There was no perfectly inane conversation. But most of all, as an amateur psychologist, I got interested in the personalities, the jealousies and rivalries, the efforts made to keep certain people completely out of things. All that side really was most interesting . . . I'll tell you about it some day as we walk round the Parks . . .

Julian Bell was the only Englishman there. He is from Kings Cambridge. He knows Roger and Margery Fry, is a friend of Lytton Strachey. He is the kind of Englishman I dislike. Very affected, paradoxical and dirty. I have known a great many Cambridge aesthetes like him. He wore a dirty ragged beard. He had one suit of filthy grey flannel which he wore all the time and there were large holes in it. He was the worst kind of inverted snob . . .

I wrote to Porquerolles but got no reply . . . I stayed 4 or 5 days in Paris working at the library and then came on here. I had heard of this place a few years ago as a quiet fishing place with no one. But that is not at all the case . . . I am in the port which is noisy. You know how noisy Marseillais are. There are also a great many motors and motor bikes as the place is in very easy reach of Marseilles. In Porquerolles there were only two motors on the island. But one could not expect to find a place as ideal as Porquerolles for work.

I hope anyway to get some done . . .[3]

In her large, whitewashed, noisy room, she continued to work on Baudelaire.

In 1931, after only five years as Principal of Somerville, Margery Fry resigned; she was succeeded by Helen Darbishire, the Wordsworth scholar, who was English tutor at the College. Miss Darbishire, less accustomed to dealing with large issues, less easy in relationships with colleagues, was slow in gaining Enid's sympathy. 'Perhaps you are hard on her,' Maude Clarke suggested. 'She is so very English and lacks our quicker intuition, but she is sincere and has always been a generous friend . . .'4 Enid came, eventually, to agree with this verdict. She recorded Miss Darbishire's 'goodness when she had time to reflect'. Helen Darbishire's reserved manner concealed unexpected and sensitive understanding. In moments of personal stress she showed a fund of practical kindness.

The only likeness of Enid in these early Darbishire years is found in her correspondence with a pupil. These letters, written in her own impulsive, awkward hand, show a side of her nature which often became obscured in later life. They show her when she was still unembittered, still able to express her warmth of heart. In October 1932, her former student, Rica Jones, returned to Oxford to take a teaching diploma; she needed to support a widowed mother. Enid was touched by the thought of this girl who suffered from the familiar burden. She sent her a cheque. 'When I was a student in Paris,' she explained, 'I had no money at all, except some very small sums that I earned. I know what it feels like not to have a penny for fares, or for tea in town with friends, or even for the necessities of life. In memory of the student that I was, please accept this very small gift.'5 The gesture was repeated; and in 1933, when Rica Jones had finished her course, Enid wrote yet again. The letter shows, above all, her own persistent longing for a close relationship, her anxiety to give and receive affection.

Dear Rica,

I am writing this in the train on my way to Southampton. I'm off to spend a fortnight in Paris before term begins.

It was nice of you to write to me. I send you all kinds of wishes for your new life. I feel towards you quite differently than I feel towards any of my pupils, I feel you so much nearer. I think it is the Celtic in you. You have a very special place in my affections. I always wish I were well enough off to give you a good salary so that you did not have to teach, so that I could keep you as my own private secretary, and send you off long months abroad just to browse about and travel. You are just the person to profit from that kind of life. But alas I am no fairy godmother. The little gift I once gave you I meant to repeat each term, but things happened . . .

I hope any time you come to Oxford you will come and see me.

I hope life won't treat you too badly, but life isn't easy at your age. Mine was in many ways hell, when I was your age.

I'd love to see you in a life full of beauty and colour and I hope you won't find school life too drab.

My best wishes and my love go with you anyway.

God bless you.

Enid Starkie.[6]

Rica Jones, now Mrs Brown, was one of her first pupils, and their friendship remained alive until Enid's death; but these early letters have their special interest. They were written by a tutor to her pupil, 'at a time when her own undergraduate days were vivid, and she could recall their problems, and sympathize absolutely with their ideals.'[7] This sympathy was one of Enid's lasting gifts as a tutor. Anne Kirkman writes: 'I was at Somerville 1952–5. It always seemed in those days that there was an enormous gap between dons and undergraduates. Some of the nicer dons tried to bridge it, but she was the only one I came across who appeared entirely unconscious that such a gap existed.'[8]

The year 1932 was unsettling for Enid. Her Sarah Smithson Lecturership had already been extended for a year, but it was due to expire in July. There seemed no immediate chance of promotion in Oxford, and she applied for a post in Aberdeen. Aberdeen refused her. She also found herself obliged to leave St Aldate's, and to search for a new flat. The prospect was depressing and, on 5 September, Gustave Rudler, the Professor of French Literature, wrote to commiserate: '*Les lodgings surabondent, mais quels lodgings!*'[9]

Enid's career was decided by Somerville. They re-appointed her Sarah Smithson Lecturer for three years. As for the question of lodgings, it was memorably settled when she moved into 41, St Giles'. The splendid Queen Anne house stood in one of the handsomest streets in Oxford. Past the sober offices which belonged to the University Appointments Committee, the visitor would see a golden gargoyle, a copy of one on a tower of Notre Dame. Beside it was a scarlet door, picked out in gold. Beyond the scarlet door was the flat—baroque, exotic and, it seemed, immutable—where Enid was to spend the next thirty-two years of her life. To her friends she would remain inseparable from her décor in St Giles'—an Oxonian *quartier* Saint-Gilles. Margaret Hooper, who became her first ephemeral tenant, never forgot 'the glowing Aladdin's caves of colour and inspiration'.[10]

And here, perhaps, one might glance at the downstairs *salon*, with gold walls ('Kenneth Clark always calls it my opium den, but it's not as exotic as that'). The Chinese mandarin smiled down from his peony-pink silk hanging over the grand piano, the gilt glass candelabra, the French clock on the mantelpiece, the golden carvings from a Burmese temple, the Byzantine shrine picked up for the proverbial song in Provence. A Venetian blind across the window hid Enid's favourite treasures from casual eyes: the cabinet of Waterford glass, the French cabinet lined with rose-coloured velvet and filled with delicate goblets and decanters. Here, in a Chinese trouser suit, a chrysanthemum in her hair, she presided over her more impressive parties. One susceptible visitor recalled her 'dressed as an exotic princess from Damascus or Samarkand, and dazzling her guests with the wit and sparkle of Scheherezade'. Next to the drawing-room was the tiny kitchen (still labelled, it is said, 'Miss Starkie's kitchen'), where Enid tried out on favoured guests the ambitious recipes she had culled from the cookery books which she had reviewed. Lord David Cecil remembers that the cooking was competent, the recipes exhaustively discussed, and Enid was generous with food and wine. From time to time the guests would hear the crash of breaking china from the kitchen. Upstairs were her pink-and-blue bedroom, her bathroom, her minute spare room, and the study, lined with French yellow-backs, which became the focal point of her life. The woodwork was painted red and gold. The mantelpiece was cluttered with red and gold Bohemian glass, a red-flecked shell (a present from the Public Orator), a row of bronze medallions of French poets, scattered ikons, a galaxy of invitations, and eventually, over all, a watercolour, grey and gold in tone, of the Palais de Justice in Paris.

Enid's flat in St Aldate's had been more conventionally furnished. But she had inherited her grandfather's taste for antiques: she revelled in attending auctions, and her purchase of lacquer furniture at the Oxford and Asquith sale had started her on her search for red-and-gold. She herself explained:

As a student at the Sorbonne I had been very poor and I had suffered from hunger, want and cold. I had lived in ugly and mean surroundings and I was starved for colour and luxury as much as for food and warmth . . . Thus, when I came to furnish my rooms at Oxford, my taste leaned towards the luxury of the Renaissance rather than towards the Gothic austerity or virginal aestheticism of William Morris of my colleagues. Gold had a peculiar attraction for me—gold blended with flame colour, the tints of Burmese lacquer—and it filled my life with the richness, luxury and warmth which I had lacked in my Paris student days. It also put a glow into the long grey winters of Oxford. I used to rummage in the antique and junk shops, ferreting out of the hidden corners any odd scraps of gold wood I could see—pieces of ornamental panels, corners of moulding, little carved figures—and from these I contrived a scheme of decoration which, with all its contradictions, was curiously harmonious and vaguely oriental.[11]

One resplendent piece of furniture was not, alas, included: The Golden Bed which, in 1935, she saw in an antique shop in Broad Street.

The headpiece rose to a height of seven feet, carved like the screen of an altar. Garlands of leaves, festoons and tendrils sprang up from the base, burst into fruits and flowers, and the delicate mouldings reminded me of the carvings on a tomb by Mino da Fiesole . . . The foot was flanked by two lovely boys in short tunics, with smiling faces and delicately carved golden curls, with graceful limbs. They seemed to be beckoning to me. Over the bed was flung a coverlet of crimson and gold brocade, faded the colour of flame, which might have hung behind an altar in a Tuscan chapel.

The bed was Italian; it had been made for the first Duke of Marlborough, and it came from Blenheim Palace. It cost £40. The sum was not impossible for an impecunious lecturer, but a serious obstacle remained. The only room in St Giles' which was big enough for the bed was Enid's study. She was not yet an established don, a Fellow of her college. She wondered what authority would think of such deviation from the conventional.

Every day she went down Broad Street and gazed at The Golden Bed.

I talked of nothing else for days, but of the golden bed. It became one of the established topics of conversation in the Senior Common Room at Somerville . . . It allowed full scope for that special talent of dons, of which they have made an art, fanciful speculation, but speculation based on logical argument once the premises have been accepted. My golden bed became the motif for brilliant conversational arabesques, growing more intricate and more complicated as members vied with one another in imagining further extravagant uses which a large bed might reasonably serve in a tutor's study . . . But I did not feel that I could join in all these pleasantries. To me the problem was a real one . . .

At last, one afternoon, as I hurried down the Broad, with my usual tremulous joy, as if I were about to meet a lover, I saw no beckoning shimmer of gold across the road.

'What has become of my golden bed?' I cried, bursting into the shop. I could scarcely speak for emotion was choking me,

'I couldn't keep it any longer,' the dealer answered. 'It was cluttering up the whole window . . . I sold it yesterday evening.'

Late in 1932, Enid moved into Saint Giles' ('remember, how she never spelt it 41, St Giles'—a remnant of Catholic respect for the Saints?').[12] That November, as she hurried across the road to post a letter—she always showed pugnacious defiance of traffic—she was knocked down and seriously hurt. She remained unconscious, in hospital, for twenty-four hours, and she spent three weeks in a nursing-home before she returned to Dublin for Christmas.

⋄ 14 ⋄

Enid had written *Baudelaire* without a publisher's contract, and she had sent it to Constable's. Helen Waddell—who had known her since her student days at Oxford—was their literary adviser. Constable's rejected the book. They were perhaps alarmed by its frank discussion of Baudelaire's sexual problems. They maintained that it would appeal to French rather than English readers. Helen Waddell disagreed with their verdict, and drafted a letter to Victor Gollancz. 'I think', she wrote, 'the book is remarkable, not only as a complete reversal of the Baudelaire legend, but for its human understanding.'[1] Gollancz accepted it at once. The 'lordly, fat volume' was published in June 1933.

Looking back at *Baudelaire*, after forty years, one is aware of its stylistic weakness. Enid was rarely a distinguished writer. She became gauche and self-conscious on paper. Surprising, perhaps, in a lover of music, she did not appreciate the music of language. 'You haven't mastered the English balance and the English rhythm,' Helen Waddell told her.[2] The comment, made about *Baudelaire*, applied to most of her writing. 'You see I never really learnt to write English properly,' she herself explained. 'I wrote no compositions as a child and I had barely four years schooling and when I went to Oxford I wrote very little English and in France I wrote nothing but French . . .' And again, years later: 'I do try to be critical of my writing . . . The difficulty used to be that I used to feel in French rather than in English, from all the time I had lived in France and reading almost nothing but French.'[3] Even when she wrote in English, she clearly thought in French. She had been taught in French, in her formative years, by Léonie

Cora, she had continued to read more French than English, she was drawn to French by instinct and by emotion. All her life she would tend to use English words and French syntax, to amass clause after clause, to choose an order of words which seemed unnatural to the English reader. Except, perhaps, in *A Lady's Child*, she showed no sense of English style. She tolerated clichés, she lazily used banal expressions; she took no pleasure in the art of writing. She would often emphasize the importance of planning a book, insist—a French insistence—on logical construction. But she lacked the love of language, the artistic vigilance, the constant power of self-criticism, which make a work of scholarship into a work of literature.

Her first *Baudelaire* has all the demerits of a first book. '*Évitez le trop plein*,' one of her teachers had scribbled in the margin of an essay; but Enid always tended to be excessive. She might have condensed her first book with advantage. As a critical study, she later found it inadequate, for she revised it. But it remains an exhaustive biography and it reflects her devotion and diligence. It also expresses a view of Baudelaire which is now so well accepted that one finds it hard to understand that this book was epoch-making. For if others had already suggested that Baudelaire was not the man of the Satanic legend, it was left to her to disprove the idea completely. It was left to her to suggest the causes of his emotional problems, to indicate his depth and his significance, to present him as an idealist and a moralist, a man who had profound-ly studied society and himself. It was left to her to place Baudelaire in his literary context: to show, at a time when he was excluded from every university syllabus, that he was among the pre-eminent French poets.

It is not without significance [said *The Times Literary Supplement*] that this notable task has been performed by a woman, and by one, more-over, who has neither shirked enquiring into the least pleasant aspects of Baudelaire's life, nor attempted to palliate either her discussion of them or her interpretation of his early poems. Twenty years ago, such matters could scarcely have been treated by a woman, and least of all by one who held, as Miss Starkie does, a responsible post at Oxford, without condemning her to unenviable and undesirable notoriety. Happily, there is no question now of having to admire her courage; what we can and do admire unreservedly is the unfailing energy and enthusiasm that have supported her in the heavy labour of collecting her material and in the even heavier one of composing it into a book which contains upwards of a quarter of a million words.[4]

Enid's *Baudelaire* allowed the poet to be seriously considered by academic and literary critics. It established Enid herself as a progressive figure in French studies. It also brought her to the notice of William Rothenstein. Now in his sixties, Rothenstein had studied art in Paris in his youth. He had known Toulouse-Lautrec. He had drawn Edmond de Goncourt, Zola, Huysmans and Verlaine, and in 1893 he had persuaded Verlaine to lecture in England. Indeed, he had helped to arrange Verlaine's visit to '*le divin Oxford*', and he had earned a poem in *Dédicaces*. Such achievements lent him an aura in Enid's eyes.

Dear Miss Starkie [he had written on 18 July],

I am deep in yr *Baudelaire*. To my mind it is one of the rare convincing studies of an artist's spirit. Its insight surprises me; and the tender understanding of a heart wracked, dismayed and ecstatic, trapped between the 2 eternities, touches mine. What insight you women have, and what pity! . . . You must know the feelings of gratitude that sweep over one when in contact with a rich mind, and will forgive the intrusion of a stranger—though not quite a stranger, perhaps, since Helen Waddell encouraged me to write to you. I was telling her of my old Professor Alphonse Legros, who, as a poor and unknown young artist, was discovered by Baudelaire. It was Legros who put Swinburne into touch with yr poet; and I notice that you say little of their relations. You might some day care to hear—if you don't already know—something of what happened between them.[5]

The acquaintance grew into a warm, illuminating friendship. A further friendship was that of the French scholar, Jules Mouquet, who admired *Baudelaire* and wrote to Enid, eagerly, on literary research. Now that *Baudelaire* was published, she had turned to another poet whom she felt to be unjustly disdained.

I am glad that you liked my little book *Rimbaud raconté par Verlaine* [Mouquet told her on 2 April 1934]. I am delighted to learn that you are preparing a book on Rimbaud . . . Yes, you certainly *ought* to go and spend a few days at Charleville, it seems to me essential if you are devoting a book to him . . . You will have seen, from the article I published last year in the *Mercure de France*, that I discovered one of the poet's schoolfriends—M. Paul Labarrière. He is a delightful man, he's just entered his 80th year; I strongly advise you to go and see him.[6]

That month, in the Easter vacation, Enid found herself in France on the trail of Rimbaud. She went to his native Charleville, and visited the library which he had used. 'I hope you were able to have an interview with M. Labarrière, in Paris,' Mouquet wrote again, on 12 April. 'What an irreparable disaster that he mislaid that book of *unpublished manuscript poems*! . . . I think that with perseverance one can still discover things.'[7]

On 18 April, Denis Saurat, from the Institut Français du Royaume Uni, sent advice on Enid's research. He added: 'I was both interested and amused by your account of the feelings of your college about your possible departure.'[8]

For Enid remained unsettled in Oxford. In 1933 she had become a University lecturer in French literature; but there seemed no prospect of further promotion. She had applied for a post at Bedford College, London. She failed to obtain it. 'I can imagine the disappointment,' Rothenstein sympathized. He added: 'The great thing after all is the writing. I have faith in yr powers.'[9]

In these, her early years as a don, Enid had the Starkie wanderlust. Like her father, and her brother, Walter, she could turn from the library and travel eagerly about Europe. Like Walter, she sought the romantic, the adventurous and the Bohemian. The Connemara pony, so her family had called her, for she was small and astonishingly tough. She showed her toughness on her travels in the Long Vacation of 1934.

I simply loved my trip to Spain and I hope to be able to go back [this to Lucy Sutherland in September]. They are a very kind simple people,

very like the Irish, much nicer to foreigners than either the French or
the Italians, and they were very kind and patient with my total lack of
knowledge of Spanish. Though travelling without knowing the language leads to many misconceptions. You think a man is saying to you
'What a nice day, or nice scenery,' and you answer encouragingly 'si, si,
si!' And it isn't that at all; he has been saying something to the effect
that he likes your face and would like to spend the night with you . . .
I got to loathe having a man say to me that I was 'muy simpatica'. It
meant that very soon one had to cope with the situation . . . I had one
adventure like a film episode, with knife etc.

The Spanish people strike one as children, living in the present, . . .
learning nothing from experience, with no thought for the future . . .
One finds it hard to believe that they ever were a great people. What
was it made them great in the 16th century? I don't think it is a question
of present poverty and poor conditions, for the French, even in their
worst period, struck me as oppressed adults, not ill-treated children. I
find the Spaniards infinitely humble and infinitely pitiable. They are
like children that no one has ever done anything for, and they have not
been able to evolve any kind of decent life for themselves, because they
had not the wisdom or the experience . . .

Just before I left I discovered that I had spent in the year that has
finished £120 more than I had earned . . . One can't go on spending
like that. I did not want to give up my trip so I decided to travel third
everywhere. Certainly third in Spain is dirtier than anything that can
be imagined . . .

I started off with a few days at Santander, or rather across the bay
from Santander . . . My days there were very peaceful and lazy . . .
After that I began my trip . . . I saw Burgos, Avila, Escurial, Madrid,
Toledo, Valencia, Tarragona, and Barcelona, and I thought I'd like a
week's rest at the sea before going back to France. I first tried L'Escula
. . . There is fishing on a very large scale, and the smell pervades
everywhere. The ground floor of every house is given over to the fish.
There are wide open doors like stable doors, and everywhere you look
you see women beheading, disembowelling, salting down fish and
packing it in barrels. The streets are full of fish entrails.

But the starting out of the fishing fleet is rather a magnificent sight.
Each boat has three large acetylene lamps on the prow, and the lights
shining on the dark sea is very impressive. It is not as fine though as the
setting out of the fishing fleet in the Basque country in France. There

every boat has a brazier of burning resin at the prow and the effect of the red flickering lights on the waves is most mysterious. It is like a midnight torch procession, and suddenly far out at sea they all scatter . . .

I moved on then to a tiny place called Cadaques, a fascinating little place in a bay between two high cliffs . . . When you come towards the town from the road, you see the church only at first, high up, looking as if it were built in the clouds. The little streets are hewn out of the rock, not even cobbled . . . I left there on Sept. 16th, I spent a day in Carcassonne and came back to Paris.[10]

It was in Paris, where she now resumed her quest for Rimbaud, that Enid met a friend who would have a significant influence on her research. Twenty years later, when she spoke at the Rimbaud centenary celebrations, she recalled her first encounter with the bibliophile Henri Matarasso. Rimbaud studies, she maintained,

. . . could not exist without him, for no-one has collected such a vast treasure-house of manuscripts, paintings, pictures, mementoes . . . They make the shop in the rue de Seine into a real Rimbaud sanctuary . . .

I well remember the first time I slipped into it . . . Henri Matarasso had just arrived from Belgium, and he had only just opened his shop. He had a copy of Rimbaud's letters for sale, the Mercure de France edition, with notes by Paterne Berrichon. Or rather, I should say, he had had this volume to sell, because when I actually asked him for it, it was, so to speak, sold to somebody else. But Henri Matarasso took it out of the parcel and sold it to me; he had compassion on me in my distress . . . That was the beginning of our great friendship, a friendship which is still growing to-day.[11]

In the autumn of 1934, Enid returned to Oxford, where, at last, she was to enjoy full academic status. Mildred Pope, once her tutor, had moved to Manchester to end her career as Professor of Romance Philology. 'We can never have another *Pontiff*,' went the College report, 'and Somerville without one is something we hardly like to think of. An era of 41 years is closed.' But a new and brilliant era had begun. It was that term that Dorothy Crowfoot (the future Dorothy Hodgkin) came into residence as Chemistry

Research Fellow; and it was that term that Enid was appointed a Fellow of Somerville, and a tutor in Modern Languages. It was the real beginning of her career. As Fellow, Professorial Fellow and Honorary Fellow she remained at Somerville for the next thirty-six years, until her death.

PART SIX

✧✧✧✧✧

Fellow and Tutor
1934–1946

She was to teach French literature from the sixteenth to the nineteenth century, but there was no doubt in which period her preferences lay. She continued her work on Rimbaud, and continued to take an interest in the author who had, years earlier, 'liberated her spirit'. 'My dear Miss Enid,' Rothenstein enquired, 'have you seen Gide's private journals, wh. have lately been published in an expensive edition of his works? My friend Mme Bussy (a sister of Lytton Strachey) is a passionate admirer of Gide—I shd like you to meet her, if you don't already know her.'[1]

Enid had been drawn to Gide by his belief in the individual, by his personal faith, by the sudden illumination he had given her in her moment of perplexity. But one problem he had failed to solve: since her days at Oxford she had been unable to accept the Catholic faith into which she had been born. Yet she still needed to believe, and at times the need became acute; she analysed herself with frustration and unhappiness. Early in 1934, on her visit to Charleville, she had felt particular distress of spirit; and she had expressed her doubts and needs to Charles du Bos.

Dearest Enid [he answered],
 . . . Your Charleville letter moved me as scarcely any letter has moved me; and for having written it, and having had the courage to send it, I thank you with my whole being . . .
 Dearest, there is not one word in those pages that I do not understand, that I have not myself lived through, not one word about which, if we were together, and if God helped me, I could not be of some help to you—and that is why I beseech you to do all you possibly can to come and spend those ten days at Pontigny with me where we could see one another daily in the best of conditions and cover all the ground together . . .
 'My only difficulty is in belief, belief in essentials. That is the

tragedy.' Ah! in the year, in the very months that preceded my conversion, how often in journals (yet unpublished, but I will bring them to Pontigny if you come) did I not give utterance to exactly the same problem! I was even further then from its solution that you are, for with me it was not only a question of having belief, but even of understanding what the word belief might mean . . .

'I feel sometimes as if there were a hard core in my heart that only needed softening and then all would be well.' Dearest, it seems to me that you say there the truest and final word on your present condition. Ever since I have known you, I have always felt sure that there was not in you the slightest element either of 'carelessness' or of 'indifference, pride (of intellect or any other), egoism, fear of suffering'. As you yourself say, even when 'the canker of doubt' made its first apparition at 'the centre of your faith', your 'need for spirituality did not grow less'. That need for spirituality is, as far as I can venture to judge, the *invariant* of your whole nature, and it is from the whole of my lived experience that I say to you that there can exist no better *preparation for faith* than that very need.[2]

Enid's religious doubts remained with her throughout her life. In about 1945, she assured Rosamond Lehmann: 'I know that if I now believed as I did once I should find nothing too difficult in the service of God. I've never understood anything except complete yielding—if one really believes. I am no longer a believer . . .'[3] In 1965, when she thought that she was dying, she had a conversation with a former pupil, the Rev. Dr Gordon Roe.

It is difficult [he writes] to talk of her religion. My impression is that she had not moved far from her position as she expressed it in *A Lady's Child*. In our frequent discussions of theology she always called herself a Catholic agnostic, one whose life and outlook were formed by the Catholic Church and who would always think of herself as a Catholic, but who could not believe. She once said, 'I am a good Catholic in everything but faith.' Since a Catholic is one who prays with his eyes open, that seems just . . . She was mystified by the Church of England. She claimed that she knew few Anglican clergymen and that I was the one she knew best (although I cannot believe that that was quite true, in Oxford of all places). She said she had been put off them by the intellectualism and modernism of W. R. Matthews, then Dean of St Paul's.[4]

Dr Roe added a more controversial comment:

I am not sure that Enid's Catholicism was really for emotional release. I never had the impression that she was emotionally any more than intellectually involved. I think it was a part of her very conscious Irishness, and that it provided a range of symbolism and imagery which she was loath to cut herself off from. She seemed to have no personal commitment to it, and yet she felt that, almost despite herself, she was a part of it and it was a part of her. Nothing but Catholicism could, I think, be regarded in this way.[5]

In the summer of 1935 Enid felt particular need for the strength and consolation of religion. Maude Clarke, her colleague at Somerville, was dying. That spring, the doctors had found that she had incurable cancer, and that she could not live for more than a year. At forty-three, Maude Clarke had established herself as a mediaeval historian; and, had she lived, she might well have been elected Principal of Somerville. As it was, she told Miss Darbishire of the doctors' verdict, and spent Trinity Term at Oxford. Then she resigned her Fellowship, and went home to Carnmoney.

Early in the Long Vacation, Enid went to see her. Maude Clarke, reserved and beautiful, witty but austere, inspired intense devotion in her pupils and colleagues, and Enid's feeling for her had no doubt been all the stronger because their Irishness drew them together. Now, for the first time since her father's death, Enid watched the process of dying. Maude had accepted her state with philosophy: she was almost superhumanly composed; but for Enid, who could not believe, who lacked philosophy, who was violently emotional, the meeting was painful.

I knew that your heart was full when you left here and *of course* I did not mind [Maude wrote to her on 5 July]. The strange thing about worry and illness like mine is that though the worst part is the sorrow they cause to those one loves, it would be intolerable if it were not so.

I am distressed that you have been going into the medical side of this illness . . . I think that I have a clear understanding of the position in a general way. There is nothing that makes me afraid about it and I think of it very seldom . . .

Dear Enid, your visit was such a help to me. I was thinking so much about Oxford and all my friends that it made all the difference to have you there.

The visit to Maude had been doubly distressing for Enid. Carnmoney was near Cushendun where, fifteen years earlier, almost to the day, Dr Starkie had died. Canon Clarke, Maude's father, took her briefly to see Cushendun. Enid must have felt that she was re-living old experience.

On 18 July, Maude assured her:

It is always lovely for me to have your letters. They are just like talking to you, only more intimate. I appreciate that intimacy, because only rarely are we able to express it in words when we meet. Last year I felt, rather than knew, all the time that you had understood the gravity of my illness and that, most delicately, you were trying to share the burden with me. You did share it, I am certain. Your seemingly casual company at dinner was the greatest pleasure to me—not only for yourself, but because you had realized that it was just at that time I was bound to think of myself as cut off from everyone by the habits which illness makes necessary. Of course, I did not know that you came deliberately from your house and looked at my bedroom light, but I am quick as well as you, and from something you once said I knew at least that you always passed under it when you were coming home and looked up at me. I used to wonder sometimes, when I could not sleep, if you had seen the light and whether your goodwill had been sent quietly up from the pavement. I never said anything to you, as we are both deeply reserved people (like most Irish who have anything in them), but I am very glad now that you told me. I am sure that I always have your love and good thoughts, without the lights which were a sign of them.

As always, when she was distressed, Enid turned to Sibyl Eastwood. She asked her, as a friend and doctor, what she could best send, by way of comfort, to Belfast.

Enid dear, what a problem [Dr Eastwood answered]! I can't think of anything but your idea of champagne sounds to me good. If I were dying I should want you to send me silly things if you sent anything at all—a penny toy one day, a single daisy in a matchbox another,—a huge armful of some lovely flowers another . . . Most of all I should like to get letters from you, letters that made me realize you loved me a little but especially that you still thought of me as understanding, realizing, enjoying, living vividly if more in the spirit than the body. But there. Anyway I rang up my wine merchant just now, and he thinks you can make arrangements for getting drink out of bond delivered in Belfast.

'The very thought of champagne exhilarates me,' wrote Maude. Soon afterwards, she added: 'I began my regular course of champagne yesterday . . . You must imagine me having it at dinner every night, with always a thought of you. About the future . . . One thing I am sure about is that it will be rich and happy for me, because I am one of the lucky people who are served by events and have a deep confidence in what God is doing for me that nothing can destroy.'[6]

She died on 17 November.

⋄ 16 ⋄

The year which followed the death of Maude Clarke was a troubled year for Enid, and at times she felt acutely lonely. Once more she thought of leaving Oxford. At the end of the year Helen Darbishire wrote: 'I was myself glad that you were not appointed to Sheffield—(obviously they wanted a man) because I should be very sorry to lose you from the College. I think you know how much I value you and rely upon you.'[1] On 7 January 1937, she wrote again: 'I have had it very much in my mind that you ought to get a break-away. I shall be very glad to talk it all over with you.'[2] The discussion proved to be unexpectedly rewarding. 'Your note to me gives me real happiness,' she added, on 9 February. 'It is dear of you to say what you do. I am sensitive to what you feel, all the more perhaps from being reserved in my own nature. I am very happy to think that you will have this long time of freedom and peace to get well and to bring your work to fruition.'[3]

Enid was given sabbatical leave for two terms. She escaped to Ischia; and 'I must say,' wrote the classics tutor, Isobel Henderson,

'I laughed at the contrast between most of my colleagues ("I am going to write a book, so I must be somewhere where there is a library") and you ("I am going to write my Rimbaud, so I must go somewhere with warm moonlit nights").'[4]

Early in September, Enid went to Rome. She lived there for three months for £20. That autumn, in her tiny flat in the via Maria dei Fiori, at the bottom of the Spanish Steps, she worked on her biography of Rimbaud.[5] Late that year the Clarendon Press published her monograph *Rimbaud in Abyssinia*. She had drawn on seventy-five volumes of unpublished diplomatic correspondence and documents in the Public Record Office. *Rimbaud in Abyssinia* filled in the unknown years of Rimbaud's life; it was also a study of the struggle for power in Africa during the last decades of the nineteenth century. It had its topical interest, its relevance to the recent Italo-Abyssinian War.

Payot, in Paris, later published *Rimbaud en Abyssinie*: an enlarged version of the book. Both monographs were by-products of the major work on which Enid was engaged. One or two points remained to be settled, but by February 1938 *Arthur Rimbaud* was virtually finished, and she sent the typescript, for criticism, to Helen Waddell.

My very dear Enid [answered Helen, on 11 February],

I finished *Rimbaud* in bed last night—in fact, most of it has been read in bed before I went to sleep. It's most profoundly moving, and it must have shaken you to write it.

Once or twice I've suggested lowering the intensity a little . . .

Again, I've cut the adverbs now and then . . . The nearer the bone, the better the prose.

My dear, forgive me laying down the law like this. It is my own eternal struggle, to combine feeling *and* austerity of expression.[6]

On 5 May, from Dublin, Walter wrote to Enid: 'I hear your new *Rimbaud* comes out on the 19th: well, . . . I drank a toast to it to-day.'[7]

My dear Miss Starkie, . . . What a book [exclaimed William Rothenstein]! Surely one of the [most] remarkable studies of a poet ever written. Only I say to myself, no one could so write who had not herself suffered; and my heart went out to you as I read. Strange it was for me to read; for when I was in Paris in 1889 and onwards, I heard so much of Rimbaud's poetry from the young poets, but he himself was a vague legend, of whom no one knew anything certain. Now you have drawn a complete and convincing portrait; I can *see* him, as he turned up at the Verlaines'; what a chapter that is! Having known Toulouse-Lautrec—a very different character from Rimbaud—I can understand his desire—his instinct—to rid himself of all inhibitions. It is something an Englishman wd find difficult to understand—the sense of exile from a vulgar world that vice and sordidness can fire, a sense of pride and bitter separateness wh has its own exaltation. I think yr comparison between Rimbaud and Verlaine extraordinarily searching and convincing—of their different attitudes to Catholicism especially . . . I still remember yr *Baudelaire*; but I think this even a profounder work.[8]

The reviews of *Arthur Rimbaud* were many, and large, but they showed little critical judgment. Reviewers could not appreciate the importance of the new material; they knew little of Rimbaud, or his work, and they remained shy of his reputation. They were impressed by Enid's courage in discussing sex and sin; they were impressed by her diligent collection of material. They were less impressed by her style, and by what they considered to be excessive sympathy for her subject.

Enid's first *Arthur Rimbaud* is a more mature book than her first *Baudelaire*. Though she is again prolix, though her writing is coloured by French, and is frequently banal, though the Verlaine episode is not, perhaps, entirely accurate, her assessment of Rimbaud has authority. It is the authority of a biographer who is aware of the facts, and marshals and interprets them with a clear and searchng imind. It is a mind impatient of *idées reçues*, determined to find the truth, however distasteful and however obscure. Enid— as in all her books—does not show herself to be an instinctive lover of literature. She is more concerned with the genesis of a poem, far more concerned with its author, than she is with the work of art itself. Certainly, when she comes to express her appreciation of literature, she is clumsy or inarticulate. But though she lacks intuitive literary sympathy, though she seems to lack artistic sense, she understands the human condition; she writes with sharpness of intellect, and with compassion. She is not blind to the weakness and the vice in Rimbaud's nature, but she makes them understandable. We cannot comprehend the workings of genius; we cannot, when we have read this book, define and explain the quality of Rimbaud's achievement. But though his genius continues to defy definition, we feel that we can appreciate him as a man.

If Enid felt any disappointment with the reviews of *Arthur Rimbaud*, it must have been short-lived. Long before they had all appeared, she was concerned with her next work. In Baudelaire and Rimbaud she had chosen to discuss two poets who had been maligned, who had ruthlessly chosen their independent ways, who had suffered in spirit. In Gide, again, she found a noble and significant writer, suffering for his personal beliefs, seeking to be his essential self despite the criticism of the conventional. She had sent him a copy of *Arthur Rimbaud*, and told him that she would like to write a book on him.

On 15 May, from Pontigny, he answered:

Chère Madame,

I am absolutely delighted by your letter. I hope you are not too mistaken about the importance of my writings! England has so far been one of the countries where they have had least effect and where they are least known. The plan that you propose is therefore of great importance to me. I shall be happy to help with it and to meet you when you come to France. I shall be in Paris myself in a few days' time . . .

Believe me, I shall be glad to make your acquaintance, and you may rest assured of my best wishes.

André Gide.

No doubt the book on Rimbaud which you mention is waiting for me in Paris—I look forward very much to finding it there.[9]

He returned to Paris, and found the book. On 1 June:

Chère Madame,

I should like to be able to write to you at length; I have no time—and no strength, for I am very tired. That is why I have entrusted your book on Rimbaud to an English friend, until I may make its acquaintance myself. He tells me, this morning, of his lively satisfaction. 'Very well done,' he writes to me, 'plainly, courageously and carefully.' There follow numerous compliments and he ends by expressing great satisfaction that you are undertaking a book about me.

I wish I could have sent you my *Œuvres complètes* in the large edition —of which, alas, I have not had a single copy, even for my closest friends! But perhaps the collection would be in an Oxford library, and you could consult it there. My *Journal* would certainly be most useful (I would even say indispensable) for you . . .

It goes without saying that (as soon as I am a little rested) I shall be glad to read your *Rimbaud en Abyssinie*; and, of course, your English *Rimbaud*, which my friend in London should soon return to me. Let me say how happy I shall be to make your acquaintance when you are passing through Paris. Please don't forget to give me notice . . .

Your attentive
André Gide.[10]

The thought of the biography continued to occupy him. A few days later he discussed it with Mme Simon Bussy. On 6 July, from Gordon Square, she wrote:

Dear Miss Starkie,

Please may I introduce myself to you as André Gide's English translator and also as a personal friend of his? When I was in Paris a little more than a month ago he told me you had written to him for permission to do a study of him on the lines of your *Baudelaire* and *Rimbaud*.

He has since written to me that he has lost your letter and your address and he doesn't know what to do about it! I think perhaps you may like to hear that he seems to me very favourably inclined towards your plan and I very much hope it may come off. The ignorance of the general English public about Gide seems to me quite lamentable. They are alone, I think, in the civilized world, [in being] totally unaware of Gide's importance and standing as a thinker and writer.

Gide has been very much shattered lately by the death of his wife, which accounts for his having mislaid and neglected to answer your letter. As a rule he is most punctilious about such things.

May I add too that I have been reading your book on Rimbaud with

profound interest, and a great deal of admiration? I should be so happy
to make your acquaintance if possible. We live in Nice as a rule, but I
am in London for the summer . . .[11]

The Rimbaud biography led to Enid's meeting with Dorothy
Bussy; it also brought her the acquaintance of Marie Belloc
Lowndes. The sister of Hilaire Belloc, she was a venerable *femme de
lettres* and a link with nineteenth-century France. On 9 July she
congratulated Enid on her *Rimbaud*.

I knew Verlaine [she added], from the early nineties (his last visit to
England) till his death. He used to talk to me somewhat intimately of
his early life. He never mentioned Rimbaud. But he again and again
spoke of his wife and son—with deep remorse and distress . . . As a
result of our first meetings, and my seeking him out whenever I went to
Paris for work, I became deeply interested in everything that concerned
him . . . It would give me much pleasure to see you.[12]

The invitation was not to be missed.

Mrs Belloc Lowndes urged Enid to write a life of Sainte-Beuve.[13]
But, in the summer of 1938, Enid was once again dreaming of
escape. Some years earlier she had found what, to her, was the
perfect island: Porquerolles, off the Mediterranean coast of France.
'Enid dear, . . . will you allow me to come and play with you a
little on your island?' Sibyl Eastwood now enquired. 'I only want
very very very little society from you! I want to sleep and swim
and do some work, and very little else. But I don't want to be quite
alone. I shan't stay more than a week.'[14] Dr Eastwood went to
Porquerolles; and there they discussed the question of Enid's
memoirs.

Enid was thinking of her memoirs; Gide was still thinking of his
biography. On 7 August he sent a postcard to her in Paris. 'How
sorry I am not to be in Paris! It would have been so delightful to
meet you! Let's hope that in September . . .'[15] But on 27 September, from Cuverville, he wrote again: 'These last days have been
so disturbed that I haven't been able to give you notice, I was too
uncertain of my movements. I very nearly invited you to come
and find me at Cuverville; but I wasn't sure that I could be there

myself. I shall return to Paris on the 29th. Will you still be there? I should be desolate to miss you . . .'[16]

It was, perhaps, this September that Enid first met Gide. In October the new academic year began, in an Oxford to which she did not seem, even now, to belong. She had hoped to be appointed University Reader in French Literature; but she had failed in her application. At the end of 1938 she applied for another post, again without success.

'Enid, my dear [wrote Rothenstein on 18 January], I was so pleased, sitting next to T. S. Eliot at dinner, to hear him single out yr. *Rimbaud,* to speak of it in the highest terms. Praise of you always warms my heart.'[17] On 18 February, Rothenstein wrote again, this time about Irish men of letters:

This evening I had a visit from Joseph Hone. He told me of his friendship with yr people—how as a child you had sat on his knee. He has been writing a life of Tonks: he wd like, I think, to write on Yeats. But who cd portray Yeats? I had 2 letters from him a week or 2 before he died, and Dorothy Wellesley wrote an account of his last days. He had been vital up to a week before; then he suddenly weakened and finally sank into a coma. I fancy there are few living who knew him earlier than I, or who continued the intimacy to the end. I don't know how well you knew him. His going, after AE's, marks the end of the period I knew in Dublin. Now it is for a new vision to help a new Ireland into being. You and Helen [Waddell] have a great part to play.[18]

Since they had met, soon after the appearance of *Baudelaire,* Enid had felt a respectful affection for Rothenstein. 'Your friendship for me is something that I value highly,' she had told him. 'I felt in you the first time I saw you at your party at Campden Hill, that goodness, that warmth and that genuineness which I have found in you ever since. Your kindness to me at our first meeting and ever since, had a quality that I am very unused to . . . With you I have looked at regions of myself that I don't look at except alone.' And again: 'I have rarely met kindness and goodness like yours and I feel a better person from contact with you, more hopeful about everything.' She admired Rothenstein's tolerance, his wide experience of life; she appreciated his generosity, sympathy and wisdom. 'It is a great pleasure to me,' she assured him, 'that you also consider me a friend, and that you understand the real tenderness and trust I feel for you.'[19]

Rothenstein was increasingly fascinated by Enid. 'Darling Enid!' he scribbled. 'When am I going to see you?'[20] 'Sleeping badly last night [14 March], I took up *Rimbaud*. And all the while yr image, yr fragrant mind and understanding person, came between me and the pages. I have such a desire to see you, to be with you again.' He planned to go to Paris for a few days after Easter; it would, he thought, be pleasant to meet there. On 22 March he wrote: 'I do want you to come to us for a week-end later. And we may meet in Paris, though my plans are less certain . . . I lunched with Gogarty to-day—a joyous, wise, libidinous companion, with a Rabelaisian note, wh. I like . . .'

Enid was in Paris in April, but they failed to meet. On the 29th, back in Gloucestershire, Rothenstein continued:

I found yr letter on my return yesterday. What a bore that you shd not have been well in Paris. I had a morning with Gide and a long talk abt you: he knows yr *Baudelaire* but not the *Rimbaud*—of the *Bre* he thinks highly. I was delighted to be in touch with him again. He looked strong and well, a little stouter than when he was here with us some 20 yrs ago, and was full of fire and energy. He was distressed to have had his name removed from the membership of the British Academy—did you know of this?

Rothenstein and Gide had recognized Enid's distinction; so had Professor Rudler. He encouraged her suggestion that she might apply for a D.Litt. Late in June, she was awarded the first Doctorate of Letters in her Faculty. The honour was announced in the Principal's speech at the Somerville Gaudy—a pleasant honour to publish on the sixtieth birthday of the College. Beatrice, the Somerville cook, marked the occasion by making an ice-pudding inscribed 'E. S. D.Litt.'.

Enid welcomed the doctorate, as it would have pleased her father, and it established her in the outside world. She took a childlike pleasure in wearing her scarlet and French grey. Rebel though she had always been, rebel though she remained, she delighted in walking in the doctors' procession at Encaenia; but not the least of the benefits conferred by her 'grand doctorate', as she called it, was that of enjoying the refreshments provided under Lord Crewe's Benefaction. In her memoirs of Oxford, she planned to devote a chapter to Encaenia, and to the hospitality given by successive Vice-Chancellors. She noted with approval: 'Bowra Champagne and Strawberries. Always three glasses.' Another chapter heading goes simply: 'Bowra best Vice-Chancellor in my time.'[21]

Enid my dear, where are you resting yr head, in what country [Rothenstein enquired on 10 August]? . . . I never see you as an arid don, wasting yr sweetness in the College air . . . How I wish I cd join you somewhere. We supped lately with Helen, and talked of you; she shares my feeling abt you and Oxford—and others too! and lately I wished you had been with me when I went, at Sir Sidney Barton's prompting, to call on Haile Selassie at Bath. He told me that Rimbaud's old friend, Bishop Cahagne, is still alive—living I think in Paris. There was something that touched and irked me, sitting there with this exile, with his suffering eyes and delicate features. And I only saw in him a sensitive nature, scandalously wounded, a Prince barbarously dragged from his throne . . .[22]

Enid had escaped, inevitably, to Porquerolles; and there she had begun to plan the first volume of her memoirs. Writing to Sibyl Eastwood, she asked to dedicate the book to her; and she told her of Porquerolles in the shadow of imminent conflict: of the Second World War so soon to begin.

I wonder if you will have stayed on [Dr Eastwood answered on 30 August]. There is no need for you to return and it might be better not, but one is apt to feel cut off when the world is in a state of so much tension. Your last letter was written on Sunday night. It is somehow sad to me to hear of troops of any colour in your island . . .

It will be a great pleasure to have that book dedicated to me. That early part of your life has always seemed in some curious way to have been transmitted to me much more intact than anything you actually told me, when we first came into close contact at Oxford—as if you had conveyed the essense of it.

To-day is a day of waiting here. We have not heard yet what Hitler has replied. I have an ominous feeling about it.[23]

War was declared on 3 September. Soon afterwards Enid returned to Oxford, and on the 16th Rothenstein confessed: 'I am relieved to know you safely back. Alas, the future is menacing for us all.'[24]

❖ 17 ❖

For Enid, quite apart from the War, 1940 was a year of much significance. In January she became involved in a love-affair with another woman. It was not, for Enid, the first affair of its kind, but it was clearly the most intense and disturbing liaison in her life; and she was, no doubt, recalling it when, years later, in her lecture on Joyce Cary, she said:

I told him many things about myself, which I would not have told to anyone else—nothing shocked or startled him—but I told him only facts, what I had done, but not the reasons which had led to my actions, nor the feelings which had come in their wake. He did not interpret these facts, nor consider their implications, and did not take into account the moral principles involved, nor the struggles and feelings of guilt resultant from them.[1]

Enid was well aware of the principles which were involved in this liaison; she had been born a Catholic, and she could not escape a feeling of guilt, sometimes a sense of degradation. But, as she explained—in some notes which she clearly wrote about herself—'she needed emotionally what a man gets from women, understanding, gentleness, sympathy. The men who could give her that could not give her the violence.' Now she remained enthralled and entirely committed. 'I thought that I had really found the perfect relationship', she wrote when it had ended. 'I was less lonely than I've ever been in my life before. I valued the intimacy and understanding far more than the love. I thought the friendship would outlive love. I saw no reason why it should end.'[2]

In August a more permanent figure entered her life. Alyse Gregory, the American widow of Llewellyn Powys, lived in a coastguard's cottage at Chaldon Herring, near Dorchester, in Dorset. Far from the bustle of the world, she lost herself in literature and philosophy. She and Enid were to meet only four times, but they were to correspond for twenty-seven years, until Alyse died in 1967.

Letter-writing was Enid's natural means of expression. It made her feel refreshingly uninhibited. She was not consciously composing, as when she wrote a book; she was talking without interruption, sharing her pleasure, releasing her indignation or self-pity, her latest collection of gossip, her fears and griefs. Seated at her typewriter she abandoned herself, sometimes to letters of ten and thirteen pages. As she once observed, if she had lived in the eighteenth century, she would have been an inveterate letter-writer, and written twenty pages to her friends. Her correspondence might perhaps be called a conversation—though sometimes it appears more like a punctuated monologue. Now, in Alyse, she found the perfect listener. Their epistolary relationship was to grow so close that Enid wrote to her, almost without restraint, about her literary work and her private life. Sibyl Eastwood had been an essential guide in her early years. Alyse Gregory, so far from the tensions and problems of Oxford, became, now, a still centre for Enid: a centre to which she could return, sure of consolation, of almost uncritical admiration, and of deepening affection.

On 29 August 1940, Alyse Gregory sent Enid her congratulations on *Arthur Rimbaud*. 'My dear Miss Gregory (or should it be Mrs? ,' Enid replied,

. . . Your letter particularly pleased me for it showed such understanding and sympathetic penetration . . .

I found the writing about Rimbaud's conversion difficult. Firstly because I really do not set much value by it intrinsically for he was not really making a free choice, he was most of the time under morphia and was not capable of clear intellectual decisions. That is from the onlooker's point of view. On the other hand I believe that Rimbaud himself got peace from giving in at the end to a will greater than his own, giving in in the struggle against blind belief, got peace from the sacrifice of what my confessor used to say to me when I was a child was 'Pride of Intellect'. I believe these were the two great impulses in Rimbaud, longing to believe, and also longing for personal intellectual liberty, '*la liberté dans le salut*'. I think that without the certainty of belief he was in a certain way maimed, for one side of him needed certainty in order to be able to fulfil himself, some, like Baudelaire and Pascal, can do that better in doubt . . .

My *Baudelaire* I wrote under poor conditions, I finished it when suffering from concussion after being run over by a motor bus and so it has many faults that I can now see. Then too Gollancz produced it in six weeks and I had no time for alterations. But the subject is a very good one, a better one than Rimbaud and so I regret I did not do it justice.[3]

On 16 September, Alyse Gregory wrote again, expressing her admiration for Sainte-Beuve. 'And now,' she added,

. . . may I ask, since I am sure you are still a young woman—and even more sure that I am an old one—though I have not yet quite reached that age that George Sand said was her happiest just over sixty—if you live alone and if you are still a Catholic and what your brother has written and how you got your taste for letters. I am married, but my husband died a little less than a year ago—and I have any way always kept my own name since my marriage including the Miss—so you addressed me correctly. I live very far up on the downs—in a very isolated house—with my two sisters-in-law in a separate house that still forms part of mine—but made like two houses. We see no-one from sunrise to sundown except the postwoman . . .[4]

6 October 1940.

Dear Miss Gregory,

. . . I am a Fellow and Tutor of Somerville College and a University Lecturer in French literature. I am not really suited for the academic profession, but I have to earn my living somehow as I have a mother and sister dependent on me and the university is willing to pay me. I find the work most terribly tiring and it gives me very little leisure for writing except in the vacations. It is then that I do my research and my writing.

You ask me about my brother . . . He it is who writes on the Gypsies . . . He is at the moment in Madrid, head of the British Council there. I did not agree with him about Spain and never agree with him about politics so I never talk to him about that. Otherwise I am devoted to him and as a child I loved him better than anyone else.

You ask about myself. I was born and bred a Catholic . . . Now I am what is called a bad Catholic, I no longer practise, I suffer from the sin of 'Pride of Intellect', but I still, in a way, feel myself a Catholic and I certainly have not lost my need of spirituality.

I live alone in a flat. All the Fellows of Somerville live in college, but I made it clear that I could not do that and so as a great concession I am allowed to live out. They put my desire for living alone down to the fact of my being a wild Irishwoman and to the fact that I was a student in Paris. I lose financially by the arrangement but I could not bear to live in a community again and I hate a lot of people around me; I particularly hate a lot of women around me. I never feel really at home with my colleagues . . .

I was much interested in what you said about Sainte-Beuve, for I too very greatly admire him and I mean some day to do a full-length study of him. I was waiting until his complete correspondence was published.[5]

On 25 November, when she had finished *Baudelaire*, Alyse Gregory sent her appreciation and certain criticisms of the book. 'But these', she added, 'are small things, though I think when you write of anyone as fastidious in matters of style as Baudelaire a particular care is expected. Then I am always puzzled by the word "sin" as Christians use it—and the word spirituality, but I imagine we would reach the same conclusion by different routes.'[6]

Dec. 21st 1940

Dear Miss Gregory,

. . . I was flattered to read all the nice things you say about my *Baudelaire* and I agree with your criticisms. I regret the faults it has for I like Baudelaire as a poet better than Rimbaud and I wish that I had done better . . .

When I have talked of *sin* in *Baudelaire*, I was not really giving my own opinion, I was taking my stand on what I thought was Baudelaire's position, and what is the Catholic opinion which I believe Baudelaire could not shake off . . . I understand that perfectly well for . . .

psychologically I am still a Catholic, I have a Catholic emotional make-up . . . When the conception of sin and struggle against sin and human weakness is left out, I find something lacking, something taste-less. You will say that the Church has cast its spell on me, that there is something morbid in me and you would probably be right . . .

I talk too much about myself and you say so little, you are so reticent.[7]

The friendship with Alyse Gregory deepened, and other friend-ships remained. 'You must, like myself, have been deeply con-cerned at the French débâcle.' This from Rothenstein in September 1940. 'I saw friend Saurat in Town; he is closely engaged with de Gaulle, of whom he speaks highly . . .'[8] On 2 November, from the South London Hospital, Sibyl Eastwood sent touching com-ments on London in wartime. 'London is beginning to look rather hurt . . . In the mean streets, round here, in Battersea, between here and Brixton, I don't regret the houses, only the lives . . . If you can get it to me safely,' Dr Eastwood added, 'I should like to read your memoirs.'[9]

In August and September, soon after the fall of France, Enid had finally written the book which she had conceived at Porquerolles. In eight weeks, she had set down her impressions of her childhood, and of her early Oxford years. She had recalled them with sharp-ness, delicacy and emotion: her vivid but unhappy life in Ireland, her adolescent growing pains at Oxford, and, finally, her depar-ture for Paris. Much remained unsaid in her book; much was set down with prejudice and perhaps with injustice. Some events were out of focus. Yet those who knew Enid must recognize, in *A Lady's Child*, her unmistakable voice. In its pages she remains as she was: vulnerable, tough, enquiring, perceptive, stubborn, warm, amus-ing, sometimes coarse, and intensely and indubitably Irish.

By May, the book was accepted by Faber's.

Now that her volume of memoirs was finished, she turned again to the novel which she had written in her Exeter days. She revised it, and showed it, chapter by chapter, to a pupil at Somerville, Liselott Haynes.

It was originally to be called something about a Running Hare—a quotation from T. S. Eliot I believe [this from Liselott] . . . Enid said she had chosen the title because she wanted to convey the hunted feeling of the girl . . . who wanted to pursue a career and was forever running away from the love-affair and having it catch up with her again. She told me that it was autobiographical. She had changed an art student into a violinist, if I remember rightly, but the central character was herself in Exeter and the whole novel really a sort of continuation of *A Lady's Child*. 'If you can find me a better title, one that will convey what I mean, do,' said Enid, and I turned up one day with *All Remedies Refusing*, taken from the Oxford Dictionary of Quotations, I regret to confess, where I found the lines 'Love is a sickness full of woe, all remedies refusing, a plant that with most cutting grows, most barren with most using etc. etc.'[10]

The heroine of the novel is Enid, in her twenties. She is ineffectively disguised as Sheilah O'Hara, an Irish doctor's daughter. The dates have been invented, the colour of the eyes has been changed from blue to grey, but the likeness remains unmistakable.

It was in the winter of 1924 that Maude had first met Sheilah who must have been nineteen at the time, though she seemed far younger for she was immature and insignificant in body. Her head, with its sleek dark hair, was large, almost too heavy for its slender neck which seemed ready to snap beneath its weight like the stalk of a flower. Her eyes were grey. Strange eyes that at times were light as if unseeing, but which turned almost black when she was moved.
Maude's first vision of Sheilah was seated at the piano at a students' club where she was playing, unconscious of everyone and everything around her . . . That was what first struck Maude, the way she could isolate herself in a crowd and cut all connection with the people around her. She was struck also by the tense and strained expression on her face, by her curious, staring eyes . . . Maude had to close her eyes beneath that burning and fixed gaze.[11]

The character of Maude, a woman doctor, was based on that of Sibyl Eastwood. The book begins with Maude in search of Sheilah in Paris. She calls on a mutual friend, a Russian artist, Velimir Velimirovitch, for news. (Velimir Velimirovitch was in fact a Russian whom Enid had known in her student days.) Maude and

Velimir discuss Sheilah, the pianist. Here, again, is a self-portrait of Enid.

'There was such a mixture in her,' said Velimir, 'and one doesn't quite know how it will all turn out. Emotionally she was utterly un-awakened, unaware of everyone. I suppose it was her Catholic up-bringing, for she came straight from her convent to Paris. She never noticed the feelings of others towards her. She seemed utterly alone and inviolate. The only people I've heard her speak of with emotion were her father and the old housekeeper who brought her up, Brigitte.'

After a pause, he continued: 'Yet her playing was different. There was something untamed in it which mystified me. When she played you realized the possibility and the promise of passion, as if this wildness burst out in spite of herself. I could never explain to myself that desper-ate and anxious tenseness, that fear of letting herself go. I was more interested in this problem than in her playing itself' . . .

Was this why she kept herself so much aloof from others, Maude wondered? Was it because she was afraid of being deflected, afraid of her own weakness and sentimentality? One felt in everything she attempted this mixture of strength and weakness, this mixture of pur-pose and drift. One felt her terror of giving way to weakness, the fear that if she relaxed her hold on herself she would be carried away to destruction by her natural impulses and emotions. There was something wild and untamed in her, Maude thought, something fiercely shy . . .[12]

And here one recalls—perhaps Enid recalled—a letter from Helen Waddell:

Always from the first moment I saw you I respected you, and divined something in you almost fierce—not your shyness, which is also fierce, but your power and your spirit. And I also thought of you as a terribly shy little animal, not a hare, but something like a little white ermine, with eyes blazing out at you out of the dark, and I used to feel that if I lifted my hand suddenly or spoke too quickly it would be out of the door and tearing down the passage before I could stop it . . .[13]

Enid saw herself through the eyes of others. She also observed herself—or, rather, Sheilah—with fascination.

When she played [the piano] she became someone different. Then one forgot that she was only a girl for there was something masculine and purposeful in her playing which surprised one. One felt the tenseness there, the desperate wildness, as if something imprisoned were trying to escape. But one felt the possibility of escape which one did not usually feel with her. There was in it at the same time something unresolved as if she were trying to discover something in herself, but did not yet know what it was.[14]

Sheilah—like Enid—had suffered from privations, and she had gone to a sanatorium in the mountains to ward off tuberculosis. Sheilah had depended on Maude for stability in her life in Paris; Enid had sometimes relied on Sibyl Eastwood. Sheilah had left Paris to teach the piano at Castle Park School, Padbury; and here is a reminiscence of Enid, teaching at Langford Grove. At Padbury the heroine of *All Remedies Refusing* falls in love with a married man, Archibald Mortimer. He teaches the violin at the school, and ekes out his living by playing at the local cinema. Sheilah, in her blindness (and Enid was often blinded by emotions), sees him as a violinist of international stature, whom she can inspire and rescue from obscurity. They dream of escaping to an island—clearly Porquerolles.

The love-affair remains an adolescent romance, largely a dream; and perhaps it indicates Enid's own emotional pattern.

Was it perhaps—Maude wondered—some deep instinct in her which impelled her, when she fell in love, to choose a man who could never really be hers, who could never have any claims on her? Perhaps this was her secret safeguard, a desperate and unconscious effort to protect the weakness in herself which she always feared, to protect her art and independence from destruction.[15]

Archibald remains with his wife, Mabel (it was the name of one of Enid's colleagues at Exeter). Sheilah is knocked down by a bus, as Enid had been, and she dies—the book demands it—of her injuries. As she lies dying, she says to Maude:

'What do we ever know of any other human being? Nothing, absolutely nothing. We can't really help them, nor draw on their help either. We can only reach truth through ourselves alone. I thought once that there could be the fusion of perfect love. But there can't be that in life. That would only be annihilation and death. One has to accept solitude. When I was younger I was afraid to leave my early solitude for fear of temptation and weakness. But that was only cowardice and I came to see that it was only an arid solitude and I left it. I've been driven back to solitude, a solitude of understanding and compassion. Perhaps that's the strong solitude of which you speak. Perhaps this is real freedom. I understand many things now I think.'[16]

It was a strangely logical and coherent statement, coming from a girl about to die. But Enid had forgotten Sheilah O'Hara. The Somervillian had taken over.

⋄ 18 ⋄

In September 1941, Enid herself was driven back to painful solitude. Her violent love-affair abruptly ended. Quite suddenly, she was abandoned for another woman. She had believed that her relationship was permanent.

To those of her colleagues who were concerned about her distress, she explained (an implausible explanation) that she was mourning the death of a relation. To Liselott Haynes she appealed for sympathy—though apparently without telling her the facts. Liselott remembers:

A friend whom she had regarded as someone to rely on completely, someone with whom she shared great intimacy, happiness and presumably also sadness abandoned her suddenly. I don't know who the friend was or anything about the precise circumstances of this major upheaval, but I know it . . . drove her to withdraw within herself and sort of distrust the whole world and everyone in it for a long time . . . I have never understood why she chose to make a friend of me at that moment. It may have been because she needed just someone far enough removed from her normal circle of friends and colleagues who would listen occasionally and make sympathetic noises without committing her to any real confidences.[1]

I have quite a few friends, but what I am is often very lonely [Enid wrote to Alyse Gregory]. Indeed I have been lonely since I was a small child. Few people have penetrated into complete intimacy with me. I have a very high standard of intimacy. I have always been lonely—very very lonely—in Oxford where no-one really knows me—or indeed would care to know me—and now I cannot get abroad amongst people who more easily understand me. My last intimate relationship was one in which my friend penetrated more deeply into the inner core of my loneliness than anyone before, and I now feel a chill emptiness. I feel a weariness towards everything—a distaste. I know this will not last, but at the moment it makes me very unhappy. You ask whether there is an essential spring broken in my being. I think not, I have power of resilience. But I am very violent inside and I find it difficult to submit. I find resignation well nigh impossible. I put a great deal into this relationship and the blow was very sudden, when I did not expect it. But I have largely pulled myself together now. It is only '*Un seul être vous manque et tout est dépeuplé!*' [2]

'Unhurt people', Enid wrote, 'are not much good in the world.' She was more hurt, now, than she had ever been: 'hurt out of the littleness of oneself. Hurt out of one's disgust of oneself, one's pain at one's own inefficiency and weakness.' She was overcome by 'terrible black floods of lack of confidence, self-depreciation'. She set down her feelings in her notes for another novel—a novel which, this time, remained unwritten. 'Roger used to talk of impermanence. But we broke when he wanted to make permanent. . . . talked of permanence and only meant—impermanence. I thought in terms of spending life beside her.'[3] Enid was left, now, with only a sense of inadequacy and rejection. She felt more lonely than ever. She felt betrayed. 'Love implies the power of constancy at least once. Love implies getting to the end of the personality and then being still welded together. Love implies more than getting into possession of personality. It implies a certain steadfastness.'[4]

The bitterness remained with her long after the love-affair had ended; on the back of a mark-sheet of July 1942 she wrote:

When you are gone. All will think of past with you. The way life was experienced [with] you and then all the pain. All the bitter hurt in memory . . .

You have no gift of friendship . . . Only to the present lover do you give anything. Yet the others continue to love. For they had with you an illusion that nothing else comes up to.[5]

The comment was pitiful. Enid, in middle age, could still be led astray by illusions. 'I'm not a bit young,' she told Alyse, 'and it seems to me very childish that I should still mind disillusionment so much.'[6] But she was still desperate for understanding. She still longed for a permanent relationship. Her nature made it impossible for any one person, man or woman, ever permanently to satisfy her needs.

On 30 October 1941, *A Lady's Child* was published. It was acclaimed as a period piece, a likeness of the Castle Catholics, of a vanished social stratum. Irish critics found the Irish atmosphere intensely vivid. Elizabeth Bowen observed that,

as a study of Edwardian and post-Edwardian Dublin—its wide, silent, tree-planted residential roads, its chintz, muslin and marqueterie drawing-rooms, its *élégantes* in Paris and Vienna models imported by Switzers of Grafton Street, its delicious extensions along the Bay, with talkative Sunday luncheons in dining-rooms within sight of the sea, its aesthetes, its scholars, its musical parties, its glitter reflected from Vice-Regal society—*A Lady's Child* could have had, purely, the charm of a pastiche. But the relentless quality of Miss Starkie's vision and the deep melancholic trend of her memory have gone to make this a very disturbing book. Here are comfort, culture and stylishness seen, as it were, through a dark glass pane, by someone who seems to have had, since her infant years, an adult faculty for unhappiness.[7]

There was striking agreement among the critics about the bitter tone of the book, and Evelyn Waugh declared in the *Tablet* that 'this is the long, sad story of a little girl without a sense of humour . . . [Miss Starkie] has the national trait of nursing a grievance, and is determined to resent her adolescence—she seems at times to believe it was positively injurious to have been carefully reared and liberally educated.' The *Listener* went deeper:

If we judge *A Lady's Child* by the standards of more conventional memoirs, we may well find it a shocking and painful book . . . At first, we suspect malice; but after a few chapters it becomes quite clear that Miss Starkie is doing this not to hurt, nor to pay off old scores, nor to look clever herself, but to lift a burden at last from her shoulders by putting it, as exactly as possible, into words . . .

The burden was family life . . .

It was an understanding comment. 'It seems to me,' was Enid's observation to Alyse, 'that there is a lot of truth in this.'[8]

In Dublin, not unexpectedly, the book created a furore. The *Irish Times* dismissed 'this very naked picture' in anger. 'Just why she should choose in her early forties to write a book which only extreme adolescence and immaturity might condone could be better explained by a student of psychology than by a literary reviewer . . . Most Dubliners will dismiss the book as an unpardonable piece of disloyalty.' *A Lady's Child* was prohibited, but prohibition increased its attraction. Joseph Hone, the friend and biographer of Yeats, told Enid: 'I *bought* your book, I did not go to a library for it. Hodges and Figgis were hiding it, but they had 84 copies!! Don't tell them I told you. Mrs W. B. Yeats said she was so absorbed in the book that she sat up reading it until 3 a.m., but would rather it had not been about people she knew . . .'[9] 'Dear Enid,' wrote Shane Leslie, 'I managed to borrow a proof copy and read your book otherwise unobtainable in Dublin. I retired to the Nunciature and never went to sleep until I had finished it in all its shifting strengths, beauties and sordidnesses. No book has affected me more as literature and as a revelation of the Irish life that we all lived in.'[10]

A Lady's Child was reprinted. It was by far the best written of Enid's books; and, in certain passages, it showed subtle understanding, and a natural style which she was not again to attain. For, despite her knowledge of French literary figures, she remained her own favourite subject. She was passionately self-absorbed. *A Lady's Child* shows what she could achieve when her heart and intellect worked together: when she set her mind to self-analysis, when she set her remarkable memory to summon back and reconstruct her past. The real loss to posterity was not her projected book on Laforgue, but her recollections of Paris and Oxford: the two further volumes of autobiography which she meant to write.

As it was, the reception of *A Lady's Child* made it impossible for her to continue her recollections for many years. While the critics admired the book, her relatives resented it fiercely. The autumn of 1941 brought Enid not only the unexpected end of her love-affair. For a time it also brought estrangement from her family.

⋄ 19 ⋄

In her distress she turned, as usual, to her confidantes. She seems to have told Sibyl Eastwood the name of her lover—and, perhaps, even asked her to mediate. Dr Eastwood tried in vain to bring about a reconciliation.[1]

To Alyse Gregory, Enid wrote in general terms of her distress.

> I go into everything with fanaticism and violence [this on 3 December], I never leave myself any loop-hole for retreat and so each time I have a complete débâcle. I take things very hardly always for I've never learnt resignation and I have to wait until the fires burn out and burn me up with them . . . I am far from being a strong character and I've never felt it more than now. I am lamentably weak and I have little discipline or control of myself. I cannot prevent a common thing like an emotional crash [from getting] me down. But I'll get over it, I've got over as bad things before. Also I do not believe that the life of an adult can be wrecked by any one else than themselves, and if one does not despair of living one finds a way of building one's pain into the foundations of one's life so that it becomes a strength and not a cause of destruction. I've never really despaired of living. But I'm too impatient and violent . . .[2]

Alyse, devoted and distant, continued to be an ideal listener; and Enid continued to talk to her. 'With you I'm more free than I've ever been with any other human being, . . . I've revealed, without any shame or reservations, all sides of myself.'[3] This was not quite true. She did not dare to confess that she was in love with a woman; she repeatedly said that she loved a man. The deception was significant. But Alyse Gregory was wise; and the name of Enid's lover appeared so frequently in her letters that perhaps she surmised the truth. On 11 December, Enid wrote again: 'I hope . . . that my academic work will not destroy me. It may quite easily do that if I don't get a Chair, that is what my career has been planned for . . . I hope that this letter doesn't strike you as too grossly egotistic and selfish. I seem to be brooding too much in the last weeks on my own troubles . . .'4

I long to draw you out of this pit [answered Alyse]. I have been in so many pits myself . . . If you were ever able to get away and felt that a weekend on the wild Dorset coast would benefit you I would be happy to entertain you. But you would have to be prepared for a very bare and simple life. I live in a *very* small cottage and almost entirely in a small whitewashed chamber with mice, spiders, and moths—at the top of the house. My cottage is exposed to the wild winds and rain. I have no servant—and no-one ever comes up here—except the woman who works for my sister-in-law. It is rough and simple—though I have a small bathroom. But you could remain as still as a stone or walk along the wild sea cliffs . . . Think of it as a possible momentary escape in a time of desperation.5

Dear Miss Gregory,
. . . As a matter of fact for a long time I've thought of the possibility of going to see you . . . I even went to the length of looking up trains . . . I'd like to go to see you and to spend a night if you really think you could do with me . . . By myself I live very austerely, almost the way I lived as a student in Paris, but a Don can't offer such treatment to her guests! I only say this to show you that I'm a very simple person . . . I'm not a bit ascetic because when I do spend then I'm very extravagant and luxurious. You'd realize that if you saw all the gold and flame and lacquer of this flat. I've always thought it rather silly to pay a lot to get adequate and uninteresting living conditions. I'd rather have really bad ones and have a bit of money for extravagance on things that really give pleasure. So I sit in the midst of my gold paint and my flame coloured lacquer and have a piece of bread and cheese and a cup of milk for supper. Sometimes I think I've made myself a golden cage here, because it will be very difficult ever to leave it, firstly because it is not paid for and secondly because I think it beautiful. For a

long time I had no possession whatsoever, then I got the Grand piano
on the instalment system and having been tied by the leg to the piano
and then to 3000 books I thought I might as well have all the rest. In
any case I can't give up my profession as I've too many family responsibilities . . . But I've never really liked Oxford except when I
was an undergraduate and I've never liked academic people. I don't
think many of my colleagues dislike me but they don't take me to their
bosom, they feel a certain mistrust of me, as if I were a different breed
of animal. I would never have got back to Oxford if my moral tutor,
Miss Pope, for some unknown reason, had not had a belief in me. Now
that I myself am on appointment boards I see that they never appoint
people like me, they are afraid to. I've always been very lonely here,
indeed I think I've always been very lonely, except when I was a student
in Paris, . . . and now I feel a chill emptiness and I feel no taste for
anything and more distaste than ever for academic people and for the
academic life. What a lot of boring stuff I'm talking, please forgive my
self-centredness. But if you really think you could do with me for a
night I'd love to come.[6]

'May I not say for two nights?' enquired Alyse Gregory. She
added a reminder: 'But you must be prepared for a wild place . . .
Since my husband's death I have let my garden go to seed and my
house lies as stagnant as the crocodiles in the aquarium I used to
watch as a child.'[7]

Dear Miss Gregory [this on Boxing Day],
 . . . Could I come as soon after Jan. 1st as possible, I could come that
week-end. You see I feel a great desire to get down to a bit of writing
before term begins . . . I have six books in my head that I could write
if only I had leisure—three novels and three works of scholarship. I also
want to find time to play the piano a bit now that I have taken it up
again. The thing that I would like to give up is the thing I cannot give
up, my academic teaching, and I am even obliged to add to that in the
vacations the marking of examination papers. The only thing that
would save me would be to get a Chair before I am too old. What I
would like best of all would be the Chair of French literature at Oxford.
Firstly because you have to give only 2 hours lecturing a week for six
weeks of the term, 36 hours a year . . . Secondly I would like the
Chair at Oxford because it would have pleased my father—not that

that matters much now, but it would give some sense to the sacrifices I have made for my academic career. But they will never give the Chair at Oxford to a woman . . . I think of all these things particularly now because I am very tired and discouraged as I see years ahead of this terribly hard work that leaves no leisure to enjoy living, or friendship and love. I feel it particularly now that a relationship has ended and when I reflect how little time I had to enjoy it as I should and put into it all I could. I put into it all I had, but I was torn away from it by too many things . . . I am very tired and would like a little leisure and rest, I feel what Baudelaire used to call *un découragement mortel*. I am not really as weak and spineless as this would lead you to believe. There is a good bit of fight in me yet. I am small but I am terrifically tough. If I wasn't tough I wouldn't have survived all I've survived. It is only every now and then that things get too much for me. Things have been too much for me these last months. I've been overworked at Oxford, I've had an emotional débâcle and I've had this rift with my family. Then there is ever present the war and the tragedy of France.[8]

'What a correspondence we seem to be having!' wrote Alyse on 1 January. 'I shall have another week to look forward to your coming . . . I shall expect you then by the four o'clock bus next Saturday—the 10th of January—and will be in the village to meet the bus.'[9]

Enid came to Dorset, and went; but in her brief visit to Chaldon Herring she and Alyse took a further step towards each other: towards a relationship of intimacy and trust. Yet Enid left with her sorrow still unspoken and unresolved. 'You must not think of yourself as of no value,' Alyse admonished her, 'you are a very rare person . . . But you did not quite trust me so I could not touch the real secret of your trouble. . . . I wish I might have given you even a little ounce of comfort—shifted that weight even for a little moment.'[10]

My dear Alyse,
. . . I thank you very much indeed and I enjoyed my visit very much and was very glad to meet you after this lengthy correspondence. I don't know that you are vastly different from what I imagined . . .
I think that, though your taste in literature is very similar to mine,

you are different to me in that you are more ready to speculate and to study from a distance than I. I want to be in the thick of people who are feeling and living, whether I like them or their life does not matter so much, I want to find out what there is in human hearts—I want it through books and authors, but I want it through life as well . . . I want to write of that quite as much as I want to write of artists whom I study in their works. When I have had my fill of being this tumultuous being then I want one place for reflection and creation. Baudelaire used to call his descent into the city his '*bain de multitude*' and then he used to appreciate solitude. '*Enfin seul!*' he cried. I have the two cravings in my nature. The people who bore me are the academic people with whom my lot is thrown, because they don't live as I understand living. I think you would be fairer to them than I am.

You must not think that I am always sad and unhappy. I was happy and at peace most of the time when I was with you, except when I stopped to think. When my mind is not otherwise occupied it gravitates back to my central pain. It is like a soreness that is always there, that I forget at times. It is a wound I hold together with my mind but sometimes it breaks out again. A lot of the pain is not just loss of love, but disillusionment, the discovery that where I thought there was frankness, there was pretence . . .

My wild heart will not resign itself to its loss . . .[11]

She could not resign herself, even now, to the end of the affair. 'I'm not finding things getting any easier [this on 11 February]. I don't seem able, whatever I do, to reach serenity and peace of mind . . . It was all so sudden and I am so bankrupt . . .'[12] And again, on 15 April:

My dear Alyse,

. . . I have been going through very bad months and I have been fighting with myself, trying to conquer myself. I did not want to write until I had reached some sort of stability . . . I thought things were getting better but then I have these desperate relapses of despair . . .

Don't be too impatient or disgusted with me. Some time I'll show you better what I am. You [have come] to know me at an unfortunate moment for me, when I am rudderless. I've had twelve or thirteen love-affairs in my life—some sordid, some cheap. Only three were really genuine and of these three it is the first and the last that have meant most. And into the last I put everything. It filled my inner loneliness entirely. You have learnt, I know, that one cannot fill that loneliness of the heart, but I thought one could and I thought I had and in the process I lost the former strength I had in my solitude.[13]

Some months later, she added: 'It is all over really except in my heart.'[14]

Enid sought not only comfort in her distress, but advice about her still unpublished novel. She had felt that she could free herself of the episode in Exeter once she had crystallized it in a book. She also felt that she canalized the pain of this last disillusionment as she contemplated her earlier grief. She had shown her novel, chapter by chapter, to Liselott Haynes; she had shown it to Sibyl Eastwood, and submitted it to two literary friends, who pronounced conflicting judgments. One of them dismissed it as worthless, and Enid was hurt. Now, in June 1942, Alyse read the novel, and—more devoted than critical—she found it 'deeply moving'; she offered to show it to a friend for a further opinion.

My dear Alyse [wrote Enid on 7 July],
      Thank you very much for sending me your friend's criticism . . .
      The more I think of the reports I've had the more I'm convinced that I ought to try to publish the novel . . . My childhood didn't give me any peace until I'd laid the ghost of it by writing the [other] book. In the same way this episode won't leave me in peace until I've made something out of it.

And, thinking once more of her recent betrayal:

I don't want to push all that down into the subconscious . . . I want to sublimate it in some writing, then perhaps I'll get peace. The older I get the more I come to believe that the only thing that really gives meaning to life is creative work of some sort. I think that is something [which] remains longest worthwhile. It is I imagine the thing that betrays one least. It need never if one goes on believing in the value of what one is doing. I don't exactly mean value so much as honesty and sincerity, genuineness, of its own kind.

I think if my novel had any kind of success it would do much to give me back courage and interest in life.[15]

Early in September, Enid announced that she had sent her novel to Faber's. Nothing shows her lack of self-criticism more clearly that this persistent longing to write fiction. She was not a novelist even of the meanest order; she was a creative writer only when she wrote of her own life, or re-created the life and emotions of Baudelaire or Rimbaud. Autobiography was her natural *genre*, biography was her métier. But she could not recognize her limits.

If I'm only a scholar [she told Alyse] then I'll never escape and the sooner I get used to the idea the better and the wiser it is and cease tearing myself to pieces with longing and frustration. If I'm only a scholar then the sooner I settle down to find happiness and peace in being a don the better it is for as a scholar there is no better position than being a Fellow of a college—except for being a professor. I know we've all got our *violon d'Ingres*, that many of us hanker to be doing what we are most unsuited to doing. But Ingres had another means of self-expression, he had his art, he didn't need the fiddle. But I'll have nothing, for I've given up the hope of making anything of music in an executant way. I've always hoped that I could eventually get out of teaching and be able to write as I would like. But maybe I haven't creative power. Anyone, with diligence, can be a 'scholar' and I've never much regarded things like my *Rimbaud in Abyssinia* etc. I've always considered the ferreting out of facts only a preliminary step to having material for deeper and more psychological judgments.[16]

And again:

I know perfectly well that when I look back I'll think that I've wasted my life . . . I think that you were probably right when you thought that it would ultimately be a good thing for me if I were disgraced at Oxford and had to leave, then I'd really be a writer. As soon as the war is over I'm going seriously to consider whether I'll throw up my academic work altogether.[17]

Faber's rejected Enid's novel, and she sent it to Macmillan's. On 4 October she wrote again to her usual correspondent:

If Macmillans refuse it I'm not yet going to give up hope. I'll try quite a lot of people first . . .

I have another novel in my mind—in fact I've two—and it would be a kind of continuation of *A Lady's Child*. It would be about student life in Paris during the middle twenties, a kind of twentieth-century *La Bohème*. It would be less psychological than the novel you've read, it would deal more with externals and I think that it would be more popular with English readers. I think that I could make something interesting of it. I think it would show some of the characteristics which eventually led to the disaster of 1940. In a way I wish it was my first novel for I think it would be much more popular. Though the other novel—if only it were good—is more the kind of novel I'd like really to write. It is taking shape in my mind in little scraps, but God knows when I'll be able to write it. Term begins this week.[18]

Alyse continued to give wrong advice. 'Of course you are a novelist,' she insisted, when Macmillan's in turn rejected the book. 'Even if this novel were not taken your next one would be. I would try Constable after Gollancz—then Harrap, . . . then John Lane. Have you a carbon copy I could send to America?'[19]

Soon after Christmas 1942, Enid went to Dublin. It was her first visit to her family since the appearance of *A Lady's Child*, and she felt apprehensive about her reception. She had another source of disquiet: a year and more after the end of her love-affair, she was still disturbed by the thought of the woman who had left her. 'I think some natures are born to torment other natures,' Alyse wrote on 3 January. '. . . I do hope, dear Enid, that all this trouble that revolves in your mind may be turned sooner or later into your creative work.'[20]

For the moment, her creative work was far from fortunate. Alyse had asked yet another friend for his opinion of the novel. The anonymous friend (soon identified as the novelist Louis Wilkinson) sent a frank condemnation.

That egotistic weakling of a half-man and that half-developed masochistic girl! To me they are both extremely unpleasant, and I recoil in disgust and contempt . . . from the thought of all those continual physical symptoms of frustration that must have gone on, for both of

them, week after week, month after month—how repulsive! . . . Of
course it was Archie—what a name, but how it suits him!—who was
chiefly, indeed almost entirely to blame for this. But the girl is of the
breed that is sure to get fixed on the first man she meets who is sure to be
able to make her unhappy: she wouldn't take to any other kind of man,
partly out of masochism, partly out of a love of dramatization, partly
out of false sentiment, and the need for self-pity, and partly out of a
weak egotism . . .[21]

'I *must* warn you once more', insisted Alyse, 'not to take this
criticism too seriously.'[22]

The topic turned from literature to religion, and they exchanged
long letters on questions of faith.

I haven't been to confession or communion for twenty years [Enid
explained]. I haven't been to mass or any of the services except for
aesthetic purposes for about the same length of time. I went to mass
last Easter Sunday in order to get the sequence of things correct in my
mind for a chapter in my novel. One cannot say that religion has any
effect whatsoever in my life or that it has any effect at all on my
thought . . .

But when I've set down thus my agnosticism, when my reason has
found satisfaction in that, there still remains something in me that isn't
satisfied . . . I know that something deep in me turns towards that
spiritual sun which I cannot see, that it eventually finds its way into the
sunlight wherever it is grown, even in a cellar.[23]

The moral and religious questions which they discussed so often
were raised once more in Enid's edition of *Les Fleurs du mal*. First
published in November 1942, it was reprinted the following
August. In her introduction, she again claimed Baudelaire as a
moralist. 'That is something from a Fellow of Somerville College!'
declared *The Times Literary Supplement*. 'One cannot but applaud
such boldness in a Fellow of Somerville. What she says is true.
Baudelaire was a visionary, but he was a passionate moralist as
well . . . How the water has flowed under Magdalen Bridge!'[24]
It had, indeed; and Enid was aware how much she herself had done
to change the climate of opinion. Writing to Thomas Higham in
1947, she added: 'Would you believe it I was not only the first

person to lecture on Rimbaud in this university but also on Baudelaire. When I came here there was a totally erroneous conception of Baudelaire. I notice, now, everywhere, that people are coming round to my view that he was one of the great spiritual poets of France and of the world.'[25]

The scholar who edited Baudelaire with courage and compassion remained incurably lonely. 'Loved or unloved we are always alone in ultimate things, alone on what Gide calls *"cette commune mer intérieure"*, that waste of loneliness . . . And yet I don't feel that I want to cast away the goblet. I want to drink to the bottom . . . There's so much still that I want to know and understand, so much to see.'[26]

Alyse wrote to her with sympathy. She also sent congratulations on her industry. Driven, perhaps, by the need to lose herself in work, Enid had written five articles in three weeks. In May she also wrote 'Nostalgie de Paris d'une Irlandaise'. It appeared that month in the review *Aguedal* at Rabat, in Morocco. Written in the depths of the War, when France was occupied and liberation seemed a distant dream, the article vibrates with an emotion which is now hard to recapture. But Enid's intimate sorrow had not blunted her sorrow at the degradation of France, and she expressed her love of France with intensity. She recalled Léonie Cora's descriptions of the French countryside, and her nostalgic accounts of French cooking (now, in wartime, Enid could only dream of Œufs Mimosa and Crabe Jambalaya). She recalled her own childhood interest in French clothes, her early affection for French literature. As she grew to adolescence, she had felt that only in French literature, in France, might she discover

that clearsightedness without illusion—and without disillusion, too—that intellectual courage which I sought so ardently. I virtually read nothing but French authors. The quality which already struck me most in the French was this adult character, or, rather, this maturity of people who had known how to come to grips with life, and had made their peace with it . . .

As for me, the French authors whom I most often read [to-day] are those who have studied human grief, the abysses of sin and remorse: Racine, Pascal, Flaubert, Baudelaire and Mauriac. These authors have not always been fully appreciated, even in France; but abroad they are masters who are not understood. Baudelaire and Rimbaud were not understood; I have tried to make them understood in my country, and one day I hope to do the same for Gide.[27]

Enid remembered how, as an Oxford don, she had returned to France every vacation, to plunge again into its atmosphere.

Once I was back in Paris, . . . I hurried off to rediscover my favourite *quartiers* on the Left Bank, the sixth and seventh arrondissements, those little streets, those tiny squares, so calm and so peaceful, just like the streets and squares in a provincial town . . .

Next morning I set off on foot for the Bibliothèque Nationale. It was, so to speak, my club, and there I knew I should meet all my friends from the Sorbonne who had not yet been swallowed up by life . . .

At the Bibliothèque Nationale, . . . I immediately went the round of the reading-room tables. On the right side, the tickets are green; on the left side, they are white. Each side of the room had its clientèle, and we should have thought it disloyal to change over. I wanted to see what still remained of the happy band who had begun, so bravely, at the same time as I had, to prepare their doctoral theses . . .

'Well, how is Rémi Belleau? Joubert? Chênedollé?' I asked, as I leant over the table, and saw the thesis in preparation.

People soon abandoned their books and came to smoke and chat in the little square opposite the library—it was no bigger than a small drawing-room. It had witnessed many literary and artistic discussions. It was there that, as a young student, I used to lunch off a roll and a bar of chocolate, and end up with a coffee at the bistro on the corner . . .

I had plunged back again into this Paris atmosphere. I forgot that I had become a serious person, a lecturer; I became once again the *gamine* of the Quartier Latin with her little student's beret.[28]

And here, unconsciously, Enid revealed herself. Emotionally, she refused to grow beyond her student days. She still needed a sense of community, she still needed not to feel different; and in Paris, as a student, for the only time in her life, she had felt that she belonged. She could not bear to lose that feeling. When she returned in later years, it was not to enjoy the place as an adult, to appreciate it in maturity. She would always stay at the Foyer in Miss Watson's lifetime; she would always impose the familiar conditions on herself. She did so not from financial need but because she could not adjust herself to the present. She would always try to re-create her past.

One rigorous habit stayed with her from her Paris days. In time she became a woman of wealth—she died worth some £70,000—but she kept the habit of poverty. She wrote her letters on odd scraps of paper (some of them on the blank pages of examination papers which she had corrected); she used envelopes which had already done service. She filled postcards and airmail letters to the outermost edges; she delivered her countless local Christmas cards by hand, to save the stamps. She often said that she kept her telephone for incoming calls; and, on her list of outgoing calls, she noted local conversations which lasted under three minutes. Her stringency achieved at times Balzacian proportions, and she owed it, largely, to her Paris days. Even when she enjoyed a solid and regular income, she refused to buy herself a meal. 'When I am in Paris,' she told Alyse, 'I of course never go to the extravagance of going to a café alone, except to take a cup of coffee.'[29] Instead, she arranged for invitations. In 1955, remembers Mrs Hamilton-Meikle, she suddenly appeared at a friend's house in Paris for lunch, 'and made no bones of the fact that she was cadging meals!'[30] 'I hope', wrote Enid to a pupil, 'that circumstances will never drive you to too great depths of scrounging and sponging . . . Perhaps you wouldn't mind that as much as I did.'[31] She may have minded it, but in time, as an Honorary Fellow of Somerville, she would slip a slice of Common Room cake into her capacious handbag at tea-time, with the comment: 'That will do for my supper.'

◆ 20 ◆

By May 1943, Alyse Gregory had become closer to Enid than many people whom she had known for years, and saw every day.

'You mean more in my life than I could ever tell you,' Enid wrote
to her.[1] And again: 'Tuesday night late. Dearest Alyse, I've just
got back from London and I'm going to write to you because I
must talk to someone. I'm tired and unhappy and lonely and who
is there to talk to if I don't talk to you? . . .'[2]

Alyse was, above all, a friend for moments of despondency, a
companion in moments of distress. On 18 June she reassured Enid:
'I think of you so much—of all that you have suffered, all that you
have come through—and still as ardently seeking truth as ever. It
is the one pursuit that can never terminate—that can never really
destroy us or break our hearts.'[3]

> I agree with you [Enid answered] that the pursuit of truth is the one
> thing that can never let us down . . . But I do not think that by itself
> it necessarily brings peace of mind . . . I think that the pursuit of truth
> alone is a confession of loneliness of spirit . . . I think that the pursuit
> of truth is an interest, an occupation, an urge, a passion, but I think that
> what really gives value to life, gives the nearest approach to happiness
> one can reach, is the getting near another soul in compassion and
> sympathy, not only to feel the need and the power to give, but for
> there to be someone who trusts one and needs one enough to be able to
> take . . .
>
> What do people do, who have no power of expression, when pain
> becomes too heavy, I often wonder. I feel always that I must make
> something of it, canalize it, use its strength for something. I used to
> think, when I was young, that this urge not to allow pain and experi-
> ence to go to waste, to evaporate, was a sign that I was going to be a
> writer, but I'm not so sure now.[4]

On 8 August, she wrote again:

> I always hope that I may extract some grain of gold from our vulgar
> modern world, I think that you feel that there is none there. Then too I
> think that I can find some pleasure—indeed quite a lot—in the more
> vulgar sensual pleasures, drink and food. I can for a moment cease
> analysing and observing and enjoy riotous eating and drinking, with
> 'good' companions, whom in my heart I really despise. I'm not very
> proud of that, but there it is. Though I'm capable also of great austerity.
> I can also, as you do, enjoy nature, the sun, the sea, music and books. I

don't think however that enjoyment is enough to make life worth living . . . The things that I think give price to life are the search for knowledge—I know you think that too—the satisfaction and development of the creative urge of whatever kind it is in the individual, and finally the getting close to others in sympathy, understanding and compassion.[5]

On 18 August, Enid was forty-six; and her birthday brought her still more cause for reflection. She unburdened herself once more: expressed her doubts, unhappiness and regrets. 'Most people don't need to talk about themselves when they are confident', so she once confessed.[6] But she herself perpetually lacked confidence, and her introspection was unending. Early in October, she wrote again:

. . . I've changed and developed in some ways so much during the last two years, that it seems to me sometimes as if I were only just beginning adult life . . . Since I've known you, since 1940, things have happened that have altered me and I feel that more strongly now than I felt at some earlier metamorphoses, almost as strongly as during adolescence, when I began to discover myself, when I was fifteen. And what I owed to you during this very difficult and very unhappy time, I could never tell you. I know that I clung to you spiritually as to a safety raft. I know that you helped me to believe in myself when I was completely lost.[7]

'Thank you, dear Enid, for the charming and consoling things you say to me. The fact that I could give you confidence gave and gives me confidence. We met at a time in both our lives when we could respond, with open hearts, each to the other.'[8]

The correspondence continued: indeed, the private conversation. 'I'm terrible when I begin to talk on paper', Enid admitted. 'Nothing seems to stop me.'[9] She still concealed the central truth, as she did from nearly all her friends. But, this fundamental truth apart, she spoke of everything; analysed herself continually. In this aftermath of crisis, she set down her stream of consciousness. It remains a revelation of her nature. 'I know well what is really most wrong with me is instability of the nervous system. Almost nothing puts me out of gear and almost nothing upsets my sleep.'[10] She was conscious not only of her instability, but of the warring characteristics within her. She was aware of her own confusing double personality, of the two different people who appeared to inhabit a single skin. One of them she respected, the other seemed to be dominant, and this was the one that she deplored.

I hate my personality. I wish I could understand it. On the one hand I think clearly and realistically. I think then my judgment is fairly good . . . On the other hand I'm impetuous, impulsive, gullible, clumsy and crude. These two personalities are never in harmony, and it is the gullible, clumsy and crude personality that comes out with close friends so I suppose that must be the true me. And the person I'd like to be is a very civilized person, sophisticated, sensitive and incapable of clumsy and crude actions . . .[11]

On 22 November, Alyse returned to the themes of love and loneliness. 'I think each human being lives alone in his or her illusion . . . Even friendship, the best of our illusions—would I dare to tell my secret fears to any friend? No, because I know they would be driven deeper in.'[12]

My dearest Alyse,
    I don't think that I agree with you . . . I do tell all my secret fears to those whom I call my close friends . . . I think that friendship is one of the best things—if not the best thing—in life. It is not so blinded as is love, sex love. You may get love and friendship with the same person, but not necessarily so. I think that it is particularly hard for women. I think that women have very greatly evolved during the last hundred years or so and that men have not kept pace with them, have not evolved in what they would like their women friends to be, their loves. It may be all right for the undersexed women—like some of my colleagues who have married—they can find all they want in marriage with a rather dried-up intellectual; they are satisfied with intellectual companionship and accept the rest with it. It is all right, of course, for those who are completely feminine. It is all right also for those who are largely maternal. But for those who are complete women in the physical sense as in the other, but who have at the same time complicated intellectual,

Enid at age three

The Starkie children, Dublin, 1916. Standing are Muriel and Walter. Sitting, from left to right, are Enid, Nancy, and Chou-Chou. Humphrey Robert is held by the nurse

Enid at the time she arrived in Paris, about 1921

Enid in academic dress in her study in St Giles', 1947

Andre Gide, Doctor of Letters, Oxford, June 1947

'A voluble, flamboyant humming-bird': Enid in 1950

Enid Starkie with Edyth Rackham's bust of the nurse who appears in the photograph of the Starkie children

Enid in her drawing room at 41, St Giles', 1959

imaginative and emotional natures, it is very hard for them to find a man who will satisfy them physically and at the same time understand them intellectually, spiritually and emotionally. The virile man, unfortunately, is very rarely interested in the deeper nature of the woman he loves . . . If a complicated woman desires a virile man she has to pretend not to have very much brains, she has to keep large stretches of her nature for ever hidden from him, she has to accept not to be understood. I know you will say 'who is ever understood?' I know that is true, but this kind of woman has to give up entirely from the very outset any hope that the man she is 'in love' with will ever begin to understand her, or would even like what he'd find if he did understand her. I like men friends and I have many of them, but I've never yet fallen in love with any man who could begin to try to understand what I was really like . . . I feel sure that this problem exists for any woman who is not purely an intellectual.[13]

Enid could be rational and perceptive on paper; but the writing of letters did not lift the burden of bewilderment and regret. She continued to be unsure of herself, unremittingly introspective, desperately self-absorbed. On 11 January, after a visit to Ireland, she explained:

When I was in Dublin I walked a lot through the streets alone, along those streets where I went as a child, on my way to school, on my way home. There was the faint rain that there so often was when I was a child and the damp pavements shining in the light of the lamps. All my childhood seemed to come before me with its weight of pain and uncertainty. I wrote *A Lady's Child* I think to try to find out the cause of all this uncertainty and pain. I think that unconsciously I blamed my mother for never having given me as a small child any feeling of personal security and value. As I walked last week it seemed to me that I understood so much better now what was wrong, but of course I don't know any more why it was. I always seemed to have too heavy a weight to bear of what people wanted me to be, too many difficult things, as if I couldn't be myself until these were done. I thought that it was only the burden and responsibility of being a Lady's Child, but I think there was more than that. That has gone on all my life and I'm now over forty—forty-two [she was in fact forty-six]—and I still feel that I cannot do anything for myself until I have carried out all that is expected of me . . . When I was a child I thought that I must first grow up, and get away from the responsibility to my parents' wishes. I went to Oxford to please my father. In Paris I thought always of what was expected of me to get my doctorate. Then in Oxford I think of what college will expect of me for the salary they give me . . . This fear of not giving others what they've a right—imagined or real—to have from me eats into my energies and destroys me . . . Do you . . . think that psycho-analysis would find out the cause of all this uncertainty?[14]

'I have had many friends who have been helped by analysis,' Alyse answered, 'but I should not be analysed myself . . . I think creative work or a true love will give you your greatest consolation—and as love is usually out of the question—then I think work is the next best.'[15]

My dearest Alyse,
    . . . I agree with you that the best consolation is work, creative work . . . But I've often heard that psycho-analysis discovers the hidden reason for some inhibition or malaise . . . What I wanted to know, if I could, was why there was this impulsion in me which so often prevents me from fulfilling myself . . . I think that I've made a mess of love for the very same reason, by thinking more of what was expected of me and never giving expression to what I longed for.[16]

'If you *knew* an analyst you felt you could trust I would certainly have a try at it,' Alyse answered. 'I think there is something in your childhood in connexion with your father that causes you to feel as you do. But . . . few people have been loved as you have been loved . . .'[17]

    Wherever did you get the idea that I've been greatly loved? Nothing could be further from the truth. I've never in my life been really loved . . .
    I've been desired a few times but that can happen to anyone and it has often been by men who thought that from the life I had led in Paris, from the way I talked that I would be easy to have. It has often not been particularly flattering. I've been loved three times I think, but it was not love that stood the tests of difficulty and time. When I say I've been loved three times I mean when I reciprocated it. The first time circumstances were against it. The second time I became engaged. That was my

one attempt to be a normal girl and not to ask for too much understanding and community of ideas and interests. I broke the engagement
eventually, . . . because I didn't think that he was a big enough person,
or loved me enough, to be able to stand up to the havoc which marriage
with me would bring to his life . . . Once I thought I had found everything but that broke down and not through my own lack of love . . .[18]

The correspondence seems to have made an endlessly complicated matter out of a simple situation. Enid needed some complete
relationship: not a mere liaison, but a permanent, absorbing and
demanding relationship which gave her intellectual stimulus and,
above all, emotional understanding. Dorothy Wadham considered
that 'she would have settled for a first-class triumph in *any* direction. If in *love*, she would have had to be somebody's goddess, and
that presumably never came her way . . . Failing great love, I
think she would have been satisfied with what she considered pre-
eminence in scholarship: hence the disproportionate obsession with
the title of Professor.'[19] And again: 'Enid needed to *give* total devotion as well as to *get* it . . . Failing both giving *and* getting I think
either would have satisfied her, but I fear neither happened, and
that her considerable successes in other directions did not compensate. I would not say that she necessarily wanted husband and
children . . . [But] she did not find content. I am certain . . .
about that.'[20]

Enid herself set down some of her thoughts in the notes for her
Paris novel.

The curse of *loneliness*.
Never exchanging and renewing and giving and receiving.
We ought to toss it about.
But where is it? And who wants it? I am in despair, such despair. I
begin weeping . . .
One will never give in. But if only people understood—one person—
ever so little, but subtly—but with exquisite rare friendship . . .
One eager person to share my discovery, one person to understand
the pattern I have made . . .
What we need ultimately most bitterly of all is to be loved and
understood, understood in our depths, in our weaknesses and dreams.[21]

In June 1944, at a dinner-party at Maurice Bowra's at Wadham, Enid met Rosamond Lehmann. They had admired one another's books. Now their warmth and perceptiveness drew them together. 'Our wining at Maurice's is such a delightful friendly memory, I don't think we care to "Miss" to each other after it', Rosamond wrote on 19 October. 'You can't imagine what pleasure your letter gave me . . . I am your earnest admirer, as I told you, so I care very much to please you by my work. How lovely that you liked it!'[1] In the same letter she mentioned the new miscellany *Orion*, which she helped to edit, and she asked Enid for a contribution. '*I* would like it to be about your early days in Paris [she added on 1 November]! . . . Anything up to 5000 words, and please say as much as you can without invalidating your chances of a Professorship.'[2]

Enid lent her a copy of *A Lady's Child*.

I've only got to the Léonie Cora chapter, but I am completely enthralled by it [came the answer]. I have never read an autobiography that didn't fascinate me for one reason or another—but I truly think this is one of the best, the richest that I've ever set eyes to. It seems to pour out in a brilliant warm streaming flood, as if you'd written it in a state of intense psychological excitement. I expect that's how you *did* write it. It is inspired; and I love the personality of the teller who mirrors it all and is mirrored by it . . .

I wonder why that last photograph of you in Paris looks so sad and tense. I shall know in time . . .[3]

Twenty years after her time in Paris, Enid remained sad and tense. The fact was clear to Rosamond and to Alyse. Those who were less close to her might have been aware of some indefinable frustration: conscious of some vague unfulfilment. Social acquaintances would only have marvelled at the intensity of Enid's life. And here again one becomes aware of her dual personality. Even when she was writing her most introspective letters, expressing her most painful *malaise*, she could forget her deeper needs in the whirl of parties with colleagues, undergraduates, visiting lecturers, literary friends and chance acquaintances. To them she radiated gaiety, she seemed a powerhouse of vitality.

Since Enid spent her working life with a constant succession of people, since she was engaged in demanding intellectual tasks, since she also contrived to live a feverish social life, she sometimes had to escape the pressure, to break the tension and restore her energies. Yet though her need of solitude was real and understandable, she was still burdened by the feeling that she had no roots, that she did not belong.

I'm like you I feel a *déracinée* almost everywhere [she wrote to Alyse]. I couldn't live any more in Ireland; I couldn't bear the narrow-minded catholicism that is now prevalent there and I couldn't bear the narrow censorship. But I've never felt really at home in England, I've always felt like a foreigner. I've never felt really at one with the English, except sometimes since the Battle of Britain. Then, for the first time, I think, I felt solidarity with them. Since then I've often again felt infuriated with them—or perhaps it is really with academic people I feel infuriated—and I've always felt most at home with Latin people. I've very much liked Italians but I've admired the French more and I think that I'd rather live in Paris than anywhere.[4]

And again: 'I have no close friends here [in Oxford], men or women,' she told Thérèse Lavauden at the end of her life. 'I have never much liked academic people—especially the women!'[5] The remark was made in a moment of bitterness, and it was not wholly true; but Enid remained lonely. It was a loneliness imposed by her diffidence and by her extraordinary self-absorption. It was also the loneliness of the born non-conformist, of the *rebelle à outrance*, of the Irish rebel in the English Establishment.

She remained a rebel all her life. 'I've an interest in anti-social people: I think I'm rather anti-social myself', she told an undergraduate the year before she died. If she chose to write about the *mauvais garçons* of French literature, her own career, as he suggested, had something of the *mauvaise fille* about it.[6] She symbolized Bohemian feminism, she was independent and outspoken. In letters to the Press, in interviews, she discussed research and vacation work. She confessed that she would love to be Vice-Chancellor. She also discussed Spanish politics, abortion and the Pill.[7] She could happily espouse conflicting beliefs: her English ancestry and her British passport did not prevent her from parading her shamrock on St Patrick's Day. Her republican instincts forbade her to contribute to a book on the monarchy,[8] but they allowed her, late in life, to accept a CBE and to maintain 'that we should need Charles III'.[9] She would not vote Conservative, but (interviewed in *Nova*) she said that she wanted the right to buy her child a better education.

In 1945, after the General Election, she made one of her rare comments on politics. 'I voted Liberal in the election. I've always been Labour before—but I've only voted once. But I'm too much afraid of the foreign policies of the Labour people.'[10] 'Enid was "Liberal" in all things,' writes Agnes Headlam-Morley, 'if one takes that to mean open-minded, but she was not particularly left wing.'[11] But in nothing was Enid predictable. In 1962 she 'claimed to have been an anarchist. I was violently left-wing in my youth,' so she told the *Cherwell,* 'but I can never see much difference between the sides these days: Macmillan, Gaitskell, they all seem the same.'[12]

She showed her independence in her views, and in her appearance. Her passport gave her height as 5 ft 3, but her father recorded that she was five foot tall.[13] Since she was diminutive, she was all the more aggressive. Early in her Oxford career she had decided that conventional clothes did not suit her, and she created a style of her own, impervious to fashion. Henceforward she always wore red and blue (French acquaintances christened her Mlle Perroquet). She always wore jackets and trousers, reefer coats and slacks. She would wear a beret—a recollection of student days in Paris—and sometimes 'a cap vaguely reminiscent of a lady postman'. In later years, she wore the famous French matelot's cap, graced by a scarlet pompom and a ribbon inscribed in gold 'Marine Nationale'. Perhaps her nautical taste owed something to the fact that she had been forbidden a sailor suit as a child. 'What's the name of your ship, lady? I'd like to be a stowaway.' So a passer-by accosted her.

Enid did not venture to wear this fancy-dress in France; but she wore it at High Table at Somerville, where she also appeared in evening dress on formal occasions, insisting on every detail of protocol.

She had been formed, after all, in late Edwardian Dublin [writes her friend, the publisher Dan Davin], and, at the formal dinners she loved, her suppressed Edwardian self would re-emerge. The sort of dress she then delighted to wear would not have been out of place in her mother's drawing-room, something she might have worn when she was sixteen —a pink or a Child of Mary blue replacing the scarlet and Prussian blue of her daytime self.[14]

She was almost the only person in post-war Oxford who demanded that men wore white ties at her College dinner-parties.[15]

One Edwardian accessory in her wardrobe proved to be a grave disappointment. Enid could never resist a bargain; and, at an auction, she had acquired the largest fan ever seen outside the Folies Bergère. Alas, there had been no use for it in academic life.

Enid's independence set her apart; but her loneliness remained the loneliness of the adult without a major relationship. 'The roots of one's being stretch out underground looking for something with which to unite, to form that perfect oneness.'[16] So she wrote to Rosamond; and she told Alyse that she was never lonely when she was working, but she was often lonely with people.

But this loneliness was oppressive, and her nervousness remained acute. When she first visited Rosamond, she arrived in desperate uncertainty.

I'm very sorry that I was such a shock to you when you opened the door to me on Saturday and that you were aware that I was nervous and uncertain. I always imagine that I wear a cloak of invisibility and that no one can see me. I suppose it is because I live so much with people who in fact don't see me at all. But I wasn't miserable, honestly I wasn't. I was nervous yes, but then I'm always sick with nervousness when I've to ring the bell of people whom I know even quite well, if I've not seen them for some time. I try to find any excuse not to have to telephone to people I don't know well. And every single Wednesday—

even after all these years—I feel that I can almost not bear to go and give my university lecture. I try to get out of these nerves but there doesn't seem anything I can do about it. But I always imagine that I disguise it and that people are not aware of it. But I very soon got over my nerves with you, you must have been aware of that. It didn't at all take until after dinner for me to be absolutely at ease. I know well that, by the time one has reached middle-age, as you say, one should not need the opinion of others to bolster up one's belief in oneself. And I don't think that my nervousness comes from that cause. I don't think that I do need the good opinion of others, I don't think I ever think of it at all, it never seems to occur to me that people have formed any opinion of me at all. I think of myself as invisible here also. I think it is that there is always a fear in me that people may not want me, that they'll find me a different breed of animal. This makes me more anxious with those whom I am beginning to like. I think it goes back to the time when Mlle Cora used to say to me that I was always 'making myself different from the others'. She bred in me a terrible feeling of uncertainty of myself in front of others, the fear that they wouldn't want me. This has made me hide what I was from all except a very few intimates. This has given me the conviction which has caused so many of my unhappinesses and mistakes, that what I am is of no interest to anyone but myself, that what I want of others is of far less importance than what they want of me.[17]

The flamboyant public figure continued to hide a strangely shy and uncertain private person. I was always conscious of this when, in later years, I saw Enid at a party. 'You will find her at every party in Oxford, a small, electric figure in scarlet and royal blue, a voluble, flamboyant humming-bird, talking of anything from fashion to music, from politics to Pommard.'[18] So I wrote of her in 1956; and there, still, in my inward eye, is Enid at the height of her career. But after the party, if we went back to St Giles', there was an almost physical change in the atmosphere. It was the shedding of the persona. This persona had, with time, become second nature. But it still remained a protective shell. Enid was increasingly dependent on the company of those whom she knew best. Once or twice a lunch-time conversation continued till she went to dine in college. On one occasion we found ourselves, still deep in conversation, in the last London train at Oxford station.

Enid needed something which had eluded her in childhood: complete and undivided attention. And, like a child, she could not be denied it. She could be wayward, moody and vulnerable as a child. 'I have always felt', wrote a friend, 'that knowing you is rather like living on top of a volcano . . .'[19] Enid needed gentleness. Like a child, she also needed emotional security, unremitting reassurance of affection.

Every year she would send out several hundred Christmas cards; and, clearly, every year, she received several hundred in return. Her Christmas cards became an Oxford legend. But one cannot entirely explain the habit by her love of anniversaries, her punctilious observance of customs. There was something sad in the need to have this massive demonstration of popularity. 'She needed to know that she had this enormous number of faithful friends,' writes Liselott Haynes, 'but she didn't wait for their cards to come, she went out to meet them, all the 700 . . . She really didn't know half the people she exchanged Christmas cards with, but . . . her life was far too full of major and minor relationships and events and she was loath to admit that any of them were of necessity transient.'[20]

She was to spend the opening days of 1946 in Dublin. On New Year's Eve, halfway on her journey, she turned yet again to her usual confidante.

My dearest Alyse,

I have just gone to bed at the Adelphi Hotel Liverpool and it is just about to strike midnight, the beginning of the first year of peace . . . I've poured out a liqueur glass of whisky from my flask and I shall drink that as soon as the bells begin and I shall wish you a very happy New Year, and also all my family and friends. The bells are beginning now. The sirens too in the ships in the Mersey. It reminds me of Dublin and my childhood, when I felt so vividly and concretely the coming of the New Year. I felt sad and happy at the same time. I feel melancholy and lonely tonight alone in a hotel bed, with great noise around me as you can imagine. This is only the second time in my life that I've been alone to see the New Year in. Last year also . . .

To-day, during this long nasty journey, . . . I thought of my life and my prospects and not with any great enthusiasm, I shall never do the quarter of what I might have done if I'd leisure . . . I think it is that I've never had sufficient belief in myself. I don't mean that I lack belief in myself, because I think I have a kind of deep belief in my own possibilities, a desire anyway to do the work at whatever cost, but . . . it would always have seemed to me pompous, conceited and self-important to talk of 'my art', 'my work', and to expect any consideration for that. I think myself all this is the proof of a second-rate talent . . . Anyway it is too late now. I can't begin giving myself airs now, no-one would take that from me. Also I cannot now—whatever the personal cost—shake off responsibilities . . . There again you see Alyse the worthy sense of responsibility of the second-rate. The conflict in me is that I don't like being this way, but what can one do? The thing that might save me—indeed would make a tremendous difference—would be to get the Readership.[21]

The University Reader in French Literature was soon to be appointed at Oxford. The post was second only to that of the Professor, and Enid longed to be elected to it. 'The affair for my Readership will come up in May [this on 16 April]. There is also a Chair of French going at Birmingham for which I'm going to apply. I don't really want it, but I think it might encourage Oxford if they thought there was a faint chance of losing me . . . So please pray for me to whatever gods listen to you.'[22]

Before the month was over, she was elected University Reader in French Literature. The committee's choice was unanimous.

Enid had now become Somerville for many of her pupils—and for undergraduates whom she did not even teach. She seemed to personify the intellectual primacy of the College, its literary tradition, its vigorous independence. She was undoubtedly proud to belong to it; and, as time went on, it not only gave her her way of life, it became the centre of her existence.

It had changed much in recent years. In 1945, a few months after the end of the War, Miss Darbishire had been succeeded as Principal by Dr Janet Vaughan. The gentle, reticent Wordsworth scholar was followed by a dynamic medical scientist who served on innumerable university committees and continued her own research alongside her administrative duties. Janet Vaughan gave Somerville new vitality and purpose; and her first decade or more in office were the years when Enid reached the peak of her career. They found stimulus in each other's conversation and achievement. Miss Darbishire had been, at most, a respected acquaintance; but Janet Vaughan was an admired friend.

In the new Somerville of the Vaughan era, Enid's presence was felt. Though, as a University Reader, she did less college teaching, she remained a diligent tutor; she was a highly active member of the Governing Body of the College. She delighted in finding herself at the heart of affairs (she took an Irish pleasure in controversy and intrigue, and she revelled in collecting gossip). In the Senior Common Room, where she had her acknowledged chair by the fire, she showed all the insight about friends and acquaintances, pupils and colleagues, which she constantly failed to show about herself. She enthralled the rest of the Common Room by her wit and her splendid eccentricity. Her gaiety and gusto marked her out in an élite which included Isobel Henderson, the classical scholar, and Dorothy Hodgkin, the chemist and future Nobel Laureate.

It was a vital, changing and absorbing society. For Enid it became essential. She was well versed in the past of Somerville; she was constantly concerned about its present, and she cared profoundly about its future. She used to say that Somerville was her family; and so she loved it, criticized it, and depended on it.

PART SEVEN

❖❖❖❖❖

University Reader
1946–1965

Late in 1945, Enid had been revising her *Arthur Rimbaud* for
Hamish Hamilton. On 16 December she had told him excitedly:
'I think I've got on to something which will revolutionize the
interpretation of Rimbaud, finally make everything clear except of
course the fact of genius.'[1] She had struck the idea of Rimbaud's
readings and experiments in magic; she became more and more
enthralled by her discovery. 'I've always thought *Rimbaud* my best
book, but I was only groping when I wrote it . . . Here at last I've
got something which suddenly lights up the whole thing. Maybe
it won't be the final explanation but it is one which makes sense
and gives a meaning to the whole of Rimbaud's life.'[2] She explored it with the intensity which she showed in all she undertook.
'I've been reading masses of Magic, Alchemy and similar works
[she told Hamish Hamilton on 27 April]. It is all mad and I dream
about it at night and then, next day, I can't remember whether I've
dreamt it or read it . . .'[3] 'I work every night until 2 and 3 a.m.
[16 May]. I live in a totally uncivilized way, just like an animal, if
you can imagine an animal writing a book.'[4] She was exuberant,
and bursting with literary plans. On 26 May, she added: 'I'm not
writing a book on Flaubert and I've several other things I want to
do before I get on to that. The edition of Rimbaud, a Laforgue and
a Sainte-Beuve . . .'[5]

The critical edition of Rimbaud was not to be produced, the
life of Laforgue was only just begun when Enid died, and a boxful of notes alone remains to attest her constant interest in Sainte-
Beuve. She began but did not finish a study of the French novel in
the nineteenth century. But one work, at least, was finished now.
On 3 June, over lunch at The Ivy, she gave her new *Rimbaud* to her
publisher.

On 22 August came a moment for which she had longed since her last oppressive summer at Porquerolles. 'I am always very happy and inspired in France', she wrote.[6] Now, after an enforced absence of almost seven years, she set foot, once again, on French soil.

She had usually travelled by way of Le Havre, because there were fewer tourists on that route, and she had always contrived to be one of the first to disembark, so that she had time to enjoy her café au lait and her croissant at the station. This breakfast, her first breakfast in France, had become a ritual. Now, in 1946, she landed at Calais. She did not know the town or miss the landmarks, though she found the place largely destroyed. When she reached Paris, there was no taxi at the Gare du Nord. She took the Métro; and here, at last, the familiar smell told her that she was home. She had chosen, inevitably, to stay at the Foyer in the boulevard Saint-Michel. She got out of the Métro at the Odéon, and walked past the Luxembourg Gardens and up the boul' Mich' in the dusk, 'and everything was as it had always been. It is curious', she told Alyse, 'how 1939 just joins on to now.'[7] At the Foyer, Sarah Watson's friend, Mme Fournier, was 'touchingly admiring of England. And she sees us as heroes.' For once, Enid chose to be identified.

In a cheap school exercise-book she set down her impressions of post-war Paris.[8] Next day she wandered down the rue de Seine and the rue des Saints-Pères, gazing into the antique shops, noting the preoccupied look of the passers-by. She dined with the Vaudremers at Auteuil, where the dinner, bought perhaps on the black market, was as good as ever. But there were signs that time had passed. When she tried to take a Z 5 bus at Saint-Sulpice, they looked at her as if she had come from Mars. There had been no Z 5 since 1940.

She dined again with the Vaudremers.

The air force colonel who was there talked of the decadence of France—and indeed of all the white races—he talked of it sadly, dispassionately, as an accepted fact . . . The colonel said there were no great names—in literature, art, or anything else—since 1900. He looked forward with acceptance to the disappearance of France and the white races, and the domination of first Russia and then the yellow races. He sees Japan as in the same position as Germany at the end of the 1914–1918 war . . . [He] talked of the failure of France as if it were only a failure of diplomacy. '*S'il y avait eu de la diplomatie, une bonne diplomatie.*' Good diplomacy would have been to turn Germany and Russia on one another—'*ces deux pays qui ne demandent qu'à s'entredévorer*'—and France and England were to come in as the peacemakers, and would have settled what they liked. Good clever diplomatists would have made that world entire! What can you hope from countries with these beliefs? . . .

I find so many different political opinions. The only ones with some kind of optimism are the Résistants, the Maquis. But theirs is a kind of hectic belief, . . . more use in resistance than in construction. They are feverish and it seems to me lacking in a sense of reality. This is just the French *panache*, a gesture: '*Après vous, messieurs les Anglais . . .*' The *peuple* are just interested in trying to get food. They seem to me sensible and civilized as ever, but they are not governing the country, they are withdrawn.

The chestnuts are beginning to turn golden. I've not been able to go and see the Peace Conference as they are afraid of an attack against Bevin by the Jews.

On 2 September, she continued:

In the evening I met Sylvia Beech who is charming. Shakespeare and Company is gone. I have met Mouquet at last after a correspondence of 12 years . . . We talked of many things. I told him I walked everywhere. '*Cela vous fait perdre beaucoup de temps.*' He does not think one might gain anything by walking and looking. Research is everything. Work prevented him from noticing anything when the Germans were there. He does not even think of the Peace Conference and the future. But that is what has struck me so much with the French—or some of them—how little they think about the future, but plan, live for to-day. They go carrying on their little everyday affairs . . . Even if they've children they do not think of them as having a future. All the innocent little pleasures are gone. The little coffee with the *fine* at a café . . .

Harold Nicolson was attending the Peace Conference at the Palais du Luxembourg. They had lunch together.

He went on helping himself to potatoes with his fingers—forgot to offer to me, in the end I just helped myself too. But I was the guest. The bottle of wine near him, he went on filling up his glass, sometimes filling mine, but not always. He says he's a bohemian, but I've found good manners—courteous to women—in bohemians.

I sat at [the Café de] Flore in the evening . . .

The Palais du Luxembourg was floodlit. I saw it all the way up Rue de Tournon . . . All those flags, the red velvet over the gateway, all in the artificial light—bunches of international flags on every pillar—it looked, from the distance of the Rue de Tournon, like the final set of the pantomime. All the characters would come out of that doorway and group themselves round the pillars, the principal boy and girl last of all. Would that be Molotov and Byrnes finally suited?

Thursday 5th September . . . I met Sarah at station, home from U.S.A.

Sarah Watson told Enid how, during the Occupation, the German army had attempted to commandeer the Foyer. She had stood in the doorway, and argued with them in her atrocious French, and they had left her in possession.

Friday, 6th September. Had dinner with Matarasso, . . . one helping lobster 600 francs—30/-. Half a lobster. It was not worth that. He showed me his treasures. He certainly has a flair amounting to genius and he always goes for the right things. Now he is on to Gide and Apollinaire. He told me of his wartime life. He seems to have bought his way through fairly successfully, but it must have been terrible to be a foreign Jew under the Germans . . . He has become a Catholic but it is only emotional Catholicism. He has always had a curious feeling for me—sometimes friendly, sometimes thinking me the devil incarnate. He told me of terrible dreams he had had about [me] and thinks they reflect me rather than him. He wrote terrible things about me in his journal as a *succube*. He thinks in terms of Baudelaire, but I'm not suitable for *Vénus noire*, I have no sadism—that is my weakness . . .

Enid walked round the Île Saint-Louis where, above all, she would have liked to live. She visited the Hôtel Lauzun, where Baudelaire had been a tenant, a century ago. She had tea with Julien Green ('very modest and quiet and interesting to talk to'), and she dined with a woman who had been interned during the

War. 'She told [me] very interesting things about the camp. What a fantastic life and how much interesting stuff one could make out of it psychologically! I wish I had been there myself for a bit. I'd have made good copy out of it.' And already Enid noticed a tendency among the French 'to think that the Resistance won the war without any help from the Allies'.

⋄ 23 ⋄

The new year, 1947, started in a ferment of activity. 'I think', Alyse decided, 'you would lead a much easier life if you entered a circus as a lion tamer . . . I know how you feel about the lecture to be attended by your colleagues . . . How I wish I could hear that lecture on Gide!'[1] On 14 February Enid gave her public lecture, and Janet Vaughan assured her:

You were superb. I shan't easily forget it—and you illustrated so well your own text. The lecture was a masterpiece but it was a woman's achievement no man could have done it. No man could have been so personal so intimate and you looked so distinguished. I shall often see you in my mind your white hands with the big ring, the red scarf the blue coat the gay tilt of your cap—the sense of understanding in your voice and in your analysis the picture of you and the picture you painted of Gide the enigma.[2]

Enid happily showed the note to Alyse ('you are the only person I'd show it to');[3] she also showed it to Rosamond. 'I *am* glad she wrote like that,' came the answer. 'I think it was just the right letter for a woman to write to another on such an occasion . . . I'm always so thankful when women write and speak to women about literature. It is so rare, and so important. I've at once started to re-read *Si Le Grain Ne Meurt*.'[4]

Enid's interest in Gide had remained unfailing since the day when, as a schoolgirl, she had found *Les Nourritures terrestres* on a secondhand bookstall in Dublin. Now she was nearly fifty, she had met him, lectured on him, and she still intended to write his life. She was the natural biographer for him. All her sympathy and insight led her to him. Unfortunately the biography was not to be written. A monograph and a boxful of papers remain the material monument to her interest. But Gide had made her sure of her purpose, he would remain a powerful influence and a personal friend. He was now to enter her life in a dramatic manner.

It was in the Easter vacation, when she went to Paris, that the celebrated Gide episode began. Enid herself recalled it in 'a full account . . . written for posterity'.[5]

I had not seen Gide since the War, . . . and I thought that I would try to see him once more. I had given a public lecture on him at the University of Oxford in [February] and had found a great deal of interest in his works amongst the younger generation. I thought that I would try to persuade him to come and give a lecture at Oxford. I found that he was temporarily away in Switzerland and so I wrote to him—just the kind of letter which I knew would touch him. I got a charming letter from him in return—there is no-one who can write such charming letters—in which he half refused: '*Je suis vieux, fatigué, presque hors d'usage*,' but he ended: '*Nous en reparlerons.*' This gave me the feeling that he might be open to a little judicious persuasion. I thought that, once I was back in Oxford, I would try to get one of the University lectureships for him—the Zaharoff or the Taylorian—but I only thought of this for the next academic year—everything moves very slowly in Oxford. In any case all the lectureships for 1946–1947 had already been disposed of and the lectures, in most cases, already given. I did not answer Gide immediately . . . Then, at the beginning of the second week in May, I got another letter from him in which he said that my '*accueil*' had been so '*chaleureux*' that, on thinking it over again, he would like to come to Oxford to lecture and could he come in the last week in May. It is almost impossible to get things going in a fortnight in Oxford, and, in any case, I did not know where I was to get a fee for him. I was determined, however, to pay the fee out of my own pocket rather than refuse his offer. But, as luck would have it, the very day I received his letter we had a Fellows' Meeting at Somerville College and the Principal announced that the man who was to come and give the Bryce Memorial Lecture—Herriot—was prevented from coming on account of the pressure of political events. She said that we should have to drop it for this year as it would be impossible to get anyone else to come at such short notice . . . Then, without leaving them the time to think it over, I pushed in Gide's name explained who he was and said what an honour it would be for the College to be able to secure him . . . I was asked to communicate with Gide and to fix the date. I thought that it would be a good thing if he could be given an honorary degree and I looked into the University calendar and saw that there was a Degree Day on 7 June . . . I told him that the last week in May would not be very good on account of the Summer Eights and that no-one would then come to a lecture. I suggested the first week in June, 5 or 6 June, and he accepted for the 5th.

The Hebdomadal Council decided swiftly to offer him a degree; but suddenly, when everything appeared to be settled, Gide sent a telegram to Enid,

asking me to tell the University that he could not, after all, come to deliver the promised lecture and that a letter would follow. In the letter he said that he had shown his lecture to Roger Martin du Gard who had said that it was '*médiocre et insuffisant*', and that he did not feel that he could come and deliver it before so august a body as the University of Oxford. He said that he had not the courage to write another . . . I had to send a long wire, priority, to explain that he could not now withdraw, that everything was ready and the speeches written. I had another wire from him:

Confus et désolé me rends à vos excellentes raisons malgré grande fatigue stop serai donc Oxford date convenue précédemment mais plein de craintes pour conférence stop prie amis et autorités universitaires excuser indécision passagère stop chaleureuse reconnaissance à vous.

One speech was indeed already written. The Public Orator, Thomas Higham, had asked Enid to draft his oration in English so that he could translate it into Latin.

It is not far from sixty years [she wrote] since André Gide's first work —a book of poems—was published, and since then each of his works— fiction, criticism, satire, autobiography and journals—has been awaited with eager interest. He is the greatest living French writer—some would claim the greatest European—and there is no writer in this age whose influence has been so marked. He occupies in the first part of the twentieth century a position very similar to that occupied by Rousseau in the 19th—an all-pervading influence—and we can speak of *Gidism* today as we spoke of *Rousseauism* a hundred years ago.

Opinions may differ as to the literary form in which Gide reached his highest achievement, but all would agree that he is pre-eminently a moralist—as the term was understood in France in the 17th century—concerned with the analysing and clarifying of moral values. This makes him the writer of journals *par excellence* and his journals rank among the greatest in the French language. He is however no mere moralist, he is a great artist in French prose—the greatest of our day—whose style equals that of the great masters of the *Siècle du Roi Soleil*.

Gide is no statue in the Pantheon of literature; he is the simplest, gayest, most witty of companions who has never grown old. Those who have been privileged to be with him at the literary *Décades* at the Abbey of Pontigny, will remember how, when the serious work of the day was done, none surpassed him in verve, extravagance and power of invention in the Charades which were a feature of the lighter moments of these famous literary gatherings. None will forget either his inimitable talent for mimicry.

Gide is a Cosmopolitan, a great European who has striven always for international understanding and friendship. The breadth of his knowledge of European literature is rare, and he knows especially well the literature of Germany, Russia and England. His translations of Shakespeare are well known and his *Hamlet* is now running in Paris.

Gide is also a great individualist, standing against encroaching collectivity, the symbol of the crisis of our time. The main problem as he sees it—the real crisis of our age—is how to reconcile the inalienable right of the individual for self-development and the necessity for the diminution of the misery of the masses.

Finally he is himself the great enigma, the Sphynx whose secret has not yet been solved—not even by himself—for all his self-analysis and autobiographical productions.[6]

On 5 June the *Oxford Magazine* observed: 'This week the University honours two very distinguished French writers. M. François Mauriac received an honorary degree on Tuesday, M. André Gide is to receive one on Saturday.' Enid later claimed that she had been responsible for securing Mauriac's degree; there is no proof of this among her papers. But the honouring of Gide was much more controversial, and she considered it. rightly, among her triumphs.

Janet Vaughan had agreed to give him hospitality. As Enid remembered:

Gide arrived [in Oxford] with Mme Bussy—an old lady of 81—his daughter and son-in-law, . . . on Thursday 5 June, and I met them at the station. I was surprised to see Gide looking so vigorous and robust . . .

I took Gide and Mme Bussy to the Principal's house and dropped the Lamberts at the Maison Française in Beaumont Street. We had lunch quietly, the Principal, Mme Bussy, Gide and myself, then Gide went to rest before his lecture . . .

The Hall at Somerville was crowded to overflowing and the Reading Room next to it and all the passages. There were people massed all the way up the stairs hoping to get a glimpse of him as he passed above on his way to the Hall. The people were even packed in the quad outside. I never saw such a crowd. Hundreds were turned away.

It is difficult to give an impression of his lecture. I suppose it was not very new or world-shattering—but one could not expect that kind of lecture from a man of 78. What would be impossible to convey in words would be the beauty of his voice or the infinite charm of his personality . . .

The theme of the lecture was based on a verse from the *Æneid* of Virgil, in which Æneas is described as leaving the burning city with his father on his shoulders. Gide said that he interpreted this symbolically, that Æneas was not merely bearing his father on his shoulders, but the whole weight of his past which he was trying to save. In the same way, said Gide, we were fleeing from the burning city of our civilization with the whole weight of our Christian past on our shoulders which we must attempt to save. He said that he was an unrepentant individualist who still believed in the Christian doctrine of the supreme value of the individual, of each individual human soul, which was greater than all ideologies or abstract conceptions, that he protested with all his power against the forces which were likely to destroy it . . .

Gide was very much pleased by his reception—though he was very tired afterwards. He said to me, when I was taking him back to the Principal's house: '*Je crois qu'il était tout juste temps pour Oxford. L'année prochaine il aurait été trop tard.*' He had recovered his vigour again by the dinner and it was a very gay affair where he captivated everybody by his charm and his wit. He left before the main body of the guests, and

I took him home and made him his 'tisane' and saw that he went to bed.

He was, she later told Thomas Higham, greatly liked in Somerville; he even charmed Janet Vaughan's maid by carrying down his own breakfast tray.

The next day the Modern Language Faculty gave him a lunch at the Randolph Hotel and there was a short speech of welcome by the *Doyen* of the men Fellows—Mr F. A. Taylor of Christ Church, seconded by the Professor of French Literature, M. Rudler. Gide replied and he was obviously very much moved. He said that it was the first time he had ever allowed his name to be put forward for an honour—'*Regardez je n'ai pas de rouge à ma boutonnière*', he said—I believe he imagined it was the Faculty which was granting him the degree. Rudler, who had recovered much of his former irony from the state of depression in which the death of his wife had plunged him two years ago, said to me: '*Il est bien sensible, n'est ce pas?*' and there was the utmost sarcasm in his voice. Certainly Gide had to wipe his eyes when he had finished speaking. But he is easily moved and that is, I think, one of the secrets of his charm.

When lunch was over I made Gide walk down Broad Street, I wanted him to have a look at Blackwell's window. I had secured some photographs of him and had asked Blackwell to do a 'Gide window' and he had set out the books as a grand display with the photographs. Gide was very much pleased and flattered by the window and said that there were books there which were unprocurable in France. I know the German assistant at Parker's over the way—he manages the foreign section—he is a great admirer of Gide's and was at the lecture; he too had done a 'Gide window'. Gide stopped to look at that also. He paused at Thornton's as we moved down the Broad and I could see that he was childishly disappointed not to find there another window with a display of his books. But Thornton does not do that kind of book trade . . .

In the evening I gave a little private dinner in College for some people who could not fit into any of the other categories—Faculty or University . . . I was allowed to invite six people—including Mme Bussy and Gide—I eventually had seven as I pretended to have forgotten myself . . . At ten o'clock I took Gide back to the Principal's house and I thought that Mme Bussy would accompany him. But not at all! I think she was having a wonderful time, a real holiday, and she insisted on accompanying the rest of my guests to my flat . . . We did not break up until after midnight.

The next day was the degree ceremony when Gide was to get the Degree of Doctor of Letters (D.Litt) *Honoris Causa*. We had lunch beforehand with Austin Gill, the new Modern Language Fellow at Magdalen College. He had known Gide when he was at Tunis during the War and Gide was very happy to meet him again . . . We arrived nearly half an hour late for the lunch as Gide would look at everything on the way, every college garden. He is mad about flowers and wanted to know the name of every plant. *'J'aime qu'on me présente les fleurs, comme des jeunes filles, avec leurs noms,'* he said. Unfortunately I could rarely make the introductions as I was so ignorant.

After lunch I handed Gide over, at the Delegates' Room, to the Public Orator and the Vice-Chancellor . . .

Gide was much interested in the whole degree ceremony and he read with obvious pleasure the Public Orator's address about him—he must be one of the few honorands to understand the Latin. He remained quite a time watching the other people taking their degrees. He was the only D.Litt. and after him came the M.A.s. He noticed that these, during the conferring of their degrees, were touched on the head with a Bible by the Vice-Chancellor and, not knowing that this is never done to Doctors, he thought it had been deliberately omitted in his case. Turning to the Principal of Somerville College, who happened to be seated beside him in the Doctors' circle, he asked her anxiously was this ceremony omitted in his case on account of his *'idées libres'* and said he was sad if this was so. She reassured and comforted him as one might a child from whom some treat had been withheld.

After the ceremony he walked back to Somerville through the streets in his scarlet and grey silk gown. He was one of the few foreigners not to look in fancy-dress in his academic robes—he might easily have been an Oxford don.

I did not tell Gide anything about the Varsity cricket match which was taking place that afternoon in the Parks, but he found it for himself. It was twenty-seven years since he had been in England and he had never seen a cricket match. I had the impression that he wanted to see everything that he could on this visit which might well be his last. His verdict on the cricket was *'Ce doit être bien assommant!'*

In the evening he went to dine in Hall at Magdalen as the guest of Professor d'Entrèves. Tom Boase, the new President, who is not yet officially in residence, came down especially for the occasion. All members of the University who dine in College wear their gowns—not of course the full-dress gowns of scarlet and grey silk, but the ordinary black ones with the embroidery—Gide, as a foreigner and a guest, would, of course, not be expected to have one, but he was so pleased at being now a member of the University that he was much disappointed when I could not get one for him, so I lent him mine.

In this gown, which was much too small for him, he went to Magdalen, and asked to see the room which had once belonged to Oscar Wilde. A cricket team were having a party there. They watched in silence as he gazed round. They did not learn his identity till he had gone.

⋄ 24 ⋄

When Trinity Term was over, Enid escaped to the pine forests and beaches of Porquerolles. While she was there, she discovered a lump on her breast. She was afraid that it might be malignant; and, as there was no doctor on the island, she wrote to her doctor in Oxford, and asked if she should come home. It took ten days to get the reply, and during those ten days she became convinced that she had cancer.

I decided then that I would keep at my job . . . When recurrence occurred—as I was sure then that it would—I would resign my post, . . . and try to get the most essential books written . . . Well, that is what I planned during the ten days I was waiting for my doctor's letter. When it came she said that she thought my symptoms as described by me were nearer to mastitis than cancer and she advised me not to cut short my holiday but to come and see her when I got back.[1]

The doctor's opinion was reassuring, but Enid needed drama. When drama did not exist, she created it, and made herself the focus of attention.

I waited to get [the doctor's] letter to write to you [she told Alyse on 8 September]. I got it this morning. She says that without seeing me she can't say anything definite . . . It might be mastitis . . . It might be a non-malignant growth and of course—one must say it—it might be cancer. My doctor says that, on my description, she favours mastitis—maybe she says this to encourage me . . .

I'm not afraid of dying—the actual moment is made comparatively easy—but of course I don't want to die until I have to. I'm not even terribly afraid of pain. I'd willingly buy time at the price of pain—time that I can use . . . As long as one can use one's suffering I believe one would not yet want to die—a spiritual being wouldn't . . . Pascal wrote the largest number of the *Pensées* when ill to the point of death . . .[2]

The growth proved not to be serious; but, years later, when she had every reason to think that she was dying, Enid behaved as she had planned.

'Darling Alyse, here is the advance copy of *Rimbaud* which is coming out on 24 October . . . I'm already caught up in the whirlwind and whirlpool of term. The life that is really suited to me is the life on Porquerolles. I wish I could live there . . .'[3] Enid wrote on 8 October. Three days later, Alyse acknowledged her copy of the new *Arthur Rimbaud*, which was dedicated to her. It was, she said, 'a sure little footpath for me down to posterity'.[4]

George Painter explained in the *New Statesman*: 'Possessors of the first edition will wish to know what material is in the second. They will find, among much else, an additional 30 pages, 2 more portraits, an enlarged bibliography, new discoveries on Rimbaud in England, especially the mystery year 1874, and on his readings and experiments in magic, an exciting piece of news . . .' Maurice Bowra told Enid: 'I admire your work and scholarship and think you are one of the few people in Oxford in our kind of subject who has made a real contribution to knowledge, and made it in a graceful and imaginative way.'[5] 'During the last few days,' wrote Gide on 25 October, 'I have spent a number of hours with you—or rather with your *Rimbaud*. Why haven't I time to talk to you about it at leisure! There would be so much to say . . . Your fine book constantly invites me to take the digressions of the *Saison en*

Enfer more seriously than I did. I had seen them as poetic invention rather than confession or personal revelation . . . And no doubt you are right.'[6]

Enid had been entirely right in her championship of Gide. He was seventy-eight, but the Oxford doctorate had been the first honour that he had accepted. Honour at Oxford brought other recognition in its train. Soon afterwards he was awarded the Nobel Prize for literature.

The year 1948 brought Enid herself the recognition which, next to her Oxford doctorate, was to please her best. The news appears to have been public property long before the official offer was made. 'I am *so* happy about your Légion-d'honneur,' wrote Rosamond on 15 March. '. . . I think it is *very* flattering for a foreigner, and all your friends will be rejoicing.'[7]

That June, in Oxford, at the opening garden-party of the new Maison Française, the French Ambassador invested Enid with the cross of Chevalier de la Légion-d'honneur. It was characteristic of her that she hurried off to see Beatrice, the cook at Somerville, 'to show myself to her in all my glory and to show her my decoration'.[8] So, in her childhood, she might have run to the kitchen to show off a new dress to Lizzie O'Beirne.

A fortnight later, the King's Private Secretary sent her restricted permission to wear the insignia. Enid did not choose to restrict herself. The cross was kept for state occasions, but she wore the ribbon in her buttonhole all day and every day. The tiny, coveted flash of scarlet became part of her legend.[9]

'I feel a great longing to get away from people and to have some peace and rest.' This to Alyse on 11 July. 'I want to get the little book on Petrus Borel finished during the summer if I can. I don't suppose for a moment that I'll get it done as I'll only be a month in the country.'[10]

The country retreat to which Enid went was a cottage in the Forest of Fontainebleau. Sarah Watson had lent it to her for September. She arrived on 1 September, spent three weeks there, led a simple, solitary life, and dashed off the first draft of the book.[11] 'I feel very envious and inferior', Rosamond confessed. 'I *hoped* to have had a first draft of my new novel done by the end of the year, but there's not a hope. It will take another six months at least.'[12] 'Amused to know you're busy with the curious figure of the romantic lycanthrope,' went a note on 11 October. 'Yours most affectionately, André Gide.'[13]

Enid claimed that *Petrus Borel* was meant as an introduction to *Baudelaire*, which she planned to revise. There seems only a frail connection between the two. Both men were Romantic at heart, both suffered from a philistine society. But Petrus Borel cannot be considered, seriously, as a poet; and Baudelaire owed nothing to him. Enid had chosen Petrus Borel, so one surmises, because he was a remarkable eccentric, and because he was misunderstood. In her study of Petrus Borel, as in all the biographies she wrote, she seemed to analyse not only a poet or novelist, but herself.

There appears to be the same tendency in the books she hoped to write, the biographies which remained unwritten. She thought of writing on Charles Cros. He might have deserved a monograph, but she planned a critical study. Cros was a minor writer of verse in the 1870s; he was also a brilliantly versatile inventor, who was not recognized by his contemporaries. Enid saw him, one suspects, as a classic misfit, and it was this which ensured her interest. She was drawn not only to the eccentric and the misunderstood, but to the bimetallist and to the homosexual. She was interested in Gide's sexual deviation, which she considered to be much exaggerated, both by himself and by his critics, 'and whenever I write a book on him,' she assured Thomas Higham, 'I shall show that.'[14] She thought that someone needed to study the Lesbian aspect of George Sand; and she herself wanted to work on the Sapphic poet Renée Vivien, the friend of Natalie Barney.

These ideas remained in embryo; but they are illuminating. These social rebels, these controversial figures shaped Enid's contribution to French studies. 'The only people who really interest me are the individualists', she told Alyse.[15] A rebel herself, she was drawn by instinct to other nonconformists. 'I know [this again to Thomas Higham] that people are inclined . . . to judge me adversely on the authors I study. They do not realize that in Baudelaire, Rimbaud and Gide there is one quality which has attracted me and moved me and that is the pursuit of spiritual values . . .'[16] This was only part of the truth. Enid also sympathized with those who had stood out against convention, with those who had been rejected by their contemporaries.

◇ 25 ◇

'I shall try to make a point of being in London to hear your paper on May 4th—though I confess I grow more and more shy.'[1] So Alyse wrote on 28 March. The paper in question was *Flaubert's Madame Bovary*, which Enid delivered at the Royal Institution. Alyse duly noted in her journal:

Enid's talk at the Royal Institute—my ridiculous consciousness of not being smartly enough dressed and nervousness at seeing her again after all these years, my absorbed interest in watching the people, so anxiously earnest and impressive. Enid standing at the rostrum with the light flooding upon her in her brilliant blue dress—what is there to say new about Flaubert and Madame Bovary. She came up to see me [in Hampstead] in the morning in her blue velvet beret and her bright red coat, as flashing as a red breasted woodpecker. One feels no obligation for she does all the talking. She took whiskey in her coffee. I felt fond of her and at ease with her and admiring of her—her integrity, spirit, vivacity, courage, ability.[2]

'I did indeed love seeing you and marvelled at your resiliency,' she wrote to Enid after the lecture. 'You flashed in and out of my vision like a bird of paradise.'[3] On 28 May, she added: 'I do keep my fingers crossed and pray to all my unorthodox gods and hold my breath. It will be a showdown if you do not get it and a triumph if you do—and I can't help thinking you will.'[4]

The triumph for which she was praying, now, was the Marshal Foch Chair of French Literature at Oxford. This year Professor Rudler was to retire from the Chair which he had held for thirty years: since it was established in 1919. Within the next few months his successor was to be chosen. He himself would have liked to see Enid elected.

I naturally hope [went her official application] that the Professorship might give me some leisure to write the books for which I have material collected—but I realize that this is problematic. My main reason [for applying] is however that it would give me a wider scope to further French studies and research in this country. Since childhood my chief interests have lain in France and its culture—I spend a third of every year in France—and I would like opportunity to increase their appreciation and understanding in England. Modern Languages are tending, more and more, to become the Modern Humanities, and French culture, with its Greco-Roman roots, lies at their heart. England, to play her part in this movement and gain widely from it, . . . needs to produce an indigenous school of French scholars who can rival the French school of English studies so brilliantly represented by Legouis, Cazamian and Delattre, whose full influence came from the fact that they were Frenchmen speaking to Frenchmen. There are signs to-day in British universities that this is beginning and I would welcome the opportunities a professorship would afford of encouraging and fostering such a school of French studies in England.[5]

Enid's feeling for French literature was no mere professional interest: it was perhaps her most consistent love, her driving force. Agnes Headlam-Morley adds: 'Her knowledge and appreciation of German literature were greater than is generally supposed. She had in fact a wide range. I am not competent to speak of her knowledge of Italian and Spanish. She certainly loved Russian literature and regretted that she never had time to learn the language.'[6] To one of her pupils, at least, Enid showed no wide range of sympathies. Certainly, with an Irish twist, she underestimated English literature—indeed, she knew astoundingly little about it. Her devotion to French culture had, at times, a political undertow; it was aggressive, and it was exclusive.

Her application for the Chair was not, however, made from disinterested devotion to French studies. Enid had never wanted to teach; she wanted to do research and to write.

Perhaps it is really better to be doing teaching, which is of some general use if nothing else, than wanting to express myself [this to Alyse]. But I know that I'm living on my intellectual capital and that terrifies me at times. And the truth is—and I'm not very proud of it—that I'm selfish and I'm really far more interested in finding things for myself, in using my discoveries for myself and my writings than in teaching others . . .

I've been thinking quite a bit in my *moments perdus* about the Paris novel, quite a bit too about odd articles I might write . . . I'm afraid that a lot of my thinking just evaporates in thin air. It gets lost in my teaching.[7]

Enid wanted time to write. She also wanted the title of Professor as the ultimate insignia of success. She had planned her career on the hope of it. 'What I always hope for is a Chair of French Literature, for that would give me leisure to write,' so she had explained to Alyse. 'I'd get the assistants to do most of the work . . . If I don't get a Chair then I've bought an empty Surprise Packet and academic work has nothing for me.'[8] Now, in 1949, there seemed a chance of winning the Chair that she wanted most of all.

'If I don't get it this time I'm not likely to get it another time so it will be farewell to it,' she confided to Hamish Hamilton in June. 'But I'm not going to allow it to blight my life if I don't get it.'[9] In August she added: 'Although of course I'll be sad and perhaps a little disappointed in one way if I am not elected, I shall certainly not be surprised. I'm building nothing on it and I shall certainly not throw myself into the Isis, or go into a decline . . .'[10] Enid had come to recognize that she had small prospect of election, but she did not consider it a matter of academic life or death.

As the election approached, one of the causes of her persistent ill-health was discovered. She went into the Acland Home for a minor operation, and she was found to have early uterine cancer. A hysterectomy was performed. 'I rang up after lunch,' wrote Rosamond on 7 September, 'and a pleasant voice answered with the usual bland ambiguousness that you'd "had the operation" and

were "going on well, so far". . . . All I can say to console you is
that thank goodness, if they *did* find trouble, they have removed it.
And perhaps you won't look so deathly white and get so ex-
hausted.'[11]

On 26 September, back in St Giles', Enid wrote to her surgeon,
William Hawksworth. He and his family were to be her friends
for life; yet even though she clearly felt gratitude for his care, her
letter is more than a letter of thanks. It is a confession. Mr Hawksworth had been the perfect listener; he had shown her the understanding for which she longed. She sent him nearly six pages of
close typescript. They suggest, more than anything else, her desperate need to confide.

Dear Mr Hawksworth,
    . . . I wish that I could make you feel my very deep gratitude for
your care of me . . .
    I believe that you have antennae which allow you to feel people and
how to treat them. I only know your way of treating me has suited me
exactly and admirably. I have liked and appreciated your honesty and
directness for these are the qualities I most like and admire in human
beings and I have met them too little in English people—or perhaps it is
only English academic people, Oxford people, who lack them . . .
Since the very first day I have felt that I could trust you. I hope that you
will allow me to continue to do so . . .
    You must not run away with the idea that I am worrying about
myself. I am not, and I feel that I've been damned lucky. I feel the
same sort of happiness at what I've escaped as I felt for months in 1932
when I was run down by a motor bus and taken to hospital unconscious.
I might so easily have been killed because a bus is a big thing . . . I can
promise you that I shall not worry about my health nor about what has
happened to me. In any case I faced something much worse two years
ago and made my peace with myself so that nothing can ever be so
hard again . . .
    When I talked to you about the Professorship in the Acland Home I
professed a confidence which I do not really possess in my chances. I got
excitement out of it—like a ticket in the Irish sweep—and it kept my
mind off other things. I think that the odds are too heavy against a
woman—and, even if I were a man, I'm not the kind of person that goes

down with the academic mind . . . I think the chances are that I shall not be appointed but I have had a lot of fun out of the election, noticing and nosing out all the intrigues. One of my friends, Maurice Bowra, the Warden of Wadham, is supporting a Frenchman who is a professor from Harvard. He told me that he put me first of all the English candidates but that he thought the appointment ought to go to a Frenchman on the grounds that France was so low that this would be a blow from which she would not recover. As a matter of fact Maurice Bowra is not on the committee so he has no direct influence, but he has indirectly—especially on the two men from All Souls who do not care for the members of my Faculty . . . Anyway I've got fun out of it and I'm not going to jump over the net and shake my opponent's hand until the election is made! As a matter of fact I do think Maurice Bowra's candidate good and if I don't get the Chair I'd like him to get it.[12]

The appointment to the Chair was made on 6 October. It was made by a small committee, and she lost it by one vote.

My dear Enid [wrote Maurice Bowra],
    I fear you must be very disappointed about the professorship of French, and I can well understand your feelings. Of course one likes to be recognized and to get more time for work. So for personal reasons I am very sorry. But I have felt throughout that this is one of the rare cases where I must sacrifice personal loyalty and affection to something else. The French attach the greatest importance to having one of themselves in the Chair, and I have felt that they are right and that it would be almost wicked now, when France is so spoken against and despised, to deprive them of this key post. France is one of the great things in our lives. We owe much more to it than we really know, and it is vitally important not to let respect for it diminish . . . Please forgive me if you think that I have behaved badly. If I did, it was after full consideration of the facts, and with considerable distress to myself. You will remain a great figure in Oxford and England, and that is what really counts.[13]

    'You don't need consolation or encouragement. None, that is to say, that does not spring naturally from the sympathy, devotion and admiration of your friends—and these you always have.' This from Rosamond on 14 October. She added:

I think that in your place there is only one thing that would make me feel a sense of failure: that is, if I had inner qualms about having failed to serve the University to the height of my powers and abilities. That will never never be said of you—not even your severest critic could ever say that. For the rest I should feel that far the most important thing was to go on writing books. No other French scholar, Professor or no, can give the world just what you have, and will, in that way.[14]

Three days later, Enid herself told William Hawksworth that she felt 'a bit sad. It would have been a nice crowning to my career. My father would have liked it and I only took up academic work to please him . . . Also I don't think that I would have disgraced the Chair.' She added: 'My failure has had a curious effect on me so far. I do not believe that I have ever lectured with more confidence and assurance, with more hold over my audience and more humour, than I have this week—although no one yet knows that I've not got the Chair. It was as if unconsciously I wanted to prove that, although I had failed to be appointed, I was good.'[15]

She certainly retained her hold over those who saw her. That month, a new undergraduate arrived in Oxford.

'Who is that extraordinary woman wearing pink pyjamas?' This question from one of my family who had driven me up to Somerville on the first day of my first term there implied that the figure passing on the other side of the lawn was no more than was to be expected—just the first of a succession of extravagant people who would in future be waiting to dazzle me with exhibitionism and lead me into bad ways. I looked more closely, and immediately warmed to the pyjamad one, realizing that there was more here than met the eye of my scornful relation: this was not exhibitionism; this lady didn't care whether we saw her or not. In 1949 pale pink trousers were unusual day-time wear, it's true, but they looked brisk and comfortable as they did a sort of twinkling lope down the path—the roll was nautical but the strides were shorter and more purposeful than the average sailor's. The sailor hat and navy blue reefer jacket might have looked odd on anyone else, but didn't on her. She just looked full of grit and vitality . . . Such hair as was visible was obviously thin and a suspicious colour, the lipstick was very red, but, oh my, those eyes! They could have frozen a rear-admiral to the mainmast if he'd said something stupid. She had an aura of France; this might be hindsight, but was probably suggested by the name of the French boat on her hat-band; there was also something reminiscent of Mistinguette and Édith Piaf—but positive, not waif-like. I think a number of fleeting impressions of her have gradually rolled into one; but I *do* remember an instinctive feeling of being prepared to take up the cudgels on her behalf that first day. Of course I soon came to realize that was scarcely necessary. Most of my impressions are visual: the very energetic walk, the blue and red clothes—even to the resplendent academic gown that put the rest of Somerville in the shade; the sailor hat, the bright blue eyes, the thinning hair, the occasional appearance at High Table hatless and evening-dressed with a short fur something round her shoulders, her hair apparently marcel-waved—on these occasions she looked like an apparition from the gay life of the thirties, but such a strong-minded one that she cracked the mould.

That strong-mindedness was what emanated from her: a brisk trenchancy—the very way she walked to High Table, stood through grace and plumped down on her seat . . . One occasionally caught the blaze of her blue eyes or the crackle of her Irish voice and wished one's own tutor would burn as brightly. I think the only time she spoke to me directly was to offer to get some wine cheaply from the SCR buttery when she walked past a group of us undergraduates and overheard talk of a party. That too was unusual in 1949.[16]

Somerville watched Enid with astonishment and affection. Her pupils continued to be fascinated.

She really *was* Somerville and Oxford for me and I was very, very fond of her [writes June Barraclough, now Mrs Wedgwood Benn] . . .

I took to her immediately and yet I never felt I wanted to presume too much. Later, I had her for tutorials in 19th-century French literature and Flaubert (special author) *and* the Symbolists (special subject) *and* for the University Prose Class. She always gave her pupils a Turkish cigarette and a glass of sherry: at least I presume so, as I always got them . . .

I savoured all my talks with her; she encouraged me—and made me feel life so supremely worth living. I've kept just a few of her little typed notes. I don't expect my memories and emotions are any different from so many others'—and I did not know her *well*—just enough for her to come up at a dinner and mutter 'Don't blame me—*I* didn't choose *your* wine. It's better stuff on High.'[17]

Enid had founded the College cellar, and she remained its steward. She probably knew as much about wine as any woman in Oxford, but her attitude was both professional and romantic. Sending Hamish Hamilton a bottle of Tokay, she confessed to him: 'I never myself think Tokay one of the best wines, and the only fun is thinking about its associations. This bottle, being Imperial Tokay, was bottled while there was still an Austrian and Hungarian Empire, and it was romantic to think of.'

She was a lover of wine (she had a special affection for Montrachet) and a lover of good food. During the War, when food was rationed, Boulestin had been her favourite bedside book, and she had browsed over his nostalgic and impossible recipes 'involving tumblerfuls of fresh cream and glasses of old liqueurs'. She delighted in the more sophisticated College dinners; she was one of the first women to dine at Magdalen, and she described the ritual with the enchantment of a child.

⋄26⋄

On 19 January 1950, Alyse thanked Enid for *The God That Failed*. In this symposium six intellectuals described their disillusionment with Communism. Enid had persuaded Gide to contribute to the book, but finally he had felt too ill to do so, and, with his help, she had written his narrative for him.[1] He was indeed failing. That autumn, in Paris, she was to see him for the last time. 'I thought he looked ill and old', she reported to Alyse. 'He was a very poor colour and he was very short of breath and he told me that he was having injections to stimulate his heart. But he does not live as a delicate old man should and he is dashing about going to the rehearsals of the play he has made out of *Les Caves du Vatican*.'[2] He died a few months later, in 1951.[3]

Gide had given Enid her first political triumph at Oxford. She was now preparing for a second. She found herself involved in a new activity which was to bring much benefit to Oxford—and considerable publicity to herself. She had begun to 'meddle'—as she expressed it—with the Chair of Poetry. 'When I started meddling with it, . . . there was no real election at all', so she told a journalist years later. 'They just used to put critics in. They hadn't had a poet since Matthew Arnold, and he was a critic, really.'[4] The Chair of Poetry was the oldest Chair in Oxford. It had been established in 1708 by Sir Henry Birkhead as a protest against the small number of lectures given by dons. The salary was £350 a year for three lectures a year; the Professor also had to deliver the Creweian Oration, in Latin, at Encaenia in alternate years. He had to judge the entries for the Newdigate Prize and the Sacred Poem Prize. The Chair of Poetry was unique, for the Professor, elected for five years, was elected by Convocation: the 30,000 Masters of Arts of Oxford University.

The election seemed to Enid to be a matter of importance which reached beyond the confines of Oxford. It was a matter of Oxford politics (and she was a power in politics) but she felt that it gave scope for a wider literary judgment. It also appealed, admittedly, to her buccaneering spirit. Now Maurice Bowra's term of office was to expire, and his successor was to be chosen. Enid felt that a scholar should be followed by a poet, and she had asked Cecil Day-Lewis if he would stand. In the first weeks of 1951 she was fiercely collecting Masters of Arts who would nominate him. She could be, as she said, 'a veritable gadfly to everyone'. And so she was now. Her energy, and her flair for publicity, were making the post a matter of general interest; and in the Common Rooms of Oxford there arose a susurrus of speculation: would the chair go to C. S. Lewis (the English tutor at Magdalen), to Cecil Day-Lewis, or to Edmund Blunden?

The nomination lists were published, and Convocation went to the poll. Edmund Blunden stood down, so as not to split the poets' vote. He himself was the first to vote for Cecil Day-Lewis; and he was among the first to congratulate Enid when her candidate won the Chair. On 10 February he wrote: 'For my part I think it a splendid appointment.'[5]

Whatever she professed in her letters to William Hawksworth, Enid remained disappointed at her failure to win the Chair of French at Oxford. On 31 May she applied for the Drapers Professorship of French at Cambridge. She was not wholehearted. 'I don't really want it [she told Alyse], and am only putting in on account of pride so that it should be known that I consider myself "Chair class".'[6] On 1 June, she added: 'I'd be I think relieved if I heard definitely that I hadn't got it. It would really complicate my life too much—though I'd keep on my flat here.'[7] She later told Agnes Headlam-Morley: 'I always said that when I failed to get the [Oxford] Chair of French, I had shot my bolt academically and would get nothing else—I never intended to leave Oxford.'[8]

She was to leave it, briefly, now: to go to America for the first time. Sarah Watson, in Paris, had often talked to her about the United States: especially about the South, where she had been born. She had urged her to accept the visiting professorships she was offered at Berkeley and Seattle Universities.

On 6 June Enid flew to New York. She went on to Washington, and to Princeton (where she caught a glimpse of Einstein,) and, on 15 June, she left for Berkeley, to begin her work as Visiting Professor in French Literature. The course was intensive, and every other day she held a two-hour seminar, where—since the class did little work—she did most of the talking. The campus was enormous, she reported to Hamish Hamilton, and there were about 25,000 students. In the same letter, she told him that she had failed to win the Cambridge Chair. 'I was more relieved really than upset when I heard the news,' so she assured him. 'I would have hated to leave Oxford.'[9]

From Berkeley, California, she moved to Seattle, in Washington State, as Visiting Professor in Comparative Literature. 'Hard as I found Berkeley [she confessed to Alyse, on 5 August], it was a haven of rest compared to what Seattle is and I've never worked as hard as I've done since I've been here . . . One of my courses is idiotic: it is on the influence of French Symbolism on English literature at the end of the 19th century, . . . and I find that about half the class has never learnt any French whatsoever . . .

I've promised them that there will be no word of French on their exam paper. So they will, from my notes, talk of the influence of poems that they haven't understood.'[10]

On 27 September, she arrived back in Oxford. 'I got on well I think with all sorts of different Americans and liked them very much [this again to Alyse]. I found them eager, responsive and sympathetic . . . I think that some of them lack subtlety and irony, but the thing that I would find it hardest to endure would be the lack of any kind of privacy, spiritual or otherwise.'[11] Years later, when she grew embittered, she wrote with vehemence: 'The only thing that prevented me from staying there was the fact that it is so far from France!'[12]

The year 1952 brought a new figure into Enid's life. Anne Artur had been among her contemporaries at Somerville. Now Anne's brother, Pierre, was visiting Oxford, and on 2 July he found himself in the study in St Giles',

. . . where Enid sat enthroned with her typewriter on one side and a bottle of sherry on the other to celebrate our meeting. You can imagine the course of our conversation [he writes]. Charmed by her culture, vivacity and warmth, I asked her to come and see us in Brittany . . .

So it was that we had the pleasure of greeting her on 12 August . . . [Next day] we made the classic pilgrimage to Combourg, which she particularly appreciated, and we had tea at a friend's house near Dinan. A Benedictine father, a great friend of ours, happened to be there on holiday. He was a man of remarkable learning, sacred and profane. It was a godsend. I still recall the exchange of opinions on the conversion of Paul Claudel . . .

On 16 August we reached Paramé where we visited my friend Théo Briant in his Tour du Vent. Writer and poet, he was also the editor of an art periodical which he brought out quarterly at his own expense under the title *Le Goëland*. His studio, next to an old mill, was stuffed with books and pictures, not to mention a quantity of the most diverse and extraordinary things. You can imagine that Enid felt at home there. Her tireless curiosity was roused by the setting and, still more, by the man himself: a massive man, abounding with life. There was a running fire of conversation on the literary subjects which absorbed them both, while the three of us quaffed a handsome bottle of port . . . Tea at the Yacht Club at Dinard, looking over the bay, and then Enid embarked on the steamer *La Falaise*.[13]

Pierre Artur had entered her life; a figure from the past returned to it. Marianne Eyles had been taking a pre-medical course at Exeter in Enid's Exeter days; she was now working in Los Angeles. She had followed Enid's career from a distance. Now, belatedly, she read *A Lady's Child* and determined to renew her acquaintance. On 12 July, from Encino, California, she invited her to stay, and announced that she would send her a return ticket.[14] On 14 November she continued: 'I have your air ticket already fixed so that you can pick it up in London whenever you are ready. I am enclosing a $ bill and will do so in each letter I send you. Then you will have some pocket money to use *en route* . . . Your book made me write these things—and only a good book would stimulate me so.'[15] Such—inspired by *A Lady's Child*—was the beginning of a generous friendship. The offer of a car (but Enid never learned to drive), a holiday in Greece, a Regency house: henceforward, at intervals, Oxford would be amazed by the munificence of Marianne Eyles and Frances Fowler, 'my American friends'.

Another deepening friendship was that of the novelist Joyce Cary. His son, Sir Michael Cary, writes: 'He admired Enid's scholarship . . . He admired her courage and independence . . . They were very old friends, and certainly in earlier days found mutual comfort and stimulation in the exchange of ideas—on poetry in particular.' In the past few years they had grown increasingly close to one another. During his wife's last illness, and since her death in 1949, he had appreciated Enid's understanding and affection, and the Sundays in her diary bear the regular entry: 'Joyce. 6 o'clock': a reminder of their weekly meetings at his house in Parks Road or her flat in St Giles'. Their hour together on Sunday evenings had become an immovable feast for both of them. Their literary distinction, their enquiring minds, their Irishness drew them together. Joyce Cary also satisfied a fundamental need in Enid's nature: a need for a close relationship with a man to whom she could give admiration. There was little difference in age between herself and Joyce Cary, but to her he had a necessary paternal quality.

He himself felt growing affection for her. On 4 September, when she was in New York, he had written: 'I expect you on the 30th with impatience. I miss you very much for tho I see so little of you I always like to feel that you are there. There is a great gap in St Giles' when you are away.' On 20 May 1952, when she was briefly in Paris, he reminded her: 'You leave a big hole in Oxford at my heart.' Late in 1953:

I'm so glad you liked the book [his new novel, *Except the Lord*]. As you know, I am very greatly beholden to people like yourself, whose judgment I value, for encouragement in my work. I am not in fact a very confident writer, partly because I am always venturing into new country and do not myself know quite what I have done. I write venturing but really I think I am pushed or driven by forces that I myself don't understand. I had gathered from my publisher that the book had been received with ambiguous and sidelong looks—but I am perfectly happy if I know that you have enjoyed it as a serious piece of work.[16]

Enid herself had a new work which was soon to appear. On 25 January, Bowes & Bowes published her monograph on Gide. It makes one regret that she did not write the full-scale biography which she had planned. Her monograph is uneven in style, and it is of course superficial, to fit this series of essays. But it remains much more than a comprehensive introduction. Enid presents the complex problems which Gide had constantly to face; she shows his struggles to reconcile his individualism with his social obligations, and to reconcile his homosexuality with his profound devotion to his wife. The comments on this relationship are among the best things in this little book, suffused with sympathy.

Gide was not now the writer with whom Enid was most concerned. Nineteen fifty-four brought the centenary of Rimbaud's birth. On 18 February she delivered the Zaharoff Lecture in Oxford. She considered it one of the highest distinctions in her career. 'It is a great honour [she explained to Hamish Hamilton] as no-one from Oxford has ever been invited yet and certainly no woman from anywhere. Usually it is someone from France.' She added, with childlike pleasure: 'It is one of the lectures where the Vice-Chancellor attends preceded by the University Mace.'[17] She took as her subject 'Rimbaud 1854–1954'.

On 11 March she went to Dublin, where she spoke on Rimbaud to the French Centre at Trinity College. She gave a second lecture next day. 'I hadn't been to bed for two nights when I went to Dublin to give my lecture,' she told me on 21 March, 'and I gave the first in a state of daze . . .' She added that there was to be a new Chair of French at Cambridge, and that she had been urged to apply for it. But she had no wish to leave Oxford. 'I think that even a Readership is preferable here. I would hate to leave my flat, also to give up my cellar at Somerville. I would also miss all my friends at Oxford . . . Also I don't like the French course at Cambridge. I certainly shan't put in for the Chair, but if they offered me it I would think about it for a week-end.'[18]

On 11 April she went to Paris, where she lunched with Henri Matarasso, visited old Professor Rudler, now in lonely retirement, and enjoyed a drink with Samuel Beckett. Ten days later she returned to Oxford to find a letter waiting from Joyce Cary: a letter of congratulation on *Petrus Borel the Lycanthrope*. He thought it the best written of her books.

He wrote with affection rather than judgment. No-one questioned Enid's preference for original characters, her talent for anatomizing complex personalities, or her knowledge of Romantic Paris. But it was clear that she had too little material for *Petrus Borel*, and that the book was hastily put together and superfluous. It was not a true biography, still less a critical study. Enid claimed it as an introduction to Baudelaire, but it had no literary significance. It was a monograph on one Romantic eccentric, blown out with digressions on the *bataille d'Hernani*, on the dandies, on the cholera epidemic, on the carnival, on Musard and the cancan, on Roger de Beauvoir, Barbey d'Aurevilly, Nestor Roqueplan, and the Impasse du Doyenné. *Petrus Borel* was superficial, and lacking in style; it was all familiar to the first-year student of French literature.

Early in September Enid attended the international Biennale Poétique et Knokke-le-Zoute. *La Lanterne* duly reported: 'Enid Starkie, a blonde Irishwoman (red jacket and beret and blue corduroy trousers), was as gay as a sailor on leave.'[19] She was, it seems, quite as gay when, the following month, she went to France to celebrate the Rimbaud centenary. On 17 October she attended the banquet at Charleville where scholars, men of letters, government and municipal officials gathered to enjoy such local delicacies as *jambon en croûte à l'Ardennaise*, and *terrine de grives*, and to wash them down with champagne. And there, reported *Le Figaro littéraire*,' immediately after the *terrine de grives*, there was nearly a diplomatic incident. Miss Enid Starkie, who had come from across the Channel with her red velvet beret, rushed to the microphone . . .'[20] Her speech reflects her devotion to Rimbaud; it also shows her unhappy egotism, and the Irish Anglophobia which, from time to time, she felt it in character to profess.

Ladies and gentlemen,

I am very proud and very happy to have been asked to speak for England on the centenary of the birth of the poet to whom I have devoted twenty years of my life. Indeed, I have written four books on him, three of them in English and one in French.

It is true that, being Irish, I would rather have spoken for Ireland, which is in fact the cradle of modern English literature . . . I always say that I am Irish by birth and French at heart, and that I earn my living in England.

It is just twenty years ago this year that I began my researches into Rimbaud . . .[21]

The speech was curiously inappropriate; but no-one could question Enid's right to speak for Rimbaud studies in England. Her authority was attested in a massive article in the *New Statesman*, and by another in the *Manchester Guardian* on 20 October, a hundred years to the day after Rimbaud's birth.[22]

Early in the new year she marked the centenary yet again, and gave two lectures on Rimbaud in Brussels. She seemed to be in perpetual movement. Mid April found her working in Paris. On 21 April she lectured on Verhaeren at the Belgian Institute in London. Six days later she returned to Paris for a series of meetings at the Quai d'Orsay. The Foreign Office had asked her to sit on the Anglo-French Cultural Commission.

Her diary records an almost incessant round of social engagements in the intervals of literary activities and academic duties. 'She would spend a day in the ordinary work of teaching, faculty jobs, committees, etc.—then go to a party, drink abundantly, talk a lot, be endlessly amusing—go home, get into her dressing-gown and start working! For me,' writes Agnes Headlam-Morley, 'it would have been utterly impossible.'[23] To Enid's friends it was sometimes disturbing. An American publisher sent a rebuke: 'I appreciate your staying up until 3 a.m. to write to me, but . . . you must look after your health. We at least want you to write many more books.' *Petrus Borel*, one might add, had been finished at 5 a.m. one Christmas Day, after she had worked throughout the night.

Caught up in this intense and unremitting activity, Enid sometimes dreamed of escape.

I suppose you don't know anything about anything so low as building a cottage of wood [she enquired of Cecil King]? I am, at the moment, much attracted by the idea of getting something in the country not too far from Oxford where I could go for refuge to get some work done. Oxford has no close season now and one is bothered all the time. I wouldn't mean to live in it permanently nor to give up my flat here . . . But I have been told that houses made of wood were very cheap to buy and to set up. I am attracted by the thought of one painted white or cream with red shutters, and hall door. I have designed one, of two bedrooms, living room, bathroom and kitchen . . . I was thinking of something in the region of £500 but I imagine that I may go on thinking . . .[24]

She went on thinking, and she continued to feel the strain of her life. On 24 May she consulted Professor Witts at the Radcliffe Infirmary. He reported to her doctor: 'She needs at least a month's complete rest—the nearest Enid Starkie can get to going into a retreat.'[25] Professor Witts was not alone in giving such advice. 'I have come to the conclusion,' wrote Alyse, 'that the only possible way of saving you—saving you for ourselves as well as for your own sake—is to abduct you and carry you away to some Jamesian "great good place" where no rumours of the outside world can reach you . . . But you are beyond all hope, nothing can alter it.'[26] It seemed that nothing could, for Enid soon complained to her: 'The other day the Brigadier at the Oxford and Bucks telephoned to me and asked me would I look after twelve cadets from the College of Saint-Cyr in France. He said that not he, nor anyone else at the barracks knew any French. He wanted me to invite them to my house, give them drinks and show them Oxford. I asked him why he didn't turn them over to the British Council, but he said that they didn't like to be disturbed.'[27]

⋄ 27 ⋄

Enid needed rest; but she needed perpetual activity. She had already embarked on an enterprise which would keep her busy into the new year. Cecil Day-Lewis had nearly finished his term as Professor of Poetry, and another election was imminent. On 1 August she had asked Wystan Auden if he would be a candidate.

Her letter reached him in Italy on 5 August, and he answered the same day:

I am very honoured and grateful that you should think of me in connection with the Chair of Poetry and I cannot deny that it is a post which I would very much like to have held. Unfortunately, there are two insuperable objections, one from the University's point of view and one from mine.

I am an American citizen. Even if the Statutes do not automatically exclude me, this would be a fatal handicap in any election.

The winter months are those in which I earn enough dollars to allow me to live here in the summer and devote myself to the unprofitable occupation of writing poetry. I do not see any way in which I could earn the equivalent if I had to reside in England during that period.

So I'm afraid I must say no. It means a great deal to me, however, that you should have thought of me.[1]

The letter was hardly final, and Enid wrote again.

Dear Miss Starkie [he answered on 23 August]:
Many thanks for your second letter. I must say that your continued interest on my behalf is weakening my reluctance, though I still don't see how I could manage economically.

I would like to suggest, however, that the fit person for the Chair is Robert Graves . . . Has he been asked? Has he refused? If he should be a candidate I would not dream of running against him.

How does one set about getting one's M.A. when one is in America?

Enid sent advice. On 7 November, from New York, Auden confessed:

This is to tell you that, some six weeks ago, I sent the Bursar of Ch. Ch. a cheque for the sum of $98.21 to pay for my M.A. I have heard nothing since, but I presume that, if I get one *in absentia*, you will know.

In other words, I am willing to be a candidate, and I am deeply grateful to you for doing me the honour of suggesting it.

On 5 December:

Dear Miss Starkie:
I duly received my M.A. I wonder if you could tell me when the election takes place and when I shall know the results?

★

When nominations for the Chair closed on 31 January, the *Oxford Mail* announced that 'of the three nominees so far, Mr G. Wilson Knight [of Leeds University] is not thought to have a large following in Convocation. Since the contest between the other two, Sir Harold Nicolson and Mr W. H. Auden, is being interpreted as a conflict between literary ideologies, the lists of their sponsors make interesting reading. The English faculty itself seems to be split. Sir Harold has the support of two former Professors of Poetry, Prof. H. W. Garrod and Sir Maurice Bowra; Mr Auden of one, Professor C. Day-Lewis, the retiring incumbent . . . The hundred people who are sponsoring Mr Auden, however, include no less than three professors of Classics and seven of the ten professors in the Modern Languages faculty.'[2] 'He is a kind of Popular Front candidate,' added the *Observer*, on 5 February. 'He is backed particularly by those who look back on their youth in the thirties, by the left-inclined in politics and literature, and by those "who are keen on poetry". He is the candidate of Dr Enid Starkie, a small, intense, and tireless French don at Somerville. She is a great judge of intrigue.' 'Of course the professor should be a poet,' she announced on polling day. 'Auden's a bit of a gamble. I admit I've only met him once, but I think he's probably the greatest of the Oxford poets of the thirties.'[3] The campaigns continued briskly up to that morning, 9 February, 'with undergraduates prowling about painting "Vote for Auden" on any wall out of sight of the police, and distinguished dons skirmishing to the last.'[4] The walls of Oxford blossomed with slogans demanding 'Auden for Pope'.[5]

Auden was elected by 216 votes, and Sir Harold Nicolson polled 192. The *Oxford Mail* reported that, when the result was known, 'Dr Enid Starkie rushed off to the Post Office to send a telegram to Mr W. H. Auden in New York. She paid 7s. (special rate) so that he should hear as quickly as possible.'[6]

Feb. 10th

Dear Miss Enid Starkey (or in Southern Parlance, Dear Miss Enid, honey):

You've obviously missed your true profession: you should be a ward boss, and make lots of money.

How on earth did you manage it? I had completely resigned myself to losing . . .

I know the Crewe Oration exists but I haven't the faintest notion of what it is supposed to be about. In any case I must find an expert in Mediaeval Latin and use an Italian pronunciation.

Entre nous, I'm surprised that the anti-Americans didn't have the political sense to put up a really distinguished academic scholar, for, if they had, I should immediately have withdrawn.

I only hope that I can prove worthy of what you have done for me.

When we meet (probably in May) we'll have some champagne *together*.

> yours affectionately and ever gratefully
> Wystan Auden.

On 16 February, the new Professor added: 'The whole business seems to have been pure Firbank. Whoever invented such a curious method of making an academic appointment? If you are a political agitator, what, then, are the Press who are not even members of the University? . . . I shall look forward to our next meeting and *sharing* some champagne.' On 30 April, he wrote:

Dear Enid (if I may),

I can't get a word out of the Registrar about the Crewe Oration—no facts, no example. Do you think there's the slightest possibility of persuading the Public Orator to do a swop? I'll do it for him next year if he'll do it this. The whole business is a farce anyway—having to stand up and deliver what everyone knows I have had to have ghost-written,★ —but that's by the way.

My inaugural, naturally, takes a lot of time and time is short. If it's not possible to get out of it this year, I must at least be provided soon with the necessary materials.

Plan to arrive in Oxford, June 1st. Longing to see you.

> Wystan Auden.

★P.S. I'm quite willing to pay some impecunious scholar provided he is trustworthy and doesn't pull my leg, to do the whole thing.

On 11 June he delivered his inaugural lecture. It was a hot summer evening and the Sheldonian Theatre was uncomfortably full. The *Sunday Times* observed that 'before the new Professor arrived, Dr Enid Starkie hustled happily to and fro, determined to enjoy the maiden voyage of the craft she had done so much to launch in the miserable depths of winter.'[7]

Enid went from a party given for Wystan Auden to a party given for Jean Cocteau. Not content with managing the poetry campaign, she had brought Cocteau to Oxford and secured him an honorary degree.

She had, it seems, approached him tentatively in March. She later told his biographer, Francis Steegmuller:

My first step, when I wanted him to come to Oxford, was to ask him whether he would come to lecture, and say that I would try to get him made a D.Litt. *Honoris Causa*. I couldn't promise anything, but the chances were favourable—in fact I was pretty certain. He accepted and I put his name before the Board of Mediaeval and Modern Languages for a lecture—I was a member of the Board, in fact I think I was Chairman that year. I knew that the Board would accept, which it did.[8]

On 25 March, Cocteau wrote to her:

Chère madame,

I am deeply moved by the honour you do me. Don't worry about the expenses of the journey. *I shall need nothing but accurate time-tables*. I must also ask you how and where in Paris I can get the costume made.

For I too need to be certain, because I shall prepare this lecture with love and I want Oxford youth to remember our meeting.

I shall hope for a letter from you, at Saint-Jean-Cap-Ferrat (Villa Santo Sospir) Alpes-Maritimes, where I shall be after to-morrow.

I want to give everything, my lecture and my presence, in exchange for the honour which is done me.[9]

'My next step', Enid remembered, 'was to get him the doctorate and I had to get members of the Hebdomadal Council to propose it to the Council. I asked several people, among them Sir Maurice Bowra . . . French people always choose the wrong names to mention for a thing. It was an honorary degree, . . . but the Latin citation is "*Doctor in Litteris Honoris Causa*" and so the Doctor is the important [part] and not the other. Cocteau always called it the "*Honoris Causa*".'[10]

Ma chère Enid Starkie [he wrote to her on 5 April],

Everything seems to be in order—as soon as we know about the *Honoris Causa,* I am going to prepare my lecture. No doubt it will be called

La poésie ou l'invisibilité.

Give me some details soon.

Votre
Jean Cocteau.[11]

On 16 April he wrote again: 'I have begun work on the Oxford lecture but I should be extremely grateful if you would let me know if you have secured the *Honoris Causa* . . . If you don't get it, I'd rather wait and let the thing happen later.'[12]

In that letter [Enid explained to Francis Steegmuller], he was, I know, really saying to me that if he wasn't going to get a doctorate, he'd rather not come. I couldn't *promise* him the doctorate but only the lecture. The other had to go through various committees. I only thought it very likely as I have some underground influence in the University. He didn't make any conditions as of course he couldn't, but I firmly believe that if he hadn't been given the doctorate, he wouldn't have come.

You mustn't make these things too precise, it is all a question of nuance and persuasion. If you try to make it all too precise you'll spoil the whole thing. I was working very hard behind the scenes as I knew Cocteau wouldn't come without the big bait, but I couldn't say much about it. I won, in the end, but don't ask too closely how it was done. He wrote several times in the vein hinting that he couldn't come for less than a doctorate. If I'd let that be known he would certainly not have got it . . . I could only use my influence and my prestige to get him the doctorate. That is what got it for him.[13]

The honorary degree was granted to Cocteau, and on 3 May he wrote again:

Ma chère Enid Starkie,
Thank you with all my heart . . .
I should a thousand times rather come with the cap and gown. Would you be kind enough to tell me either *if you know an English tailor in Paris who could make them*—or whether, if I sent you my exact measurements and the size of my head, they could be made in Oxford for the 12th.
I should like to keep them as a memento of the great honour which I much appreciate.[14]

He continued to be preoccupied by his academic dress; on 23 May he sent a sketch of himself in cap and gown, with measurements, and the comment: 'The Honour which Oxford does me certainly deserves a new dress.'[15] On 6 June he wrote:

Ma bien chère Enid Starkie,

The die is cast. Yesterday I finished correcting the lecture and this evening I am leaving the South of France. I fought like the very devil on the telephone with the BBC, and they managed to wear me down. Just imagine that to ensure that I am not disturbed at Oxford, I agreed that the television might come and meet me at London Airport! And French television are making me present the Tower of London on the evening of the 14th!!!

This is the age we live in, . . . and I only like the style of Goethe's Weimar . . .[16]

Enid remembered:

He arrived on the evening of Monday 11 June. It was an awful day for me as I had from 2.00 to 5 o'clock the Board; then I had Auden's Inaugural Lecture at 5 o'clock and, after that, there was a party for Auden at New College. Then, at 8.30, I gave a party at my house for Cocteau . . .

He said that he would arrive with a car and a bi-lingual chauffeur and I had visions of his landing in St Giles' with them! He asked me to get two rooms at a hotel—I chose the Randolph as it was near me . . .[17]

He fizzled through the foyer like an elderly Puck, wrapped around in a leaf-green cloak [*Picture Post* reported]. With him came a middle-aged woman and a young man—she, an exotically smart hot-house orchid of the species that only flowers in the *salons* of Paris; he, in his electric blue suit and suavely-tanned smile, looking like a young gallant from *La Ronde*.

M. Jean Cocteau and entourage were in Oxford, where he received the highest University accolade, an honorary degree. The lady was Madame Weisweiller, his 'patroness'. (She runs a literary salon of great distinction.) The young man was M. Dermit, his 'fils adoptif'. (He paints.) There was also a chauffeur in a silver-grey Rolls, who spoke seven languages.

They were met in a cloudburst of French by a brilliant little lady wearing scarlet slacks, beret and duffle coat. She turned out to be Irish— Dr Enid Starkie, who was responsible for getting Cocteau a degree and bringing him over.

M. Cocteau and Dr Starkie have more in common than eccentricity of dress. They are both the most respected elderly *enfants terribles* of their particular spheres.[18]

On 22 June Cocteau sent Enid a cutting from *Le Figaro littéraire*. On the front page was a photograph of the two *enfants terribles* strolling, in their academic dress, down Broad Street.

⋄ 28 ⋄

On 4 September Enid noted in her diary: 'Go to Russia.' Since her student days in Paris, she had always felt a natural affinity with Russians. They had many qualities which she found in her compatriots. No doubt she was therefore especially pleased to be the only woman in the University delegation to Moscow. The visit was an historic event. It was the first time since their foundation that the Universities of Oxford and Moscow had formally met each other.

The Oxford delegation was led by the Vice-Chancellor, A. H. Smith, the Warden of New College, and among the other members were F. W. D. Deakin, the Warden of St Anthony's College, and K. T. Parker, Keeper of the Ashmolean Museum. They flew in a Finnish plane from Copenhagen to Helsinki. At Helsinki they boarded a Russian plane; and finally, at about midnight, they saw the red stars shining on the Kremlin towers. They were met at Moscow Airport by a University deputation, and Enid was given a bouquet 'as big as the pig in *Alice*—and which I could only hold as she held the pig, if I wanted to be seen at all.'[1]

They drove in limousines into Moscow, 'past the new University on Lenin Hills, an enormous skyscraper, of the American variety, which was built in less than four years. We saw gangs working on the skyscraper apartment houses which are springing up all round . . . They work continuously over the 24 hours . . . The streets were being washed, although it was nearly 1 a.m.—they are washed every night.' At the giant Moscow Hotel, where they stayed, they were given a feast on arrival. 'We had caviar,' noted Enid in her diary, 'smoked salmon, crab salad. There were, after that, hot soup, three dishes of hot fish and meat, which we were

203

all expected to have. Then pastries and fruit. The éclairs were more like thunder-bolts than lightning! We had glasses of tea afterwards. Then we went to bed. I didn't sleep very well.'

Next morning they toured Moscow, where she found the clumsy, peasant-like women 'all unsmiling and unresponsive . . . Every man', she added, 'has a black mackintosh, which he wears with a brown suit, the colour one sees in late 19th century pictures. They are the drabbest people I've ever seen . . . I saw only one Tolstoyan figure, in top boots and the flat military cap which one sees in Russian pictures—he must have been a relic from the past.'

She admired the old University, an eighteenth-century palace now used as a government office, and painted in that favourite Russian colour, pistachio green. She admired Red Square, 'with the Church of Saint Basil at one end, like the drop-scene of a Russian ballet, with its onion domes of different colours. Down another side runs the lovely Kremlin wall, the same pink brick one finds in Cambridge.' The delegation attended a banquet at the new University, and once again she was amazed by Russian eating habits.

The table was set with embroidered cloth, napkins and lovely flowers, and piled up fruits from all republics of the Union. The cover was laid in French fashion, with the glasses in front of the plates, and not at the side. There were many waitresses. We started with caviar, followed by smoked salmon, followed by sturgeon in aspic. I didn't like the sturgeon and I thought that he had done all that was required of him when he had produced caviar! Also the aspic is not nice, looking like slabs of carpenter's glue! This was followed by crab salad, followed by chicken salad, followed by beef patties called *piroshkis*. Then the serious part of the meal began. There was hot fish, with a rich sauce; roast chicken with allumettes potatoes; roast beef, then escalopes with tomatoes. Then came ice-cream, with every kind of cake, biscuit and sweet—the most succulent cake was called Napoleon! We had vodka and Armenian brandy in little glasses all through the meal. We had a very nice dry white wine from Georgia, called Tsinandali—this I thought the best of their wines—red wine from the Don valley and, with the dessert, a sweet red wine from the Crimea. It ended with Turkish coffee. The meal took two and a half hours . . .

After lunch we visited the University, and saw the beautiful view of Moscow from the 32nd storey . . .

The Russians certainly have justification for being proud of what they have achieved in so short a time, in their university. A young person coming from one of the central republics of Asia—I talked to many of these—must see Moscow University as more enchanting and marvellous than Oxford must seem to someone coming from even the most remote and underprivileged home—the difference is so much greater, between that and home conditions.

Perhaps they haven't freedom of thought and expression, but one does not notice this in the ordinary day-to-day living. There are no foreign newspapers to read, no foreign periodicals, no protesting papers, but actually, in one's ordinary university work, one cannot perceive the difference, and one is not aware of restriction. Of course I am not personally interested in politics. I have felt little difference here with other university milieux that I've known.

On 6 September the Oxford delegation visited the Kremlin museum, and Enid noted 'English silver of a kind I've never seen in England—Parker says that most of that period was melted down during the Civil Wars—gifts from Queen Elizabeth, very exuberant and rich in design . . . I remember wonderfully rich ceremonial carriages, and similar troikas . . . I saw some of the best Fabergé I've ever seen.'

They had tea that day with the students at the new University.

The girls, without cosmetics, looked unsophisticated and young— rather like convent girls. I saw no slacks or jeans on any of the women students. Many of them were younger than our students as they went up to the University about a year or so younger. Their course is five years against our three, but during the first two years they do roughly what is done with us in the last two years at school . . . The only activity they seem to carry on outside their studies is sport, and this is highly organized by 'authority' . . .

They did not seem to me often to change their course, and [they seemed] to be more directed than our students. Their appointment committees seem to have more powers of persuasion—or coercion—than similar bodies in England. I asked the Minister of Higher Education how the government, and other bodies, got into touch with those seeking jobs—there is

no civil-service examination—and he answered, ominously, I thought—
that there was no problem of employment, and that there were more
jobs than candidates, that the Government told the universities ahead of
time how many people they would need in industry, commerce, the universities, the schools and the government, and the universities provided
them. This seemed to me rather like ordering tractors from a firm!

On 9 September the delegation drove through a birch-tree
landscape to Vladimir, where they toured the Cathedral, and
admired the mediaeval ikons; they visited a church which had been
built for one of the Tsars: 'a lovely white church, rising like a
flower from a built-up terrace in the river.'

On 14 September, they set out for Leningrad.

We went by the same train that Anna Karenina took nearly a
hundred years ago, and it seems still to take all night. It is now called
The Red Arrow, and there is electric light, where she had a little oil
lamp hanging behind her seat . . .

I slept until 4 o'clock—we started at midnight, and were not really
in bed until after 1 o'clock—and then only in fitful snatches. We passed
through lovely forest country, with lakes here and there. In the morning
we had glasses of tea and caviar sandwiches. We were met at the station
by a deputation headed by the Rector. Then we drove in three big
limousines to our hotel. It is the Astoria, the only hotel in Leningrad
that foreigners can stay at . . . There are some elegant genuine pieces
of First Empire furniture in the reception rooms . . .

Next morning, at the Hermitage Museum, Enid was amazed by
the number of Impressionist pictures. They toured the city, and

I love the amber colour of some of the buildings and the pistachio
green of others. I suppose these colours look well against the snow in the
long winters. The statue of Peter the Great is one of the finest equestrian
statues that I know. It is more lovely than Moscow—except for the
Kremlin and the Red Square. Some of the parts are more like early
19th-century Paris, and some like the 18th century parts of the Île
Saint-Louis in Paris. A peace drips from the trees along the rivers and
the canals, which one doesn't find in Moscow. Although it is nearly 40
years that Leningrad has not been a capital, it doesn't seem like a provincial town . . .

The university seemed to me more literary than Moscow, and I was much struck by the knowledge and understanding of French literature of some of the professors. They seem to me more cultivated than the people in Moscow, and as if they still looked towards Paris . . .

I noticed many people in Leningrad who looked to me in poor condition, and as if they had suffered at some time from rickets. I imagined that it might be due to the terrible blockade during the War by the Germans. The memory of it seems to be burnt into the minds of the people, as no other event. They told me it was worse than the bombardments, than the air-raids, worse even than the famine of the twenties. People died in thousands, they died at their work from hunger—they were often too weak to go home in the evening and remained in the factories. People taking coffins to be buried died on the way, and the sleighs were afterwards found with the coffins and the drivers, all dead . . .

Sunday, 16 September

We got up late . . . We had breakfast at 10 o'clock, and, as a treat, had *blini*. These seemed to me like drop-scones, which are eaten with red caviar, melted butter and sour cream. They were very good.

At 11.15 we left for the theatre, and some of us wanted a slightly longer walk. We passed a church, and I found what I'd been looking for in vain, a 'functioning' church. There was a service in progress, indeed several. I think that almost every baby in Leningrad was being baptized in one of the chapels in the lower church, and there were burial services in another. I saw people burning candles, with great fervour, . . . and everybody was praying with the utmost devotion . . .

This might give the impression that religion was flourishing in Russia, but one must remember that there are very few functioning churches for a very much increased population . . .

Then we went to the ballet which was *The Fountain of Bakhchisaraya* . . . The theatre was as usual crowded with people, with a large number of children. Each grown-up can bring a child under five free to matinée performances and they take full advantage of this . . . It was touching to see toddlers of three and four watching and listening with a look of transfigured emotion on their faces . . .

At 11 o'clock we got to the train. We were to meet the Rector of Leningrad University there who was going to Moscow. He was in another sleeper, but we fetched him to ours, and there was singing of songs, and drinking of vodka which Bill Deakin had bought in the station.

On 17 September they arrived back in Moscow, and attended a farewell party given by the Rector. 'All the students wanted to talk to the people from England—even those who knew no English—they wanted to get near us . . . Many had just read Graham Greene's *Quiet American*, which was the first of his novels to be translated into Russian and which had just come out. They were mad about it and wanted more of Greene.' There were many speeches of farewell, and Enid was presented with an amber necklace and a bottle of Russian scent called Moscow Red. Next day they returned to London.

I have many impressions left after the trip. The strongest I think is that of the longing of everyone for culture and learning . . .

I was struck by the ugliness of everything which was manufactured, of anything which could be bought. They seem to me to have given up their old traditional patterns and all their manufactured articles are inartistic. I think that their outlet for art is in museums and theatres, and concert halls . . .

I missed the *rouspeteur*, the grumbler and protester, especially amongst the young. Yet I think it is youth's birthright and privilege to protest, to be difficult, to be cussed. I missed the ironic approach to life which is so noticeable in the French.

I didn't talk politics while I was in Russia . . . They seem to me, like sanitation, to be necessary, but not an interesting topic of civilized conversation. Only one person—Professor Akhmenova—came near the subject with me. One day she said that one naturally wants to persuade others to one's way of life and thought, and that one's teaching would reflect this . . . I answered that I'd never felt any desire in my life to persuade anyone of anything, to teach anyone anything . . . I was willing to talk about the things that I knew, that interested me, and the most I hoped was that my example as a scholar might have some good effect, but only towards preserving intellectual integrity and standards of research. I said that I'd hate to alter people as I liked them different from myself . . .

I asked myself all the time when I was in Russia whether I felt any restriction on one's personal liberty, and . . . I couldn't see that there was any. If one can fit in with the majority, if one doesn't feel the itch to protest, then I think one would not feel any difference with other places. But if one wanted to be 'agin' things, if one wanted to be 'contrariwise', or be alone, then I think one might feel cramped. But I didn't feel that the Russians minded this as much as we would, as they are a gregarious people. I would however, myself, give anything for privacy, and for going my own way. A rabid individualist like myself might feel unhappy, or uncomfortable there.

❖ 29 ❖

Enid felt a certain romantic affection for Russia. Her devotion to France remained a dominant trait in her nature, a dominant feature in her career. '*Évitez le trop plein*': the comment which her teacher had once scribbled on her essay might sometimes be applied, even now, to her writing about France. It might well be applied to the article which appeared in *Vogue* in April 1957. In 'France Éternelle', she still displayed uncritical devotion. As usual, her judgment was coloured by Irishism.

In June there appeared a more solid tribute to her love of France: her revised biography of Baudelaire. It was exactly twenty-four years since the first version had appeared, and in the interval the climate of opinion had vastly changed. Enid herself had done much to destroy the old prejudice against Baudelaire; and one of her admirers, hearing *Les Fleurs du mal* on the Third Programme, praised her, now, for her championship of the poet. 'In the resulting new historical context he does not merely seem different, he *is* different. Hence the creative force of literary criticism.'[1]

The new *Baudelaire* appeared in the centenary year of *Les Fleurs du mal*. It was dedicated to the memory of Joyce Cary. On 15 August 1956, Enid had confided to Alyse:

Joyce Cary, the novelist, is very ill and can never get better as he has disseminated sclerosis, and it is tragic watching the gradual decline—sometimes slow, but sometimes accelerated. I was the first to notice there was something wrong, and that was when he was in Paris with me in 1954, at the time of the Rimbaud Centenary, and I remarked how badly he was walking and suggested he should ask a doctor about it. I thought it was arthritis. He didn't do anything about it—not that it would have made any difference if he had as there is no cure. He traces his illness back to the time when he had the aeroplane accident in April last year, when the plane on which he was travelling to Greece, went down the wrong runway and was wrecked, though no-one was hurt. However, in that year and four months, there has been a sensational decline. Last summer he was lecturing, and up to Easter this year, he was able to walk with a stick. Now his left side is useless and he can no longer even stand. For the past few weeks he has [had] a nurse-secretary who helps him in everything, and he is carried from his invalid chair to his bed and vice versa. He still has his right hand and writes still, but that is about all. Last autumn he had some kind of treatment at Stoke Mandeville Hospital for nervous diseases, but it did no good, and, this spring he went to Bristol for another experimental bout of treatment, but again in vain. He won't try any more as it all tires him so much and he says it uses up his very small store of strength. He wants to husband that as much as possible. He won't even go out driving now as that might tire him. He only now moves from his bedroom to a room next door to it. No one can know how much longer he has, but I shouldn't say myself much more than a year.[2]

As he became increasingly disabled, Enid had given him comfort by her letters and her visits, her sympathy and invigorating gaiety. He thanked her '1000 times for the claret' in a note that showed that he was losing the use of his hand.[3] When his illness was much advanced, and he could hardly hold a pencil, he proved his courage by drawing a self-portrait. Henceforth it stood in Enid's study, on the bookcase opposite her chair. 'He was working on a book when he died,' she told Alyse, some time later, 'and he dictated it when he could no longer move, until his voice went also.'[4] By mid March it was clear that he could not live much longer, and her diary records almost daily visits to him. On 29 March she noted: 'Joyce Cary died peacefully at 10 o'clock.'

Her devotion to him had been intensified by her admiration for his stoic acceptance of illness. She expressed her feelings in the dedication of her revised *Baudelaire*, and more personally, in

Joyce Cary: A Portrait: the paper which she read that October to the Royal Society of Literature. Pamela Hansford Johnson, who took the chair for her, assured her that 'the paper seemed perfect in tone: the kind of critical tribute so few seem able to give with such honesty to anyone lately dead. It is by this kind of honesty, insight and imagination that a reputation comes to burn steadily: slop dowses it. Tristram Cary was obviously moved and delighted. Joyce would have loved it, and argued the toss.'[5]

⋄ 30 ⋄

On 7 June 1958, at the Maison Française at Oxford, the French Ambassador promoted Enid to Officier de la Légion-d'honneur. Henceforth she wore her red rosette with undisguised delight. But, Officier or not, she kept her irrepressible gaiety; and a young graduate who met her, only a few weeks later, happily recalled 'our raiding party and carrying away S.C.R. cake in triumph! I felt very much back *in statu pupillari* and as though the Dean might descend at any moment in wrath!'[1]

And so Enid's life veered between the grand and the gay, the dignified and the lighthearted. Now, at the height of her career, her effect on others was intense, immediate and unique. Sibyl Eastwood wrote from her country house near Cambridge: 'The cows often ask after the lady in scarlet boots! No other visitor has appealed to them so much.' Evangeline Olmsted, at Berkeley, assured her that she 'played equally well the parts of the intellectual bohemian or the grande dame'.[2] Henri Peyre, at Yale, remembered her as a 'dashing, cheerful, enlivening comet'.[3] The *Spectator* described her as 'a person of electric energy who smokes cigars'.[4] Michael MacLiammoir gave a performance at Oxford, his verbal portrait of Oscar Wilde, and hurried from the theatre to 41, St Giles', where the party continued, sparkling, until four next morning. In his memoirs he recalled 'the incomparable Enid Starkie. Enid was wearing vermilion and sometimes black tights that year, surmounted by gorgeous Chinese gowns: her scholarship and eloquence were only equalled by her gay hospitality.'[5] There was indeed no-one quite like her. Even E. H. W. Meyerstein, that misogynistic man of letters, recorded: 'I have never met a woman yet who has been of the slightest use to me morally or intellectually (to say nothing of emotionally) except perhaps Enid Starkie.'

Eithne Kaiser always kept a mental picture of Enid 'as met one day, . . . in St Giles', in azure and cherry, with blazing blue eyes and the wild Irish ecstatic look.' Enid's azure and cherry, her slacks and duffle coat, remained a vivid flash on the Oxford scene. Dorothy Wadham suggests that her need for drama 'probably accounted for her insistence on dressing as she did, certainly not without the consciousness of outraging the soberer dons of Somerville. When I stayed at St Giles' with her she usually took me in to college lunch, and I remember one occasion when in addition to the blue trousers and scarlet coat and cap she was literally covered with imitation diamond brooches!'[6] Enid's pupil, Gordon Roe, takes a different view. He maintains that 'her flamboyance was anything but arrogant. The first time she came to see us in Marlborough Road, she, wearing her usual outfit, approached a local inhabitant to ask the way. Before even she could open her mouth, the inhabitant eyed her up and down and directed her unhesitatingly to "Mrs Merry, Transport Accommodation". She enjoyed that.'[7] Since Enid often chose to buy her clothes at multiple stores, since she wore cotton gloves, and carried handbags and umbrellas which had clearly seen better days, her appearance sometimes led to false conclusions. David Ball, a postgraduate student, first met her when, one night, he caught the last Oxford train from Paddington. He thought she must be an elderly cleaner who had been up to London for a jaunt. Before they reached Oxford, he recognized his error.[8]

Enid could be casual about her everyday clothes; but she was vain about her appearance in academic dress. She revelled in wearing her doctoral scarlet and her Légion-d'honneur. She was delighted when Herbert Morrison told her at Encaenia: 'I like your colour scheme and you have all the rest of us knocked into a cocked hat!'⁹ She knew the impression she wished to create, and she created it as an actress created a part. Sometimes she seemed frail, and then 'she shivered in the wind like some native of a tropical country in their first English summer.' Thérèse Lavauden said that in Oxford, on a winter day, 'she looked, in the sunless streets, like a poor Irish waif, starving in body and spirit.' A few hours later, the Irish waif would become the don, and one would find her lecturing on the Naturalist novel. That evening, she might change again: the outwardly conventional don might become an Oriental hostess. Liselott Haynes writes: 'In some funny ways she was vain—endearingly so I thought. She loved the portrait of herself aged 20 at the piano looking, she thought, ethereal, and you will remember the way she used to steady the hand of anyone lighting a cigarette for her with her own hand lightly touching yours in a gesture that displayed its beauty to the full. She did have beautiful hands and was proud of them "because they were pianist's hands".'¹⁰ She drew attention to them by wearing rings of Sitwell proportions. She was well aware that she had a fine profile and remarkably expressive Irish eyes. Thérèse Lavauden found in them 'the pale, hypnotic gaze of Rimbaud's eyes'. In fact they were pale when she was tired, intensely blue when she was animated. They reflected her many moods, they shone with intelligence, and with a penetration that was some-times disconcerting.

It is strange that, for all her vanity, Enid took little interest in cosmetics. She never changed her lipstick, and she always used a chalk-white powder which emphasized her pallor. As for her hair, she attempted to dye it, with questionable success. A small child who bumped into her in the High Street was 'fascinated by this voluble lady, particularly by her hair, which was a mixture of colours and not those which nature intended!'

Enid was a strange amalgam of the vain, the naïve, the calculat-ing and devastatingly honest. Her photograph once appeared in the colour supplement of a paper, and a pupil sent congratulations. 'You compliment me', Enid answered, 'by telling me that I looked like a fast duchess. I thought I looked like an ex-gaiety girl!'[11] And, discussing a photograph of herself: 'I think that I look . . . rather like a self-indulgent prostitute, gone to seed!' In her fiftieth year, she admitted, disarmingly, to Alyse: 'Of course I'm not young though I always forget it.'[12]

⋄ 31 ⋄

'*Docteur ami vous embrasse et forme voeux pour le cher Oxford.* Jean Cocteau.' So the New Year, 1959, opened, with a telegram to '41, Saint-Gilles'.[1] On 25 February, Enid arrived in Paris for another meeting of the Anglo-French cultural commission. Before she returned to Oxford, she lunched with Sarah Watson at the Foyer. The Foyer had long been her Paris home, and in her diary she gave it as her second address. On 19 May, Sarah Watson died; her funeral was held at the American Church in Paris, and Enid attended it.

Sarah Watson had often talked about Hollins College, Virginia, where she had been a student in the late 1890s; and she had wanted Enid to visit it. Ironically it was this year that Enid went there as visiting professor. On 26 August she left for New York. Her remarkable American friends, Marianne Eyles and Frances Fowler, had quietly taken the journey in hand. Marianne confesses that she had paid the return fare, and asked the authorities 'to take good care of Dr Starkie'. The result was delightful. Enid described her journey to Thérèse Lavauden, once her colleague at Langford Grove, who was now teaching French at Roedean.

I had taken an economy class ticket on the jet. I was just going to have a rather bad seat, and nothing to eat on the journey. But when I got on to the plane I found that, without paying anything extra, I had been up-graded, and they had put me in the luxury class. When I got into the plane they gave me whisky and soda. Then I strolled around a little and saw the poor 'economy class' behind their grille, and then I had another whisky and soda to get over it! Later on, we were given coffee and all kinds of sandwiches, crab, salmon, ham and beef. And then we broke the journey in Iceland, and the people behind the grille were able to buy food and drink. Then we got into the plane again, and we in the luxury class were given dinner, and the dinner came from Maxim's in Paris. There was a choice of hors-d'oeuvre, and I took caviar which came from the Volga. There was a choice of entrées, and I had Lobster Thermidor, and all sorts of vegetables, and then a salad, and then an assortment of cheeses—I had Port Salut. Then there were *entremets*, and I chose crêpes suzette, and it was all hot. Then there was fruit. And then coffee and cognac. With the meal I had a white Burgundy, 1950, and champagne—I could also have had a Haut Brion, but it didn't go with the lobster![2]

She spent a week in New York, and then on 3 September she set off for Encino, California, to stay with Marianne Eyles and Frances Fowler. On 14 September she left for Hollins. Years later, she recalled her arrival by the local plane. The President of Hollins and his wife had met her and taken her to her own house on the campus: 'That darling little house which I loved so much and in which I gave a cocktail party every Saturday. I could not see the full beauty of it on my arrival, by night, but, next morning, I looked out on the blue glory of Tinker Mountain . . .'[3] The Blue Ridge Mountains, to her Irish eyes, recalled the hills of Connemara. Soon afterwards, with childlike excitement, she wrote again to Mlle Lavauden:

My sitting-room leads into my dining-room, I have two bedrooms, a bathroom, and a magnificent kitchen, with a huge frigidaire (with a freezing cabinet), an electric cooker, and a washing-up machine. Every day they bring me something new. The day after my arrival it was the typewriter which I am using now; then a television set; then a radio set; then an electric coffee-pot; and finally an electric grill.

It's an enormous place here, 500 acres, and there are 600 young girls who are only interested in horses . . .

There are nearly 60 teachers, most of them men, living on the campus with their families, in nice little houses like mine, and in larger ones. The campus is full of children, it encourages the birth-rate!

I have a lot to do, more than I expected. I have four lessons a week of two hours each . . . I also have six public lectures . . . On 20 November I'm going to New York to give a lecture at Columbia University . . .[4]

In the intervals of her teaching, she also found a few minutes to talk to the local paper. She wisely refused to discuss American university education. On 6 November, writing again to Thérèse Lavauden, she expressed herself frankly: 'The young girls here are very well brought-up—from the same class as the girls at Roedean —they are very rich, and it costs $3,000 a year to come here. They are more interested in horses than in anything else—there are 60 horses here—and they learn to ride, to play golf, and dance. Work is the least of their concerns.'[5]

Enid was on safer ground when she was interviewed for the student paper at Hollins. 'Questioned about the origins of her interest in French literature, she says that a French governess, and a spirit sympathetic with that of France, are largely responsible. "After all the French and the Irish are dreadfully alike. Why, some of the best French wines are Irish!" She cited Palmer and Talbot as examples. From wines we moved on to a discussion of the relative possibilities for getting rich here, and in England; burdensome taxes; the charm of the faculty children, the Abbey Theatre . . . A morning with her is an experience, to think on it is exhausting.'[6] However, Hollins could not hear her often enough. The same issue of the paper announced 'An Evening with Enid Starkie', in which she would talk informally about her life and interests and discuss writers whom she had known.

On 2 December, she informed her usual correspondent:

To-morrow I go to Charlottesville to lecture at the University of Virginia; it was founded by Jefferson, and he drew up all the plans. I am giving another lecture in the same district, and I'm going to see Jefferson's house, which he designed himself, Monticello. On Monday I go to Baltimore to give a lecture at the Johns Hopkins University. The Friday after, I go to Richmond to lecture at the University of Richmond, and at William & Mary College . . .[7]

Described as 'an astringent lecturer and conversationalist', Enid talked about Baudelaire at the University of Richmond. An unidentified paper also recorded that

A fast-talking little Irishwoman with red-streaked hair and China-blue eyes last night gave a learned discourse on 'Boudelaire [*sic*] and Our Time' before a joint meeting of Knoxville's Chapter of the English-Speaking Union and The Philological Club at Claxton Hall on U.T. Campus.

Dr Enid Starkie, . . . in an afternoon interview at the Faculty Club, said she always found lecturing in America much more pleasant than in England . . .

The colourful little professor—she wore an electric-blue suit with hosiery to match, and sparkling jewellery—said she would 'advise anybody to learn Russian. It's a language of the future', she said. 'Not so hard to learn, either, after you get past the alphabet.'[8]

Enid visited Williamsburg, which had been restored to its eighteenth-century state. On 14 December, she delivered the Washington and Lee Lecture on 'The Influence of French Literature on Yeats and Eliot'. 'I'm going to spend Christmas at Hartsville in South Carolina [this, again, to Thérèse Lavauden], and on 26 December I go to Chicago, for a congress of the Modern Languages Association . . . On 8 January I go to Knoxville, Tennessee, to give a lecture . . . The hardest thing here is that I've had so little time to myself, and I have done no work of my own. All the same, they are very nice to me, and I am very appreciated!'[9] On 31 December she confided to her Oxford colleague, Robert Shackleton: 'The people here think me wonderful and that is very flattering to my ego!! They think that every word that comes out of my mouth is amusing—I can't think why as I talk as I always talk! They elected me a member of a student secret organization as the "wittiest person of the year on the Campus"!!'[10]

The night before she left Hollins, she was guest of honour at a farewell party. It began at five in the afternoon, and each of the seven courses of the banquet was served at a different college house. Enid was taken from course to course in a car flying the Irish flag, and, when the last liqueur was drunk, the carillon resounded through Hollins College: one of the professors rang out 'When Irish Eyes Are Smiling'.[11]

Enid understood, now, that she would not get the title of professor for which she longed; she had persuaded herself that Oxford failed to appreciate her. Since her childhood in Dublin, she had wanted uncritical love and total admiration. She had found them now, at last, on this unheard-of campus in Virginia: a campus where, one day, a building would bear her name. Hollins College became for her 'the Jamesian "great good place" ' to which Alyse had once wished to transport her. To Hollins College, when she died, she would bequeath her fortune. No event in her life was to match these four months when she had been a visiting professor on the campus in the Appalachian mountains.

She arrived back in Oxford on 17 January 1960. But the thought of Hollins remained with her; assurances of devotion flowed in from pupils and members of the staff, and she herself recalled the college with such affection that she considered returning there during the Long Vacation. An apartment was made available for her.[12]

In the meantime, she immersed herself in her Oxford work; and in February, reviewing *The Women at Oxford* by Vera Brittain, she recorded her own feelings on the higher education of women.

There are many Oxford women whose gorge rises at the thought of the sordid and shaming beginnings of their intellectual emancipation, who ask for nothing better than to be allowed to forget them, and to disappear into a sexless mass of academic records . . .

But perhaps this is not a fair view, and the fact that women today, in learning and scholarship, are allowed to forget their sex, . . . may be due to the efforts of these eager and earnest, silly and scuttling women. True, all were not silly and scuttling. Some, like Dame Emily Penrose, had dignity and decorum, diplomacy and discretion; and it is probably due to her objective integrity that Oxford University granted degrees to women nearly thirty years before Cambridge . . .[13]

Enid was recalling not only her student days at Oxford; she had occasion to recall other places in her past. Exeter University had offered her the honorary degree of Doctor of Letters. It was only two years since Exeter had achieved university status. On 4 May she was among its earliest honorands. A fortnight later, on the first anniversary of Sarah Watson's death, a memorial plaque was unveiled at the Foyer. Enid gave an *oraison funèbre*:

I am one of the old, old students of the Foyer—perhaps not of the *tête de cuvée*, but not far off it . . .

No-one will ever be able to say what Miss Watson was for us students thirty-five years ago . . .

Miss Watson possessed a wonderful spring of youth which never ran dry . . . The youth of others flowed through her . . .

One could not claim that she was really beautiful . . . [But] in a gathering, when she passed, one noticed only her. Without any impression of self-satisfaction, she radiated that essence which is personality itself.[14]

The observation might have been made about Enid Starkie. That June, at the annual garden party at the Maison Française in Oxford, 'she wore not only her D.Litt. robes and insignia of the Legion of Honour, but also a pair of unmistakably blue stockings.'[15]

On the last day of the month, she went back once again into her past: beyond Exeter and Paris to her childhood. She was already a member of the Irish Academy of Letters ('Starkie by all means', Bernard Shaw had written to Helen Waddell). Now she became a Doctor in Letters, *honoris causa*, of Trinity College, Dublin. The Public Orator expressed the hope that 'she will find as much joy in receiving honour and acclamation in Ireland and Dublin as we now feel in offering them to her.'[16]

❖ 32 ❖

On 21 March Hutchinson had published *From Gautier to Eliot*: Enid's study of the influence of France on English literature, 1851–1939. It is the least successful of her books. Literature, to Enid, was French literature; and, writing to Alyse, she confessed: 'What has made [this book] so hard for me is that I've not studied English literature since I was a girl.'[1] Nor had she ever read it for pleasure.

She had depended on concentrated reading to fill the lacunae of a lifetime. She had amassed abundant facts, but she had clearly felt no enthusiasm. The result was unhappy window-dressing. In her conclusion she discussed Anglo-French relations, and the significance of French culture. It was her set piece on France; it was also the only chapter written with feeling.

From Gautier to Eliot was criticized for misquotations, factual errors, and meaningless judgments; reviewers regretted that private quirks should spoil a study of such potential importance. *The Times Literary Supplement* assessed the book succinctly:

One rejoices that, day by day, at Somerville and more largely in Oxford, and, perhaps, intermittently in France, young women are absorbing the doctrine without, one hopes, its Irish joke on the side. Alas, Dr Starkie's new book does not quite represent what she so importantly feels. In large part, it is merely another book on Yeats— Eliot and the *symbolistes*, with Dr Starkie's extra understanding of Rimbaud and Baudelaire thrown in, and a useless top-dressing of Irish Anglophobia.

The reviewer was not alone in observing Enid's Irish joke. It recurred frequently in her conversation. Anne Kirkman's comment might have been made by any of Enid's pupils: 'She once challenged me to name a really great British playwright since the days of Shakespeare who had not been an Irishman, and was almost childishly delighted when I failed.'[2] Sir Michael Cary, writing of her relationship with his father, said that 'in later years and particularly during his illness, one had the feeling that her Irishism grated, and that he found her excessive devotion to certain well-worn nationalist themes a bit hard to bear.'[3]

Less attractive than her Irish joke was her Irish Anglophobia, which permitted her not only to ignore English literature but to assume the natural and undoubted superiority of all things French. Enid's Anglophobia might be displayed in an interview with a Cape Town journalist ('Don't you call me English! That would be frightful!'), in an article in *Vogue*, at a Rimbaud celebration in Charleville, on receiving a degree at Aix, in social conversation in Oxford and Paris. In 1947 she had written to Alyse: 'I think the

English are probably a lot to blame . . . for having always prevented European unity . . . We prevented Louis XIV, Napoleon.
I know they were aggressors but I think eventually that a unified
Europe under French influence—or even domination—might have
been a good thing.' In 1959 she had written to Eithne Kaiser: 'I'd
love to be able to live out of England. I don't like—and have never
liked—English life.' Enid's Anglophobia was a rather stupid
quirk. She herself had chosen not to be naturalized French, or to
live in France.[4]

However, the question of the two cultures remained in her
mind. For, in 1961, Wystan Auden's tenure of the Chair of
Poetry would expire, and she thought of standing as his successor.
On 25 June she explained to Agnes Headlam-Morley:

> There have been several mentions in the press recently—both here
> and in U.S.A.—that I was going to be the next Professor of Poetry. But
> one does not apply for the post and one cannot nominate oneself, but
> must wait for other people to do it . . . Please do not tell anyone what
> I'm telling you here. I would hate anyone to think, to know, that the
> matter had ever crossed my mind. It hadn't until I saw the mentions in
> the press, and until the reporters began pestering me. If I was invited,
> I'd accept nomination and, if I was elected, it would be the greatest day
> of my life, and would make up to me for not getting the Chair of
> French.[5]

It was a clear enough statement that she wished to be nominated;
and it was a clear explanation why she wished to have the Chair.
She must have known that the Chair of Poetry could not compare
for value or prestige with the Marshal Foch Chair of French
Literature. But she was prepared to delude herself. For the Chair
of Poetry would give her, if she were elected, the title of Professor
at Oxford. It would fulfil her persistent ambition. 'Is there anything one could do to get you elected?' Agnes Headlam-Morley
enquired. 'Of course I would gladly propose you but I don't think
that would help you as it should be a big gun on the literature
side?'[6] On 19 December, Enid confessed again to Alyse: 'If I was
elected it would be the greatest day of my academic career, and
would make up to me for having failed to be appointed to the

Chair of French.'[7] Alyse answered: 'I will certainly keep my fingers crossed on Feb. 16th and have written the date down in my new little diary for 1961.'[8]

On 8 January, Atticus of the *Sunday Times* turned his attention to the contest. 'All hands are looking forward to a nice clean fight for the Oxford Chair of Poetry next month. Members of the fancy give Robert Graves as favourite, but may hedge their bets when they hear that Dr Enid Starkie (Somerville) and Miss Helen Gardner (St Hilda's) have now agreed to stand against him.' On 20 January, *The Times* correspondent at Oxford noted an unexpected complication. A clause in the University statutes said that no professorship should be held with any other professorship or readership. Under this regulation, neither the Reader in French Literature nor the Reader in Renaissance English Literature would be eligible to stand in the election. An amendment to the statutes was published that day, proposing that the clause should not apply to the professorship of poetry. If, however, this amendment was not soon passed by Congregation, Robert Graves would be left as the undisputed successor to Auden's Chair. Such university politics now made headlines in the national Press, and created interest abroad. As Walter Allen suggested, in the *New York Times Book Review*: 'Miss Starkie is probably responsible for having rescued the Chair of Poetry from the respectable torpor into which it had fallen.'[9]

On 31 January a fourth candidate entered the contest: F. R. Leavis, the Reader in English at Cambridge. His nomination had been signed by over a hundred people. Professor C. L. Wrenn, who was one of his supporters, assured the *Daily Express*: 'To have him as Professor of Poetry would brighten up Oxford enormously . . . As far as I know he has not written any poetry. But that doesn't matter. He is such an outstandingly important critic.'[10]

Nominations for the Chair closed on 7 February. That day Congregation approved the promulgation of an amendment to the statutes, to enable the two Oxford Readers to stand. One difficulty was removed, but, for Enid, another arose. On 9 February the *Gazette* published the list of her nominators. There were sixty-two, but there was no Fellow of Somerville among them. However her colleagues voted, this public lack of support must have made her angry and bitter. Perhaps it marked the beginning of her stormy relationship with her own college. She could not accept that academic judgment must sometimes go against personal feelings.

On 10 February, in the *New Statesman*, Louis MacNeice observed:

> To vote for the Chair of Poetry, an institution described by the out-going Auden as 'comically absurd', you need not even know the English language. Nor need you to occupy the Chair; nothing in the statutes would prevent the election of a Chinese botanist who would give three lectures a year, in Chinese, on Leninist botany. But Enid Starkie, when first she started canvassing at the Oxford and Cambridge cricket match, . . . started a lot of March hares which are still rampaging not only through Fleet Street but Manhattan; and it now seems to matter bitterly who succeeds to the throne . . . It all began with la Starkie clutching her brandy in front of the Tavern at Lord's with her back to the cricket, her stockings out-blueing the sky and her blue hat loftily pinnacled at a height of around five feet.

Two days later, the *Sunday Times* gave Robert Graves 'as the hands-down winner, with Starkie the best each-way bet'. On 16 February, election day, the *Daily Mail* reported: 'Dr Starkie thinks Graves will win and that she will be second.' Robert Graves polled 329 votes, exactly half the number cast, and was 212 ahead of Helen Gardner. Dr Leavis polled 116, and Enid 96.

'Life pushes us on whether we will or no', wrote Alyse to Enid. 'As Dr Johnson said: "Grief is a species of idleness", and I think idleness is something you are never allowed.'[11]

Enid was hardly idle. In April she explained to a pupil:

> I am in a desperate state at the moment with work . . . I am examining for Finals at Glasgow in May, and I've had to set the papers during the vacation; I have to mark them early next month. I have also to go to Exeter to give a paper on 3rd May. I am examining for Finals at

Oxford, and had to set the papers for that during the vacation. What is worst is that I'm Chairman and that entails constant writing to 21 examiners. At the moment I'm struggling with the Time Table and there don't seem to be any limits to the permutations and combinations possible. I've had to do it several times as there was one 'late entry' in French and Modern Greek and another in Italian and Russian. I don't know what else may happen before the actual examination . . .[12]

Despite her protests and complaints, Enid delighted in being Chairman of the Examiners. She enjoyed the prestige, the authority and the very complications of her position. She revelled in the play of personalities, and, no doubt, in the taste of university politics. She corrected papers with diligence, and she was a shrewd examiner in vivas. She was a competent administrator, and for a time she was Chairman of the Board of Mediaeval and Modern Languages: presiding over discussions of curricula and research. She combined such faculty work with tuition of undergraduates, supervision of graduate students, college committee work, and her own writing.

Her first *Arthur Rimbaud* had appeared in 1938; it had been revised and republished in 1947. But the Rimbaud manuscripts had not then been available; in 1960 she had seen them, and had had to re-write most of the book. Now, on 10 November, the third version of *Arthur Rimbaud* was published. She was disappointed in its reception.

So far there has been a kind of conspiracy of silence [she told Alyse on 17 December] . . . It is probably considered merely a reprint although there is masses of new material in it . . .

I am spending Christmas in Oxford and, then, on Boxing Day, I am going over to Paris to do some work at the Bibliothèque Nationale . . .

As usual I have two Christmas dinners on Christmas Day, and I have a Christmas tree party on Christmas Eve. The day before that I'm going to the Astors at Cliveden to dine. They are always very nice to me, and it is the kind of world I never see otherwise. The first time I was there I was beside the millionnaire Gulbenkian and it reminded me of something out of Edwardian days, and he is a little like Edward VII. He had a gold cigar case from which he offered me a cigar, and he addressed me all the time as 'my dear young lady'. He wore an orchid in his button-hole and he told me that he wore two every day, and changed half way through the afternoon. One of his problems was to have the second one delivered at the right time wherever he was.[13]

On Boxing Day, she reported on her latest visit to Cliveden.

The old lady, Nancy Astor, the mother of the present Viscount, was there, and I'd never met her before. She is still very wonderful for her age, which is well over 80. She still has her sharp tongue. When the men came into the drawing-room after the port she said: 'Did you ever see such a foolish lot of men? Let's laugh at them.' And she added: 'I hate men. If you had been as long in the House of Commons as I, you would think them all dreadful.'[14]

Dinner at Cliveden was a peak in Enid's social life. She revelled in the richness of the décor, and in the celebrity of the guests. There remained an element of the Lady's Child in her nature, and Clive-den took her back to an almost Edwardian world. She liked to live, for a moment, in the grand manner. On such occasions, one sus-pects, she felt the wonder of the Dublin girl.

But her social range was wide. In Oxford, she dined with Lord David Cecil, Roy Harrod and Nevill Coghill. She had cooked a famous dinner for Janet Vaughan, Joyce Cary and Maurice Bowra. She had invited Rosamond Lehmann to St Giles' to meet the Carys, and Rosamond had found Joyce 'a fascinating fountain of observations and ideas'. Now Joyce had died, but his friends the Davins were Enid's own close friends. She went regularly, on Saturdays, to the Lamb and Flag in St Giles', where Dan and Winnie gathered round them a group of talkative writers and thirsty intellectuals (Louis MacNeice was sometimes among them). Dan Davin of the Clarendon Press gave Enid advice on her pub-lishers' contracts. Peter Ady, the economics tutor at St Anne's, was another of the inner circle; and in time a Sunday drink with Peter replaced the Sunday drink with Joyce Cary. Enid's friends in Oxford included not only dons, but the more original clerical figures, and an Irish admirer, Paddy Shannon, a mystery man who arrived from time to time to drink champagne, to present her with

Bohemian glass, Dresden china or Georgian silver. Enid was found at nearly every literary party in Oxford; she had met Dylan Thomas at the Turf Tavern, she had known Graham Greene when he lived in Beaumont Street, she had drunk Pommard, 'princesslike', with Louis Wilkinson. She knew Rex Warner and Kenneth Clark. She entertained the distinguished and the undistinguished, the conventional and the Bohemian. From time to time she liked a glimpse of the Harrods-of-Knightsbridge world, and she enjoyed a drink with a local tradesman. Generations of undergraduates revelled in a visit to St Giles': it was one of the delightfully extravagant experiences of an Oxford education.

∾ 33 ∾

Now that her work on Rimbaud seemed to be definitive, Enid had turned to Flaubert. She had long been drawn to him. As early as 1950 she had planned to do preliminary research on his papers at Rouen.[1] She intended to write two books on him, dividing his life after the publication of *Madame Bovary*. It was by far the biggest subject that she had undertaken. She was working on Flaubert when, on 12 April 1962, she set off again to visit Paris.

The university year ran its course. On 30 August she went to the Colloque International at Ghent to celebrate the centenary of the birth of Maurice Maeterlinck. 'The Countess, Maeterlinck's widow, . . . is certainly a fantastic looking woman, and she kept on breaking into the speeches, in agreement or disagreement . . .'[2] On 1 September Enid delivered a paper on Maeterlinck and England. Mid-September found her once again in Paris, on the trail of the author of *Madame Bovary*. 'It must be fascinating working on Flaubert,' Alyse wrote on 10 October, 'and always exciting being Enid.'[3]

It was always exciting. She spent eight weeks in Paris. On 10 November, back in England preparing for a holiday in Greece, she dashed off a letter to Brian Hill to thank him for his translations from Heredia.[4] She had, in a sense, shaped his career. 'In the late 'forties,' he records, 'I read her *Arthur Rimbaud* and was immensely impressed both with the book and its subject's history, so much so that I tried to translate one or two of the poems . . . I sent my efforts to E.S. and she was kind enough to encourage me.'[5] She sent him understanding criticism, and urged him to continue his translation.[6] Her book and her encouragement were decisive.[7] He published five volumes of translated poems.

She had her effect on others, too. Pamela Hansford Johnson told her: 'The effect your *Rimbaud* had on Dylan Thomas and myself was—I'd say "seminal", if it weren't such an awful word. It gave Dylan the misguided impression, for ever after, that he knew French.'[8] Roy Fuller later wrote: 'I think she was pleased to be told . . . how much she had done for someone like me—quite ignorant of the language—in the field of French literature. I think this is an important side of her work.'[9] Enid's influence extended well beyond Oxford; many readers were drawn to French literature by her biographies, and, perhaps, a little by her personal panache. She achieved much by her scholarship; but one suspects that she achieved all the more by her affection for the strange, the eccentric and the romantic, and by the well-fostered Starkie legend.

Now, on 16 November 1962, she left to meet Marianne Eyles and Frances Fowler in Greece. 'It was wonderful!' she wrote, later. 'I long to go again. I saw the ordinary things, in great luxury, Athens, Delphi, Olympia, Epidaurus, Mycaenae, Nauplia, Argos, Corinth . . . It was like a good summer there, . . . and, the day I left Athens, on 1 December, people were bathing along the coast.'[10] She had brought a Greek cap to add to her wardrobe, when she returned to 41, St Giles'.

⋄ 34 ⋄

As 1963 began, St Giles' was much in her mind. It had seemed, as one of her pupils wrote, a law of the Medes and Persians that Enid lived there. It was an Oxford institution. But she had recently been asked to leave the flat which had been her home for thirty-one years. The rooms were needed as University offices. 'It is', she complained, 'pure Parkinson's law . . . Every minion has a minion and the most minion of minions has a private room . . .'[1]

Both Ernst and I still feel passionately about 41 St Giles' and how they put her out [writes Eithne Kaiser]. How she took one on a tour of the place, not least of the flowered Wedgwood loo-bowl, talking swiftly all the time, in that deep voice, always so Irish. The first time we visited her together, . . . we brought her a Roman silk scarf, very large (larger than we ever gave anyone else!) in Joseph's coat colours, those 'Roman stripes', you know, a sort of stole, and she instantly flung it round herself. Reaching for the decanter, she said all in one breath: 'Will you have sherry I hope you drink sherry I don't *do* tea it's far too much trouble I just give people drinks', and kept pouring it out, and when we left, far from clear in the head, she said: 'Have you forgotten anything people are always forgetting things and having to come back five minutes later' and I firmly said no, and of course five minutes later we had to come back for gloves or something, by which time she was evidently up to the neck in writing or cooking—still entirely hospitable, but going faster than ever and therefore waving us goodbye with the faintest extra shade of abstraction as well as intensity.[2]

Enid's move from St Giles' marked the end of an era in Oxford social life. But Enid always attracted the extraordinary and the unexpected. The disturbance of her removal was wonderfully eased when Marianne and Frances, ever munificent, offered to buy her a house. Walton Street is a long, unlovely street, but the west side is redeemed by a row of Regency houses, and one of these was now to be her own. 'I longed for beautiful rooms, colours, the lovely shapes of furniture,' she had written in the notes for her Paris book. 'I wandered in imagination in beautiful rooms with rich hangings.'[3] She had always tried to make her décor match her imagination. For the first time, she had a house on which she might exercise her gifts.

It was still exciting to be Enid, and she remained a legend. Somerville now decided to commemorate the legend, and commissioned Patrick George to paint her portrait. 'I suppose I should be flattered that they want to have me on their walls in perpetuity, but it is an awful nuisance [she told Alyse] . . . I am being painted in my D.Litt. gown. I am rather glad at that because, if the face is awful, the gown will distract attention!'[4] On 27 June she went to London for her first sitting.

Enid was one of the worst sitters I have ever faced [so Patrick George remembers]. After the first sitting I thought we would not be able to go on. Each time I asked her to move her head she sprang up out of the chair. We did go on all through the summer. She came down from Oxford by bus and walked from Victoria bus station dressed in her red and blue clothes and gym shoes. In the studio she wore her gown and her medal and rushed around with her robes flying and fairly often brushing in the paint . . . After some time we reached a way of working together: she sat more or less still and talked about Baudelaire and Rimbaud. I tried to keep the conversation going to prevent her falling asleep. Between sittings I worked at my reading assignments from the books she had given me in preparation for her next visit.[5]

On 22 September, when the portrait was done, he duly reported to his sitter: 'I have finished the Rimbaud and tried hard with the poems and translations of the poems. I enjoyed the Rimbaud very much . . . This afternoon I was meant to be painting the large canvas of the corner of my room (the paint from which got on your gown) but the colours went dull grey and I found myself reading *Petrus Borel* . . . Regardless of the portrait I enjoyed the sittings with you.'[6] 'I very much enjoyed our long talks', Enid answered. 'Best wishes to you and your wife, from your ex-victim.'[7]

However victimized she professed to be, she was immensely proud to have her portrait over High Table. She was delighted when she sat below it, and saw the undergraduates pointing her out to their guests. She considered that one eye in the picture resembled her own, and that her hair looked like the inside of a mattress. She claimed that the portrait turned her into a combination of Miss Buss and Miss Beale. 'They say that it makes me look fifteen years older,' she told her American friends, 'so perhaps, one day, I'll grow to it. What I can't bear in it is the enormous humourless face, also a tired looking face. Of course I was tired sitting for nearly seven hours a day on 32 separate days, and 100 hours of sitting strains one's sense of humour!'[8]

Patrick George had not caught her animation. He had made her thick-set and heavy-jowled. But the blue Encaenia suit, the glitter of paste jewellery, the scarlet of the doctoral robes and the Légion-d'honneur: all made the unmistakable impact. Perhaps one could not ask for more; for, as Eithne Kaiser wrote: 'Really I don't believe there is anyone alive who could convey the blue blaze of those eyes. Modigliani might have been the painter to get on to canvas the extraordinary Starkie quality, though it might have been tiresome to have been elongated like a piece of elastic.'[9]

❖ 35 ❖

'I really am driven distracted with work.' This from Enid on 5 February. 'I work until 3 a.m. every night but don't seem able to keep even abreast. I've two new lectures which I prepare as I go along. This week I've the Heath Harrison Scholarships and I have not begun yet to think about my lecture on Flaubert.'[1] On 19 March, for the second time, she delivered the Tredegar Memorial Lecture at the Royal Society of Literature. She spoke on *Flaubert and Madame Bovary*.

On 8 May she left 41, St Giles'. Within a matter of weeks, she had re-created its atmosphere at 23, Walton Street. It was clearly Enid's house from the moment she opened the red-and-gold door.

The drawing-room walls and ceiling were papered in gold, and the walls were hung with Chinese and Tibetan tapestries and paintings. The mantelpiece was painted Burmese red and decorated with panels of compressed palm-leaf, gilded and inscribed, from an Eastern temple; the hearth was guarded by brass Chinese dragons. The oriental atmosphere was intensified by an eighteenth-century Chinese chair, so carved and gilt that it was like a throne. A common elaboration united such Eastern pieces with such Western ones as the sixteenth-century Italian light sconces. On the mantelpiece stood the elegant French clock which Enid had bought to mark her Readership.

The drawing-room was largely gold; the study was predominantly red. The woodwork was painted scarlet, the chairs and tables, the carpet and the typewriter were scarlet, too. Italian and Venetian mirrors multiplied a room which was crowded with treasures: among them Joyce Cary's self-portrait, and a lithograph of Yeats by Augustus John. At the top of the house was the library, where two of the walls were lined with books and one was almost hidden by a hideous oak dresser, huge and black and intricately carved. This had been sent to Enid by an admirer. On the desk was Edyth Rackham's haunting bust of a Starkie nursemaid (Enid had rescued it from a Dublin cellar).

The house was a series of stage sets, which Enid's personality held together. It gleamed with red lacquer, baroque gold carvings and Empire console tables, Bohemian and Waterford glass. The pink-and-blue bedroom was enhanced by Dresden and Staffordshire china, and by delicate engravings after Angelica Kauffmann. The study and the library were resplendent with the best private collection of books on nineteenth-century France to be found in Oxford. Among them were first editions and unobtainable volumes which Enid had bought for a franc or two on the Paris *quais*. And, since her taste was sometimes Sotheby's, sometimes Marks and Spencer's, the kitchen dresser was laden not only with Bristol glass and Georgian silver but with scarlet plastic cups and saucers; the library was enhanced by an early Italian painting of the Massacre of the Innocents, and the kitchen wall was enlivened by a caricature of a *clochard*. Enid's cellar contained rare vintages, and a bottle of splendid brandy which she was still keeping for the day when she won a Chair. It also contained Blanquette de Limoux, which she insisted on calling champagne.

The house in Walton Street was Aladdin's Cave for the antique collector and for the student of French literature. It was a constant fascination for the student of human nature. Yet few of Enid's visitors would have chosen to live in a world of almost unrelieved scarlet and gold, to use a bathroom of peacock blue and red. It belonged to Enid alone. Two rooms, above all, revealed her nature. One was the spare bedroom, which she had clearly furnished as a deterrent ('I suppose I don't really want people to stay'). The other was the kitchen, where the refrigerator rarely held more than a single egg. The house in Walton Street, like the flat in St Giles', was a backdrop and an experience; but it did not give the impression that it was lived in. There were no flowers, except the flowers given by Enid's friends, and these were often wilting for lack of care. The windows were rarely cleaned. The house was not a woman's house. It was a monument to Enid's literary taste, to her artistic flair, to her loneliness and her unreal existence.

Enid's tiredness had been evident during her move from St Giles'. I assumed that it was the effect of strain. In August, from Cape Town, where she was spending a few weeks as visiting professor, she sent me a more serious explanation.

For two years, now, her friends had been concerned about her persistent cough, and had urged her to be x-rayed. A few days before she left Oxford, she had happened to see a mass-radiography van, and, on an impulse, she had had the x-ray done. There had proved to be shadows on both her lungs; she had had tests in hospital, and further x-ray photographs were taken. The specialist had reluctantly allowed her to go to South Africa, provided that she consulted a doctor there. She had asked what the possibilities were.

He said tuberculosis of the lungs, cancer of the lungs, leukaemia, or else old scars from pneumonia, or the result of an asthmatic cough. None of these could be ruled out, and the only things that were ruled out were cancer and tuberculosis of the spine. You can imagine [she wrote to me] how encouraged I was by this diagnosis and began to think, of course, of leukaemia . . . I got in touch as soon as I could with the specialist here [in Cape Town], and further x-rays were taken . . . The photos were exactly the same as those taken in Oxford and there was no deterioration . . . So I am more optimistic than I was. The specialist in Oxford, and the one here, said that I should take a day in bed whenever I felt tired, or felt like it. I feel inclined to say 'don't make me laugh!' The work is appallingly hard and I'm lucky to get my nights in bed, much less odd days! It is the constant change from one subject to the other which I find so wearing. I dash from Baudelaire to Rimbaud, to Gide, to Proust, to Mauriac, to Flaubert, to Yeats, to Pound, to Eliot, to Joyce etc. etc. I have also a lot of social life to get in . . .

I'll be here until 13 September and then I go to Johannesburg for a week, but I finish on 20 September. After that I may go home by Ghana.[2]

On 31 August she wrote to me again:

I wish they would decide what it is so that I can have some treatment if necessary . . . I'm glad all the same that I didn't cry off, as I nearly did on my last night in Oxford as I naturally thought it must be fairly certain leukaemia or they wouldn't have mentioned it . . . At first it was always in the back of my mind and it used to wake me up at night. Now I'm not really envisaging anything bad as I think they'd have found it out by now . . .

I don't know yet what I'll do about Ghana as I've not yet heard anything from there. I'd be quite glad to drop it altogether . . . I'd like to get back to my book at Oxford.[3]

On 23 September she arrived back in England. On 27 October she reported:

I spent most of the morning at the Chest Clinic. What they are inclined to favour now is something called Sarcoidosis, which has nothing to do with Sarcoma . . . Fifty per cent of the cases cure themselves without treatment. If, in the course of a year, it hasn't cured itself then the treatment is one of the poisons which kills everything within sight—and perhaps the patient as well! A sarcoid is some kind of tissue in a bag which in fifty per cent of the cases becomes reabsorbed, and it isn't malignant.[4]

The facts were more disquieting than Enid was told. Next day Frank Ridehalgh, the chest specialist at the Churchill Hospital, wrote to Dr Herrin, her doctor:

I do not think there is any real doubt that these are metastatic deposits. The easy assumption is that they arise from her former uterine cancer but that was a very long time ago . . . I think it would create needless alarm to embark on a meticulous search for a possible new primary . . . Meanwhile Miss Starkie has asked for a diagnosis. I have told her that sarcoidosis is a condition which produces bizarre shadows in the lungs; that its course is not certainly known; that in most cases it is benign and is never treated without at least a year's observation . . . She has made a note of the name.[5]

For the moment she was reassured. Dame Janet Vaughan was told about her condition and her treatment, and on 2 November she wrote to Dr Ridehalgh: 'I saw her yesterday just before she went off to Paris. She is quite a different person—back to her old enjoyment of life. We love her very much. So you must count on College and me to help in any way we can at any time.'[6]

Enid spent a week in Paris, and noted six dinner engagements.

PART EIGHT

✧✧✧✧✧

Reader Emeritus
1965–1970

Her enjoyment of life did not last. On 2 March she complained to me: 'I never seem to work less than 15 hours per day. I'm very tired and very depressed and I never feel well. I think it is that this hard work has gone on now too long and I haven't had a rest for a long time.'[1] On 8 March she had a biopsy. It showed that she had cancer of the lungs: a recurrence of the cancer of 1949.

She was given local radiotherapy and twice weekly injections of progesterone. On 12 March, Dr Ridehalgh explained to Dr Herrin: 'She asked if this [abnormality in the lungs] was malignant and I said "no" . . . She appeared to accept this. I see no reason to interfere with her trip to Paris in April. She tells me, however, that she is booked for a three months' appointment in Pennsylvania in the autumn . . . I doubt whether it will come off.'[2]

Enid did not in fact accept what she had been told. On 14 March she wrote to him:

I am very much perplexed at the moment and it is the unknown in my condition that I find hard to accept. An academic mind cannot help working on a problem trying to find a pattern in it, but I can make no pattern out of what has been happening to me, and I cannot shake off a feeling that I am being told nothing, that everything is being kept from me.

At first when you diagnosed sarcoidosis, it seemed clear . . .

I was told nothing about the possibility of the bone swellings. I noticed the one on my collar-bone before Christmas—perhaps even before that—and asked about it, but I did not worry about it as it was never given to me as a possibility.

Then the lump turned out to need treatment and I've had radium treatment, and that, to the uninitiated, always seems serious. Then I had a biopsy. I've not been told what the results of this were: I've not been told what this lump is, nor why it needs radium treatment, and so frequently. I've not been told why, fifteen years after a hysterectomy, I have a hormone deficiency, why I need these injections . . .

As I try to figure it out odd things come up into my mind, how I once saw that sex hormone injections were sometimes given in the treatment of cancer, and I can't help wondering whether the bone lump is cancerous. If that were the case I'd much rather know. The unknown is always the hardest thing to envisage.

I can only build a pattern out of scraps. As when I asked you whether the delay in treating the lump had been harmful, and you answered that you thought it had been caught in time. Then there is the possibility of its not having been caught in time. What happens then?

What other things can there be in store for me and what can I expect, or be prepared for?[3]

Next day, after consultation with Janet Vaughan, Dr Ridehalgh reluctantly decided that Enid must be told the truth. He called on her that evening.

She knows that there are secondary deposits in her lungs which have almost certainly arisen from the old uterine cancer [this to Dr Herrin on 16 March]. She knows that this is not a lung cancer in the usual sense and she understands that there is a good chance of improvement under hormone therapy although this is not likely to be permanent. She took this news with amazing courage. She said she had faced death in the same way ten years ago [sic] and it did not happen but that in any case she now knew how to plan her affairs.

Telling people this kind of news is something I try to avoid and have rarely found helpful for the patient. This case will perhaps be the exception.[4]

Enid understood that she had from six to nine months to live. She wrote at once to Alyse: 'I have got to get used to the annihilation of so many plans and projects.'[5] Alyse answered: 'You have always risen to a challenge and this is the greatest you will have to face . . . I do blame the doctors—also I don't even now feel sure they are right.'[6]

On 17 March I saw Enid in Oxford. She told me that she had resigned her Readership. I said that I was convinced that she would recover, and I asked her if she would dine with me a year hence.

Enid accepted. She never knew the lie that I had told, but she later said how much the assurance had helped her.

> I'll try not to look on the gloomy side too much [she wrote on 19 March], but my temperament is to face the worst! . . .
> My best hope is that it can be kept down with treatment because the specialist told me it was bound to return. And what I really ask for and pray for is time to finish my *Flaubert* and I need at least a year for that— a year with fairly good health and peace to work. I shall certainly remember your hunch! I'm going to sacrifice everything to the book and I must not allow anything to stand in its way.[7]

> The only thing I don't know is how long I can count on [this to Dorothy Wadham]. I have given up all my work from the end of June and have asked for sick leave for next term. What I want to do is devote as much time as I can to my *Flaubert*, which is far behind schedule. I need a year to finish it and I don't know whether I'll be granted that. I'll go on as long as I can, and if I can't finish it I'll destroy what I've done as no-one would be able to find their way round my notes . . .
> I'm not going to the United States in September, but I am going to Paris on 4th April for nine days to do some work at the Bdiliothèque Nationale.[8]

It was hard to concentrate on Flaubert. 'The annoying thing is that my mind isn't really free for creative work [she told Alyse on 21 March]. Sometimes also it comes over me the vanity of it all and that the world won't be any the poorer if it doesn't get my book . . . I have very bad moments, sometimes, in the middle of the night, but these, I imagine, will get less when I get more acclimatized to the idea.'[9] Next day she wrote to Professor Reid, the Chairman of the Modern Languages Board:

> I'm not yet used to the idea of having no future . . . I love life passionately and I have so many plans and projects in my mind—indeed sufficient to last me another half century. However there it is and, as my French governess used to say to me: '*L'homme propose mais Dieu dispose.*' I must put the best face on it and I hope not to be a burden to those

round me. I can quite see that it won't be too easy for College, where I've been for thirty-five years.

My life was always based on the tacit assumption that I'd live a long time and that I'd become a tough old lady, that I was indestructible, like my mother!

I want certainly to go to the first meeting of the Board to speak up for some difficult cases and to answer any questions which may be put.[10]

Enid was not only in the care of Oxford doctors ('it would be foolish', she observed, 'to die out of politeness').[11] She was also being advised, from America, by Dr André Cournand. He was a lung specialist, a Nobel Laureate, and the father of a former pupil. She was also in touch with a French cancer specialist, Dr Sauvage. On 4 April she went to Paris, where she consulted him.

She returned to Oxford on 13 April. She was already thinking of another visit to France. She had been invited to be a Chevalier du Tastevin. The *intrônisation* was a pleasure for the founder of the Somerville cellar. She asked Dr Ridehalgh if she might go to Beaune. 'Dear Miss Starkie,' came the answer, 'if I had the chance to become a Chevalier du Tastevin, only the Sheriff's officer with a warrant would hold me back.'[12]

Her anxiety and depression remained; but she had already begun to make medical history. On 4 May Dr Ridehalgh added: 'Your X-ray shows a remarkable improvement. All foci in both lungs are smaller and some of them have practically disappeared. I hope this will enable you to enjoy Burgundy in all its aspects.'[13]

On 6 May, with a temperature (she recorded) of 101, Enid left for Macon; and there, on 8 May, she became a Chevalier du Tastevin. She was admitted to the Confrérie in the Château du Clos de Vougeot. She received the accolade of a polished vineroot on each shoulder and was given the silver tastevin, or wine-tasting cup, on its red-and-gold ribbon. The ceremony was followed by a seven-course banquet for two hundred people in the castle cellars. It lasted until nearly two next morning. Back in Oxford, she continued to live with panache. On 22 June, Veronica Wedgwood gave a party for her Oxford friends. Enid 'lit up the whole room

as she came in—not just the gorgeous bright colours she loved,
. . . but this undimmed, flame-like vitality.'[14]

On 28 April, Janet Vaughan had suggested the special regard
which Somerville had long felt for Enid Starkie.

Dear Enid,

I am writing at once to tell you that it was unanimously agreed to
elect you an Honorary Fellow of the College at the Formal Meeting in
the 5th Week. The Governing Body hope to see you about in college as
they do now free to come to all meals and to attend any meeting of the
Governing Body that you wish. They also wish you to have the privilege of bringing guests to High Table.

They hope that you will oversee the Cellar as long as you wish . . . I
was asked to express to you formally the admiration and affection we all
have for you and our gratitude for all you have done both for the
College and the University in countless different ways.[15]

Enid was delighted by the munificence of this gesture. 'Somerville has made me an Honorary Fellow of a most generous kind,'
she announced to her American friends, 'and they have done it so
that there is no interruption and I have no time out in the outer
darkness, in fact my status will be exactly the same . . . But the
most extraordinary thing is that they have also made me a member
of the Governing Body of the College!'[16] No decision could have
pleased her more.

For, whatever her criticism in her last years of ill-health, however bitterly she might behave, Enid remained devoted to Somerville. She owed it her academic existence and, now, her unchanged
way of life, her emotional security. No other women's college
would have produced or tolerated or held Enid Starkie. Somerville
gave her intellectual stimulus and scope, and, more, it gave her
touching understanding. It gave her a lifetime of assured affection.
Enid recognized her debt. Today the Principal's regalia includes
not only the pendant set with Ruskin's sapphires and rubies, but
the ring bequeathed by Enid for use on ceremonial occasions: the
diamond ring which is said to have belonged to Jonathan Swift.[17]

On 24 June, the Faculty of Mediaeval and Modern Languages
gave a dinner in Enid's honour at The Queen's College. They

presented her with a Georgian aquamarine cross. To some of the guests, the occasion seemed macabre; they felt that Enid had not long to live. Yet she herself must have wondered, increasingly, whether she had needed to resign.

On 12 March William Hawksworth, who had operated on her in 1949, had urged Dr Ridehalgh to prescribe progesterone. 'You realize, of course,' Dr Ridehalgh told her, 'that he is really responsible for your cure, since he produced the right hormone in response to my query.'[18] At Mr Hawksworth's suggestion, progesterone was later changed for depo-provera. For the rest of her life, Enid was to have two intra-muscular injections a week; and she learned—no mean achievement—to give them to herself. But the discomfort was a small price to pay for her new and unexpected lease of years: for what Agnes Headlam-Morley called 'that strange reprieve'.[19] On 22 July Dr Cournand, then in Paris, flew to England to consult with her doctors and to see her. He thought that the change in the condition of her lungs was 'nothing short of amazing'.[20]

Enid considered herself to be a realist; but she had always had an active imagination and an Irish sense of drama. Ever since her childhood, she had craved for undivided love and attention; and she had never demanded them more than now. Living alone, she was all the more in need of sympathy. She gaily told Dorothy Wadham that she had made medical history; yet even now, as Dorothy Wadham observed, she laid continued stress on the fact that her cancer was not cured, and that it was liable to recur.[21] She wrote in much the same tone to her former pupil, the Rev. Dr Gordon Roe. On 12 August he 'went and had a long talk with her . . . She was quite clear and unworried about the approach of death—not in any defiant way, though. It was as if she was trying to experience death as fully as she had experienced life.'[22] He added:

We sat in the sun lounge at the back and drank sherry from huge glasses and talked, mainly about the first volume of her Flaubert—she was still very much preoccupied with it—but also about facing death . . . I had the impression that she intended to fill every moment. It was largely a question of how many unfinished projects she would get completed before death overtook her. She did not want to let me think that she was *worried* by death itself, although she was certainly not averse from talking about it.[23]

Agnes Headlam-Morley writes: 'I think her outgoing nature and her love of drama (in the truest and best sense of the word) came to her help. She was not particularly reserved about that kind of thing, . . . and in an almost detached way I think she was interested to observe how one could work under sentence of death.'[24]

As Enid knew, the sentence of death had in fact been commuted.

If my state had been like this in March [she assured Alyse], I would not have resigned from my University post. I liked my work and loved my students; I liked being at the centre of things and don't care for being a back number. But, in March, I really thought that I had only six or nine months left . . .

In spite of hardships and unhappiness, I have liked my life and am grateful for it. I like it still, and don't want to die yet. I'm still interested and excited by it. I also feel full of things that I'd like to do . . . There are the two volumes on Flaubert, then the continuation of my autobiography; my student life in Paris and then, when I was very old, I was going to do my time in Oxford . . .

I am hoping, now that I am better, to get on seriously with my own work.[25]

On 20 September she finished the first draft of her *Flaubert*. Soon afterwards she confessed: 'I feel almost as if I'd come back from the dead.'[26]

Seven days later, she was involved in a car accident. She was slightly concussed, and her spine was jolted. Enid always lived on the verge of danger.

❖ 37 ❖

On 9 December she came to London. I met her at Paddington, and there, at the Great Western Hotel, before she went on to a lunch appointment, we discussed the coming election for the Professorship of Poetry. Robert Graves's tenure was about to end, and I asked her—as I had often done—if she would campaign for Edmund Blunden. He had been a candidate in 1951, when Cecil Day-Lewis was elected, but he had chivalrously stood down, so as not to split the vote. Now he was back in England from the University of Hong Kong, and it seemed the moment to enquire if he would stand again.

Four days later, Enid asked me: 'Do you think—or could you find out—whether Edmund Blunden would stand? . . . If so, I might do a campaign for him.'[1]

Dear Joanna [Edmund wrote to me],

It is nice of you to pay me a visit on this cloudy morning, in letter form, and to bring the generous suggestion of Enid Starkie with your favouring thoughts. I write in bed, getting over one of my asthmatic illnesses and hoping our Dr will let me move about a little today. My troubles are not great but they shackle me and derange plans.

The pleasure your combined messages give is deep. But the time for me to stand for that venerable Professorship is past, I am afraid. Not because I am quite incapable of some work, but the business of completing things begun and fulfilling promised designs and perhaps getting my books and papers in order at last (for new notions!) seems sufficient at my age . . .[2]

Not for the first time, Enid had to persuade a reluctant candidate to stand. On 21 December she wrote to him. On 27 December he answered:

Dear Enid Starkie,

In this house there had been a disapproval of my reply to Joanna Richardson, and your generous letter brought on a renewed protest (there are 5 women and sometimes six to advise me on everything).

In spite of them it is due to your thoughts on the Professorship and your remembering me in a particularly understanding way that I write. I shall apologize to Joanna, and at this moment only accept your invitation to write 'a better answer'. Please put my name on the list of candidates. If the others offer to lecture in Latin I will, my Chinese not being honourable.

I hope that you will not be overworked because of my coming into the contest. Even if someone else is elected, my 'image' of yourself and your constant fight for the right sort of Oxford won't be dimmed.[3]

Robert Lowell, the American poet, was already standing for the Chair. On 4 January, Enid told me:

I've only started this morning getting names for Edmund Blunden's nomination form, and I've already got the necessary six names. But of course one couldn't send in a form with only six names on it!

I met Masterman—formerly Provost of Worcester—and he stopped me in the street—he had seen the announcement that Blunden had accepted to be a candidate—and he assumed I was at the back of it and he offered me, quite spontaneously, to nominate him. He said that if I wasn't a candidate, he'd vote for Blunden—if I was a candidate he'd vote for me! I'm going to send him a form, like the one I'm enclosing here, and ask him to try to get some other names on it. He could get some at Worcester. Afterwards I met Professor Syme—the Latin Professor—and I made him sign on the spot as I had my form with me.[4]

On 8 January she dined with me in London. 'After seeing you yesterday, I am more hopeful about Blunden's chances [this on 9 January], and I think that all you have done is wonderful . . . I can't hope to get the 130 names I had for Auden, but then I don't believe Lowell will get that either—unless they have a far better canvasser than I imagine.'[5] Election fever set in. On 14 January:

Lowell's list was in the *Gazette* to-day, 36 names, and not a woman among them! My campaign is beginning to hot up and I believe that I have now over 50 names—some of my sheets are still out. Thank you for the lists received this morning. I stop people in the street and try to get them to sign as I always have a list in my bag . . . Ridehalgh offered me his vote but I don't think he's an M.A. only a D.M. which doesn't count. I got Hawksworth's on Sunday when I was lunching there. I'm going to write to Sir George Pickering today—the Regius Professor of Medicine. I've got the Dean of Christ Church . . .[6]

She also tried to get Graham Greene. Next day she dashed off a letter, sending him congratulations on his C.H., and a nomination form to sign.[7]

On 17 January, she wrote to me again:

Thank you for your two letters received this morning and for all the signatures. I've now 76 in my possession . . .

Dan said to me on Saturday 'Of course you won't get him in' and he said he was sorry I should attach myself to someone certain to fail. I suppose because, in all probability, this will be my last election. But he underrates the trouble I take when I take on something. Also the value of a cause is not diminished by its being lost. In any case it is not at all a foregone conclusion that Blunden will in fact fail. I think, on the contrary, he has a very good chance, and I have you this time to help me . . .

I got a disquieting letter from Mrs Blunden this morning, saying that he did not want to be nominated. I enclose the letter for you to see.[8]

Claire Blunden had become apprehensive that Edmund might lose the election; she did not want him, now, at the end of his career, to be rejected by his own university. Enid did not share this wifely anxiety, or Edmund's sudden moment of doubt. She sent him 'a furious letter', and told him that he could not withdraw, when so much had been done.[8] 'Dear Enid Starkie,' he answered, 'your great and (as always) valiant work for me, as you sketch it, of course keeps me in the field . . . Thank you for strong opinion and hopeful prediction.'[9]

On 23 January, Atticus explained in the *Sunday Times*:

To-morrow the nominations close for the next Professor of Poetry at Oxford. It doesn't really matter who gets in, there's no power, little work and less money.

Personally, I think the whole business is fictional. The position doesn't really exist. It's all been dreamt up by Enid Starkie.

Dr Starkie exists. To-morrow morning she'll leave her red type-writer, her red bound books and her red armchair in her red house, and carry her list of nominations across Oxford to hand it in. She doesn't trust the post, or college messengers.

She is leading the campaign for Edmund Blunden. Sir Maurice Bowra is handling the Robert Lowell campaign. 'He has a very poor little list. I hear he only has forty names,' says Dr Starkie. 'I would never be satisfied with forty names. By tomorrow, I hope to have 250 names, almost twice as many as I've ever had before.

I started lists. You only need to have six nominators. My 250 names will mean that the *University Gazette* will have to print extra pages.'[10]

Next day Edmund wrote to me: 'Whatever the voting may be at the last I am sincerely moved by the great faith Enid S. and you and other friends have shown in me by regarding me as a candidate, and the work you have done for the first stage. If the voters choose Mr Lowell, I shall nevertheless have an episode of my 70th year to think of very happily to the last.'[11]

On 25 January, Enid announced in triumph: 'The final number of nominations was beyond all expectation, 301 . . .'[12] Next day: 'Twenty-seven of Blunden's nominators turn out to have no M.A. and some even to have no degree at all! . . . So his list has fallen to 274—perhaps it may be less as some names, I'm told, are indecipherable. Still, it is very good . . .'[13] The *Financial Times* took up the story:

'I am interested in all you say about Robert Lowell and, more particularly, about Edmund Blunden.' This careful sentence is in a letter from Mr Wilson to a canvasser in the Oxford Poetry Professorship hustings; it is getting as rigorous a textual analysis as a disputed line of Aristotle . . .

Oxford is as close as it will ever be to the atmosphere of a party convention, with Dr Enid Starkie playing her accustomed rôle on behalf of Mr Edmund Blunden . . .

Ladbroke's has actually made a book on the post—Lowell 6–4 on, Blunden 5–4 against. *O tempora, o mores!*[14]

The first day of voting was 3 February. Anne Scott-James, in the *Daily Mail*, expressed her surprise that Oxford had appointed a public relations officer when it had Enid Starkie within its precincts.[15] An unidentified journalist spoke of her 'promotional genius', and added that 'Dr Starkie, in red and blue under academic robes, draped in Byzantine jewellery, was enjoying herself hugely, giving interviews to television and radio—it is, after all, quite a change from Flaubert, her current scholastic pre-occupation.'[16]

On 5 February, at the end of the second day of polling, the result was announced outside the Sheldonian Theatre. Edmund had received 477 votes, a majority of more than 200 over Robert Lowell.

That evening there was a celebration party at the Victoria Arms, a usually peaceful punters' public house near the Cherwell. Among the guests were Richard Burton and Elizabeth Taylor, who had come to perform *Dr Faustus* at the Oxford Playhouse. 'Mr Blunden, who edited the first edition of Wilfred Owen's poems, said: "My election has set the seal on my life . . ." '[17]

Next day Dr Ridehalgh sent congratulations to Enid. 'I regard your return to battleworthy condition as a clinical sign of great prognostic significance and I hope Oxford, Blunden, and all those who really care about poetry in Britain are properly grateful to the N.H.S.'[18]

On 31 May Edmund Blunden gave his inaugural lecture.

⋄ 38 ⋄

On 8 January Enid had attended the meeting of the Association of Senior Members of Somerville. A cheque had been presented to her. Nearly a hundred Somervillians had contributed to it. She returned the compliment by giving Somerville a Georgian claret jug for High Table, and two inscribed coasters for the Senior Common Room; the Common Room, not to be outdone, elected her an honorary member, with the right to bring guests. And, recognizing Enid's devotion to protocol, the Governing Body expressed their unanimous hope that as an Honorary Fellow she would always consider herself the second senior person in College, entitled to bring her guests to sit at the Principal's right hand.[1] She had helped to found the Somerville cellar in 1935, and almost ever since she had been its steward. Now she was presented with a personal key to her domain.

The tributes were touching, but she remained depressed: all the more so as her health improved, and she resented her inactivity. She regretted her teaching; she also regretted her slow progress with *Flaubert*. 'I'm not getting on as fast as I should,' she told me on 29 March. 'I'm unfortunately not yet capable of very hard work and I get most terribly tired when life does not seem worth living!'[2] She wrote in much the same terms to Alyse, and on 27 April Alyse answered: 'I suppose our real failures are known only to ourselves, failures in generosity, understanding, love—and then it is too late. *Le bonheur est le plus grand développement de mes facultés*, Napoleon wrote. So few of us have the chance to live up to this or take advantage of it when we have. I feel that you have.'[3]

As far as my disease is concerned, my lungs are still clear [Enid answered] . . . Of course I'm not cured and cannot be as the disease is in the blood-stream and it can break out at any time elsewhere. My own great fear is that it might come in the brain . . .

I can certainly hope to finish the first volume of *Flaubert* . . . Now, when I go to Paris, if the worst happened, the book could be published —with imperfections. But even though this book will be finished, I'll not say 'Nunc dimittis' as I have a lot of things that I can still do— much more than will fill my diminished expectation of life . . .

One is indeed always conscious of one's failures—especially when, like me, one has shot one's bolt and there is nothing good left to hope for. Quite apart from one's personal failure in goodness and kindness, one realizes also—in my case—that I didn't reach the top, profes- sionally . . .[4]

Enid brooded over her health, her position in Oxford, and what she considered to be her professional failure. Meanwhile, her work on Flaubert continued, and her social engagements were unremit- ting. On 6 May she lectured at the University of Kent at Canter- bury; on 5 June she went to Paris. Soon after her return to Oxford, Francis Steegmuller—writing a life of Cocteau—came with his wife to see her. Mrs Steegmuller remembers:

We took her out to [lunch at] the Elizabeth, where she filled up her capacious handbag with macaroons from a dish on the table saying, 'Don't worry, they know about me here.' The macaroons were for—I think—her [great-]nieces. It made me think (though no doubt the circumstances were different) of little Miss Noble in *Middlemarch*. She also said (perhaps had said it other times) of her typing that she had now lost all use of her handwriting except her signature as she always typed everything; then—'As I was a pianist once, typing comes naturally. I find I do the conjunctions as chords.' . . . Like my husband [Mrs Steegmuller adds], I felt she had a hunger for praise, and a difficulty in giving it. We both noticed, first with surprise and finally with amused desperation, the lengths she would go to in order to avoid referring to the fact that we were ourselves both writers (I don't remember that she ever got round to admitting it at all in my case). Of course you will know that we did not want pats on the back, but it *was* odd . . .[5]

'I think it must have been the long-time insecurities so evident in *A Lady's Child* that showed themselves in these little things,' Francis Steegmuller suggests. 'One cannot hold them against her, as she inspired a certain affection.'[6] 'One of the things I most enjoyed about her,' Mrs Steegmuller adds, 'was her true eccentricity, in a world where false eccentricity has become a kind of conformity.'[7]

One anecdote [this from Francis Steegmuller again]. She told us that when she went from Oxford to Paris it was her habit to take a bus in Oxford & not to go all the way into London, but to get off beside the highway as close as possible to London airport. She would have with her a baggage-cart, would pile all her luggage on it, and push it herself through the pedestrian tunnel to the departure building . . . My wife and I never go to London airport without thinking of Enid pushing her cart through the tunnel; we find ourselves looking for a little figure in a red tam-o-shanter . . . My wife is the novelist Shirley Hazzard. I always wonder whether a similar little figure won't turn up in one of her books.[8]

Enid scorned both buses and taxis. One evening in 1966, when she had dined with me in London, I took her in a taxi back to Paddington. 'You shouldn't have done that,' she wrote next day. 'You were encouraging me in self-indulgence . . . As far as self-indulgence is concerned, there is no difference in my taking the taxi myself and in your taking it for me.'

During the summer of 1966, she remained unsettled. She thought of spending some of her presentation cheque on a visit to Rome. Dr

Ridehalgh approved. '*Prescription*. Italy 1 month. *Ante cibos*, Punt y Mes. *Cum cibos* Chianti Classico, Soave, Orvieto . . .'[9] Eithne Kaiser and her husband, in the Via Giovanni Cadolini, welcomed the idea of Enid's visit: 'We think probably the hotel you would find as suitable as any is the Minerva, in Piazza S. Maria sopra Minerva, with the Pantheon obliquely opposite. It was a palazzo where Stendhal stayed . . .'[10]

Enid did not visit Rome, or live in the shadow of Stendhal. But Flaubert still remained with her. On 9 September she handed the typescript of the first volume to George Weidenfeld. She was already working on the sequel. 'I may try to go to Chantilly next Easter,' she told me. 'I'll also have to go to Rouen as there are a lot of papers there on *Bouvard & Pécuchet* . . . I'm also thinking of my autobiography . . . I'm getting quite excited by the new book.'[11]

On 16 November she was interviewed in the *Cherwell*, and talked with all her old rebelliousness.

Apart from Communism—I'm very anti-Communist—I'd much prefer Russian world-dominance to American . . . Yes, I'd like to be young now—I've always liked the present best . . . I do sometimes regret not having married, not having had children . . . I still feel a foreigner in England, much more than in France. The French and the Irish have always got on . . . I'd never refuse an honour: I think it's terribly conceited. But 'Dame' is so dull—such a pity. Anyway, I'm not on the right circuit . . . I'd like to be a life peeress, though: that would be nice. 'Baroness Starkie of Killiney in the County of Dublin'—doesn't it sound lovely? . . . I could wear that lovely red and grey robe.[12]

Baroness Starkie was not to be. But on 1 December Enid told me, delightedly, that she was to have a CBE in the New Year Honours. Dorothy Wadham was also told of her decoration, and instructed her to buy herself champagne from the College cellar. On Christmas Day Enid thanked her, and added that Hollins College were giving her one of the medals struck to commemorate their 125th anniversary. She was also to receive a Doctorat-ès-Lettres from the University of Aix-en-Provence.

On 1 January 1967, her CBE was announced in the New Year Honours. She was touched, above all, by congratulations from her former pupils. Many old students, wrote one of them, 'will today be thinking of the pleasure and excitement of learning which you inevitably conveyed to those you taught, and be feeling that for this alone the award would be richly deserved . . . It is nearly twenty years now since I was fortunate enough to come to your room in St Giles' for tutorials on nineteenth-century French literature—amidst icons, and piles of books—but I can still recapture the eagerness with which I came!'[13] Liselott Haynes (now Mrs Strauss) wrote from New Zealand:

It is really becoming increasingly impossible to address you correctly on an envelope! . . . For me you will always remain the private person who once took me to a Myra Hess concert, often fried the peculiar concoction we used to call omelettes in wartime in your little kitchen (you taught me an excellent variety done with grated raw potato and dried egg), let me see draft chapters, as they were written, of a (never to be published?) autobiographical novel . . .[14]

On 20 January, Enid announced triumphantly: 'My letters etc. have now reached 306 and I'm writing hard all day. I've answered between 270 and 280.'[15] On 5 March she was interviewed on television. A critic declared that she was so alert and volatile that she often seemed in danger of taking flight. 'I thought myself,' wrote Enid, 'that I didn't really have a chance with the kind of question I got, I had nothing I could sparkle on! . . . My next excitement is Buckingham Palace on Tuesday.'[16] She received her CBE on 14 March.

Her latest decoration had been one of the series of excitements which she constantly needed. When the excitement faded, she found herself again in depression.

At night in bed I think a lot about life—mostly about my wasted life, but I imagine that everyone thinks that at the end of their life, when there are no further opportunities. I realize always forcibly [this to Alyse] that I have always been in a wrong life, and that I'm a different breed of animal from my colleagues. In my more than thirty years in

Oxford, I never made a really intimate friend, though I have many acquaintances, and that is what I miss now in my diminished condition, someone to whom I could really talk . . .

When I lie awake I often wish that I believed—not in the hope of the consolation of immortality, but only to find some meaning in life, to believe that it had all been worthwhile.[17]

'I don't see how you can ever think your life has been wasted,' came the answer. 'I know of no life that has been less so.'[18]

It was now two years since Enid had resigned her Readership. She had grown accustomed to perpetual activity, to decision-making and influence, and to the social status they carried with them. She had never reconciled herself to retirement. Living alone, across the road from Somerville, she felt herself still part of the establishment; and every day, unfailingly, she had lunch at High Table. It was not the general rule for Honorary Fellows, but the College understood her dependence. They gave her rights and attentions accorded to no-one else. There was, as a colleague once observed, one rule for College and another rule for Enid; and in her retirement the fact was abundantly clear. 'I think one has to realize,' wrote the Dean, Mary Proudfoot, 'that Enid really does love the College very much. It means more to her than, probably, any of us can understand. And her status in it is the one thing left to her.'[19]

Her status was now a matter of perpetual concern. She was always afraid that it would be diminished, always vigilant in case she was not given proper precedence, in case she was not invited to a party. Her ill-health made her aggressive, and it created innumerable problems for her colleagues. In 1965, when she was elected an Honorary Fellow, she had been invited to remain on the Governing Body until July 1966: the time when she would normally have retired. She had continued to go to meetings; and, when it was discovered that an Honorary Fellow was not entitled to do so, she had been elected an Additional Fellow with member-ship of the Governing Body until October 1966. This membership, a unique concession, had been given to her so that she might help to elect the new Principal of Somerville. She was among the warmest original supporters of Barbara Craig, who was duly chosen to succeed Janet Vaughan.

In October 1966 Enid ceased to be a member of the Governing Body. She had always been at the centre of affairs, she had always helped to make decisions, she had always sat, like a spider, in her web of intrigue, aware of every tremor at the circumference. Now, for the first time, she did not know what decisions were taken. In the Common Room she sat, brooding, in her customary chair; her resentment was almost tangible. Every morning, without fail, she went into College for coffee. This regular appointment was a sadly obvious attempt to gather some of the information which she was now officially denied. The college bore with her moods and tempers, her sometimes outrageous conduct, they kept a watchful eye on her health, and provided her with food when she felt unable to eat in Hall. They listened patiently to her lamentations about ill-health, ingratitude and injustice. Enid accepted their kindness, but her bitterness remained, and she let it grow.

In February she spent three days at a conference in London, held to mark the centenary of the death of Baudelaire. On 28 March she went again to London to receive her medal from Hollins College ('Human Nature is naïve,' her father had once written, 'and, however old a man is, he is pleased with toys').[20] On 2 April she left for Paris, to work on Flaubert and lecture on Baudelaire. On 13 April she returned to Oxford. On 24 May she left for the Colloque Baudelaire at Nice, where she heard Georges Pompidou, then Prime Minister, speak on the author of *Les Fleurs du mal*. She herself gave a paper on 'Baudelaire et l'Angleterre', and on 29 May she returned to Oxford for the usual round of lectures and parties. Among her favourite gatherings was the Saturday lunchtime assembly which had now moved from the Lamb and Flag in St Giles' to the Victoria in Walton Street. Enid presided over it like a *salonnière*. When she complained that the seats were too high for her, someone bought her a Victorian footstool. It was fetched from behind the bar when she arrived.

Her activity was endless; but it remained the activity of the restless and unsatisfied. The social life often seemed to be an ineffective bromide. Someone who saw her at an Oxford party made the poignant comment that she had been invited 'because she had once been Enid Starkie'.

'I don't count any more.' The phrase became familiar to her friends. She professed, against all the evidence, that she was not appreciated at Somerville. She also brooded constantly over what she considered harsh treatment from the University. The title of Reader Emeritus, given to her on her resignation, seemed merely a public and permanent affirmation that she had failed to earn the title of Professor. She had lost the Marshal Foch Chair of French Literature by a single vote. The second Chair of French was not established until some years after her retirement. The only possibility seemed a titular professorship; Enid understood that this had been discussed and rejected. In her isolation and ill-health, this fact now assumed the proportions of Greek tragedy. 'I need as much cheering up as I can get,' she told me on 1 June. 'I'm not stupid enough to believe that my life's work is of no value because it has not been appreciated by Oxford, but . . . I would rather have had recognition from my own University, to which I've given so much, than outside recognition. If I went away to USA I would hope to come back completely indifferent.'[21]

⋄ 39 ⋄

The American visit she had in mind was a visit to Columbia University. She had been invited to spend a semester there as Gildersleeve Professor. She had at first refused on the grounds of precarious health, but they had asked her to reconsider her decision. Enid had not forgotten the adulation which she had been given in Virginia, and she longed to have it again. She felt that she might find it in New York.

This seemed the only reason for a visit to Columbia. She did not need the money that America would offer, and she did not need the prestige. If she went, she would be losing time that she should spend on Flaubert. Some of her friends had serious doubts whether she was well enough to plunge again into intensive teaching. She had asked advice from Janet Vaughan. 'I am so glad you have asked,' came the answer, 'but I am sure you should say NO. You *must* finish *Flaubert*, no-one else can do this—also your autobiography and you need care and not to go racketing off.'[1] On 15 February Enid had asked Dr Ridehalgh for his opinion. He answered: 'I couldn't honestly advise any medical reason against your accepting . . . So I don't agree with Dame Janet—I say *fay ce que voudras* and damn the doctors.'[2] It was the advice that Enid wanted. On 24 February, she accepted the professorship.[3]

The acceptance remained provisional until she had signed the official contract, and this did not need to be signed for some months. In the meanwhile, she continued to consider the idea.

I think it likely that I'll accept the Visiting Professorship at Columbia University [she wrote to me on 17 July] . . . I know that, in many ways, it will be a mistake and it may jeopardize my finishing the second volume of *Flaubert*, in which I am growing more and more interested and I think it would be more important than Book One. Of course I've another month to make the final decision. I feel, more and more, that I want to get away from Oxford to recharge my batteries, and get back some belief and confidence in myself—also get back, perhaps, some pleasure in life. The past two years have been the unhappiest and most hopeless of my life. It is not only my illness and the 'death sentence', as I could find the fortitude to bear that—and indeed did find it. But Oxford . . . has given me a wound that nothing will ever heal . . .

I never wanted to go in for academic work and I sacrificed a lot to it. I would have liked, more than anything, to have been recognized and appreciated by my own University. All the other honours I have got have meant very little to me. When you've gone through what I've gone through for the past two years it all seems unimportant and trivial. I care for very few things now—some friends whom I love and on whom I rely; my work and writing; and perhaps my house which is still for me a new toy. The CBE meant nothing to me, except in the letters which I got from friends and former students . . . But the recognition from my own University would have shown me that my life had not been wasted . . . If Oxford had done nothing at all I would not have minded so much, . . . but it went out of its way to express positively lack of confidence and appreciation of me. If I'd just been left a Reader it would not have mattered, but I have been told that the Board was asked to make me a Titular Professor but that it decided that there was no reason to change my status. It was such a minor honour and would have cost nothing, . . . and the only difference would be that I would have been called Titular Professor instead of Reader and I'd now be Professor Emeritus and it would have been visible that I had not failed in my job . . . I've worried and worried over it and I cannot see the grounds for refusal. How can one have any belief in oneself after that? If one is honest with oneself one can only admit that one was not thought good enough! This annihilates the whole of my life's work.[4]

On 26 July she wrote in almost identical terms to Alyse.[5] 'Oh Enid, dearest Enid,' came the answer, '. . . the one real failure in your life would be to lose at this juncture confidence in yourself.'[6]

It was almost the end of their correspondence. Alyse died on the night of 27 August. She was an octogenarian, troubled by her poor sight, by her ebbing strength, and by the loneliness which had oppressed her since her husband's death. She had been an incomparable friend.

Flaubert. The Making of the Master was published four days later. It was the first comprehensive account of the novelist in the making. It was based not only on Flaubert's published work and the findings of modern research but on the great bulk of his manuscripts preserved in French libraries, and on correspondence which had, until then, remained unpublished. It was the first half of a work which was to cover all his life and writing. It ended with *Madame Bovary*; and indeed, as Enid said, Flaubert's existence was divided in two by the publication of his masterpiece. Until 1856, when it began to appear in *La Revue de Paris*, all was preparation, conscious or unconscious, for the event; Flaubert was trying to find himself, seeking his purpose and his style, accumulating his material. After 1856 he was an established author, conscious of his means and of his powers. His real temperamental problem—as she observed—was the clash between the scholar, or scientist, and the creator. His stylistic precision was dictated by his academic nature, as well as by devotion to his art. He learned the power of discipline. Art became his religion. He despised ambition. He turned away from his mistress, Louise Colet, because she was vulgar and superficial. Some of the most illuminating chapters in Enid's book were those on Flaubert's liaison with Mme Colet; and, drawing on unpublished passages from their correspondence, she showed Flaubert's terror of paternity. Perhaps this almost unnatural fear owed something to the homosexual strain in his character. Despite his passionate experiences with women, he clearly gave his deepest affections to men. Here, again, she illuminated his nature. Despite its deficiencies in style, her book remained a significant contribution to Flaubert studies.

It was acclaimed; but she remained low-spirited. On 3 September, she wrote to me: 'Before my book appeared, I would have been overjoyed at the thought of having so many important reviews so quickly, but I find that I can't take any interest in any of them . . . None have been as nasty as I expected—they are still to come!!— none have done anything to give me back confidence in myself. I have found them mostly boring.'[7] A fortnight later she went to Paris to work on her second volume. On 1 October she returned to Oxford. Her gloom still weighed on her. 'The only thing', she wrote, 'that keeps me going is the hope that I may write Volume Two of *Flaubert*, that gives some meaning to my life. Otherwise I wouldn't care what happened to me.'[8] She had finally decided to go to Columbia, and she was leaving early in the New Year. On 23 November she added: 'I am without interest in anything . . . If I cannot get up some interest when I'm in America it will be hopeless, and I might as well pack up.'[9]

On 21 December she was to receive her honorary degree at Aix; but she seemed more disturbed by the thought of the journey than gratified by the *doctorat-ès-lettres*. However, on 19 December, the

Oxford Mail recalled her famous matelot cap, and reported that she would soon be wearing another remarkable piece of French costume: an *épitoge*. 'It is pinned over the shoulders', Enid explained, 'and hangs down like some enormous epaulettes. It is yellow, with white fur. I shall wear it with my Oxford cap and gown.'

On 5 January she wrote to the Dean of the Modern Languages Faculty at Barnard College: the women's college at Columbia. 'Dear Professor Breunig, . . . All my arrangements are now finalized to go to New York . . . I posted my D.Litt. gown today, to myself at Butler Hall, and it cost a terrible lot of money—£1. 2s. 6d.! . . . I'll bring my Aix *épitoge* and my cap in my suitcase . . .'[10] The problem of academic dress was settled, but another arose. Three days later, leaving college, she slipped on a patch of ice. 'Poor Miss Starkie concussed herself quite severely,' Dr Ridehalgh told Dr Herrin, later in the month, 'so that she was admitted to the Radcliffe, but fought her way out. However, she seems to have recovered from this and I am glad to say that I could find no clinical signs of metastasis on January 17th. . . . She tells me that you have supplied her with adequate amounts of Provera to cover her stay in America, and we can only wish her God speed.'[11]

On 27 January she left for New York. Next day, a Sunday, from Butler Hall, the block of flats where she was staying, she scrawled a desperate letter to LeRoy Breunig.

It was a mistake to arrive on a Saturday but I thought my friends would want to have me out on their free day, but no-one has left any message or telephoned . . . I've waited until mid-day but no-one has given a sign of life, and I must get something to eat as I've had nothing to eat since a meagre lunch on the plane at 1 o'clock yesterday . . .

I'm going out soon as I cannot bear doing nothing any longer—I've nothing to read except my notes! I didn't sleep at all last night so it has been a long time doing nothing. My trunk had come and I unpacked that, I went to bed at midnight, your time, but, as I could not sleep and had nothing to read, I got up at three which is eight o'clock our time and just sat about looking at my notes! I've still the evening to get through and not even TV, not that I have that in England!

If you have any free time to-morrow could I see you please? I must organize my life. I can do nothing as I am and I *must* have a typewriter. Can I get books out of the library to prepare my courses? . . .

I most particularly want to start work and I can't bear to have another squandered day like today when I haven't even the pleasure of seeing my friends! I don't mind being alone but to be alone without a book is hell!

I don't know what I'll do for the rest of the day—it is not a nice day, it has a London fog! Otherwise I might have walked. I might look for a movie—but I don't normally go unless there is something I want to see. However the main thing is to get something to eat—there seemed to be lots of places on Broadway . . . I never thought I'd long so much for a cup of coffee! I'll go out immediately.[12]

On 10 February she sent me her first letter from Columbia. It was already clear that her visit was a grave mistake.

My flat has only one small narrow room and minute kitchen and bathroom. The latter are adequate but the room is very depressing being so small and dark and I have to have the light on most of the day . . .

So far I can't say that I'm enjoying much being here. Except for the University it is a slummy negro quarter, and one can't go out alone at night as there are frequent murders. One is even attacked in broad daylight. One of the lecturers was attacked at 6.30 in Broadway by three youths of about 16 with knives and they took away all the money he had on him and his watch. So far people have seen me home but I don't know what I'll do if they don't or don't have cars. I don't see how I'm going to have time for my own work as my lectures—enough material for six hours per week—take so much of my time. I've done nothing but them since I arrived, about ten hours a day—and I'm only one week ahead and I only began lecturing on Thursday.[13]

Five days later:

They've now dealt with the matter of ventilation and heat for my apartment and it is now bearable, but I'm very cramped. Of course it couldn't be as nice as my little house in Hollins. I'll never be able to entertain here as it is too small and not properly equipped. Everett, who was my President when I was at Hollins and is now in New York, gave me some wine the other day—as well as Cognac and Bourbon—but I've not yet been able to open the wine as I've no corkscrew and I forget to buy one—I don't know where to buy one in this Godforsaken district. I've not yet been down to Fifth Avenue as I've been so busy at my lectures . . . I've found all sorts of other duties. In my Barnard College class I've 68 students and I have to give them an examination at mid-term and also at the end before I leave . . . This is the class that I have twice a week for two hours. I don't know yet what extras I'll have with my Columbia Class, who are graduates—there are about 30 of them.

The weather is most ghastly cold but what is worse than the actual cold is the arctic wind that blows down the Hudson from the lakes of Canada. When I wrote to you the temperature was 13 degrees Fahrenheit but, on Sunday, it fell to 7. I stupidly walked from 119 St. to 77 St. along Riverside Drive and it is an hour's walk. I arrived in a state of collapse and fainted and I had to lie down for 40 minutes to recover. I can't breathe in that weather as my lungs are bad and I suppose I don't get enough oxygen. I couldn't stop walking as the buses were all going the wrong way and there never are any taxis on Riverside Drive . . . I can't say that I'm enjoying it so far . . . I think, so far, that it is waste of my time and that Janet Vaughan was right.[14]

Enid had always found it easy to talk to a typewriter; on 14 March she unburdened herself again, this time to Dorothy Wadham.

The political situation is tricky here, complicated by the imminent presidential election. All the people whom I meet here are against the Vietnam war and some of the students are in prison for evading the draft; some have gone to Canada. The state of mind is, I think, generally unhappy. I agree that Americans, on the whole, are very undisciplined —in their ordinary life any way—and they are also so used to physical comfort they seem to me to be in poor condition and to eat too much, especially of the wrong kind of food . . . I'm still working most terribly hard at my wretched courses—about ten hours a day—I know that I'm probably giving them too much but one can't get rid of the habits of a life-time and the course as billed demands this. I've treated in the one course already 13 English and 11 French poets and that takes some chasing round for books etc. . . . Life is much rougher here than in an English university . . .[15]

There remained one oasis in this desert: Enid was to lecture at Hollins. Stuart Degginger, associate professor of English, came to New York to fetch her. On 31 March he drove her back to Virginia. After an absence of eight years she returned to the mountain campus where, like a child at a birthday party, she had enjoyed total and uncritical admiration. She enjoyed it, still. She stayed at Hollins for nearly a week. Back in New York, she reported happily: 'They had arranged so many parties for me—two every day—that I couldn't get away.'[16]

During Enid's semester at Columbia, there was a university *cause célèbre*. One of the women students at Barnard informed the Press that she was living with a man. The fact was unremarkable, but the publicity grew to surprising proportions.

Both the people concerned are really only interested in publicity [so Enid wrote to me], and the girl wouldn't have been found out if she had not talked to the Press and then Barnard had to take action. Some of the things that were said by the Senior Members struck me as extraordinary . . . One said that she considered that the girl's health would have suffered if she hadn't gone to live with the man! As a matter of fact neither is any use as a student so it can't be said—what I so often hear at Somerville and here—that this kind of thing will improve their work and morale. People now seem to think that sex never existed before this generation, and although it is a completely permissive generation, I cannot see that their mental health is better than earlier.[17]

The question of the errant students was not the only one to occupy Columbia; Enid's semester coincided with the student revolution. It was prolonged; and, even by American standards, it was violent and intense. It made headlines in the Press, at home and abroad. The student rebels held the authorities to ransom, and academic work was bedevilled by university politics.

Dear Professor Breunig [wrote Enid in despair on 3 May],
   . . . I am completely at sea at the moment, and do not know exactly what to do . . .

I missed two sessions this week with my French 48 on account of the events. On Thursday the lectures were cancelled, and, on Tuesday, only two people came. I assumed that the two classes missed this week would not be given at all and so I rearranged my two remaining lectures . . . But I did not quite understand the meeting this afternoon, are these lectures, in fact, to be given?[18]

Professor Breunig thought that Enid could not grasp the significance of the Columbia revolution. When the students went on strike she took it almost as a personal insult.[19]

She was of course at Barnard at a terrible time in the university life of Columbia [Mrs Steegmuller writes]. You will no doubt have heard how she was carried shoulder-high on the campus by students saying 'Enid Starkie, you belong to the revolution'. The Breunigs felt that this was rather more because of her habit of wearing red than for her revolutionary tendencies. However, from the brief glimpses we had of her then, . . . we felt that she had fallen into something of a depression; she complained of being immensely overburdened with work, and also of conditions in general.[20]

You made me laugh when you thought that I had less work to do with the affairs at Columbia [Enid wrote to me on 11 May]. One has far more to do as there are endless meetings of policy and no student, however rabid a striker, must be allowed to suffer, so there are courses in all sorts of odd places and buildings. The atmosphere is very unpleasant. I was against the occupying of the buildings, and to keeping the Dean as a hostage for 24 hours without food, except one banana which was thrown in to him; I was also against the President's offices being occupied, his private papers being ransacked, and the confidential papers of the University, Xeroxed and published abroad. However I do think that it was a mistake to bring the police in though they say that they couldn't have got them out otherwise, but it has certainly inflamed matters. At first the causes of the sit-in seemed trivial enough and the authorities gave in over them—I think that they give in too easily—but afterwards a lot of other grievances were added. I imagine that it is a long-standing situation. I think that the organization of Columbia needs changing. The Trustees, who are business men, are the owners of Columbia and make all the decisions, appoint the President who is their servant, and the 'dons' have no say in anything. I think that is unhealthy.

The police are now off the Campus but they surround all the gates and inspect the cards of the members of the University. This is to prevent outside people from congregating in the buildings, but I think it would have been wiser to have these tickets inspected by the Campus Guards and not by the police. I must say that I don't care to show my pass to a policeman as I don't think it is his business to ask me why I am going on my own Campus. Of course I'm wrong in this, it isn't my Campus but that of the Trustees and they can forbid me access to it if they want to. It is not over yet and one doesn't know how it will end, but it has certainly increased my work and worry . . .

I certainly have been given excitement since I've been here. First the garbage strike, then the assassination of Martin Luther King; then the resignation of Johnson from the candidature for the Presidency; then the affair of the girl at Barnard; then the revolution at Columbia, and the war in Vietnam as a constant factor. Paris, however, seems to be in an even worse situation than Columbia and the Unions are now going to take part in it.[21]

It was the time when student rebellion in Paris had grown into nation-wide dissension. There were strikes throughout France; the whole country expressed its long-standing grievances against de Gaulle's régime, and the turbulence and violence in Paris nearly reached the proportions of civil war.

They don't give much space to France in the papers here [Enid told me on 30 May] as they use up so much for the Vietnam Conference and the Presidential election—it is rather like us with Vietnam in England. I must say that things are pretty grim in France and, of course, I think about nothing else . . . As you say, it is exactly like the Commune in 1871, except that there hasn't been any great bloodshed yet. I listen in every hour to the news but there is not much change from hour to hour. Here, on the whole, people are not all that sorry about what is happening in France and there was, yesterday, decided glee when they thought that de Gaulle was finished!

Tomorrow week I shall be returning to Oxford and I shall be glad to leave here. When I stopped to think about it, I hated it, but most of the time I was too busy to think about it . . . I think that America is a sad country now and the people are unhappy, with a great guilt complex and inferiority complex.[22]

There was another moment of violence, more terrible than the rest, before she left for home. On 6 June, in a farewell note to Shirley Steegmuller, she wrote:

All the violence everywhere! I couldn't sleep on Tuesday night and I thought I'd turn on the 24-hour radio to see was there any news of the California Primary and I got on just at the moment of the [Robert] Kennedy shooting, and I got all the unofficial stress and turmoil and it was very traumatic and dramatic! Also this morning I got on just after he had died. I was never a great admirer of Kennedy and McCarthy is my candidate but this is a ghastly thing to have happened, and so senseless! When will all this violence end?[23]

On 9 June she returned to Oxford.

❖ 40 ❖

Enid had been tired by her experience at Columbia; and, after the relief and the excitement of her return, she found herself, as usual, introspective, and in need of sympathy. She returned to her familiar theme.

I don't suppose I'll ever forget what Oxford did to me [she wrote to me on 16 July], but I no longer mind—in fact there is nothing that I mind about any more for myself, except finishing my second volume now.

You mustn't think that I worry about myself or about things. I have no hopes, ambitions or expectations for myself any more and so I am at peace in that respect. My only hope for the future is to finish my book on Flaubert and that it should be as good as possible.[1]

She went to Paris for three weeks, attended a French literature conference at the Collège de France, worked at the Bibliothèque Nationale, and paid a visit to Rouen. On 17 August, back in Oxford, she wrote to Dorothy Wadham about her semester at Columbia.

Except for this money, I feel that I've wasted five months of my life,

five months which I can't afford to lose . . . I feel worse than before I
went to New York . . . I don't think that my heart is normal as I get
such a hammering at the slightest movement and I get pain when
walking . . . I know that I have a lot to be thankful for. If I don't
move I'm in no pain; I can work comparatively well; and I've got my
eyesight . . . I can read and without glasses.[2]

In this unhappy state of mind, physically frail, but driven by her
buccaneering spirit, Enid plunged again, for the last time, into
Oxford politics.

On 11 July, on the grounds of ill-health, Edmund Blunden had
resigned the Chair of Poetry; on 21 November his successor was
to be chosen.

On 18 July *The Times* had observed 'a pensive gleam in the eye
of Dr Enid Starkie . . . She has already written to Samuel
Beckett in Paris trying—with little hope of success—to tempt him
to stand.' Beckett refused that day. 'I am greatly touched and
grateful that you should take such trouble in your thought for me
and think me worth it. And it is a sorry acknowledgement to have
to reply, as I must, no to everything. To you I know I need not try
to explain and that it is enough briefly to say that such honours are
not for me.'[3]

Next day, 19 July, Robert Graves wrote from Mallorca:
'Dearest Enid: Now that you are well again why don't you go for
the Professorship?'[4]

I wouldn't expect to be put up as I've too many enemies in Oxford
and not enough friends—no real friends that I could rely on [Enid told
me on 14 August]. As you know I don't expect anything further to
happen to me! I wouldn't terribly mind being defeated this time. I
would like to be elected as it would do a lot to give me back my confidence in myself and take away the nasty taste of Oxford from my
mouth; and it would show my Faculty that there were some people
who thought me worthy of a Professorship! But I wouldn't mind not
getting it, and it would be a kind of relief as it would greatly complicate
my life. I wouldn't mind the Crewe Oration as one writes that in
English and gets someone else to put it into Latin. But I would be

nervous about examining for the Newdigate Prize and the Sacred Poem Prize as I know so little about English poetry, though probably as much as Maurice Bowra does. I can't think that I'd have glamour for the electors, and, since I began meddling with the election, people expect some glamour and excitement, and not just a local person. However, if the demand for me were strong enough . . .[5]

On 25 August, Robert Graves pressed his point: 'If you get someone to put up your name, I'll promise my written support. It seems most important to get a candidate who *is* Oxford and (for a change) someone who is not a professional poet.'[6] He was increasingly determined that she should have the Chair. On 28 September he confessed: 'Dearest Enid, I have nominated you . . . I hope this will work.'[7]

Two days later Enid wrote to Cecil King, her friend from childhood days, and told him of her nomination. He drafted an answer. 'I do beg of you not to let your name go forward . . . You have established a wonderful reputation in a quite different field of scholarship and I feel very strongly you should stand on that.'[8] Such advice was not taken. On 10 October she was announced, officially, as a candidate for the Chair.

Since the Professor of Poetry is elected by Convocation, and any Oxford Master of Arts is qualified to vote, the election was certain to seem extremely personal. Living in Oxford, where most of her friends were potential supporters, Enid felt the strain. So did her colleagues. They were not happy about her qualifications. They also considered her too frail to lecture. They felt that, if she were elected, it would embarrass the University; they knew that, if she were not, she would be hurt. For her colleagues at Somerville, who saw her daily, the conflict between affection and judgment was hard. And there was not only the problem of Enid's ill-health. She had already created a serious obstacle for herself. Many scholars had occupied the Chair of Poetry. It was she who had insisted that poets should be chosen.

The election campaign had given her a new charge of energy. Irish as she was, she was always revived by a fight; and though this time she avoided personal publicity, she revelled in being once again involved in Oxford politics.

Not the least of her achievements had been her contribution to the cause of poetry in Oxford. She had 'discovered' the Chair, and ensured the election of three poets; she had turned an almost forgotten sinecure into a matter of lively interest. It was due to her that this last election was covered broadly in the national Press, reported in the *New York Times* and the *Buenos Aires Herald*. Even a French paper carried the headline: '*Bataille homérique à Oxford pour la Chaire de Poésie*.' Enid had earned the titles which the *Listener* gave her: 'Friend of Oxford, canvasser extraordinary'.[9]

Extraordinary, indeed, For, as the *Guardian* would observe, she was helped in her campaigns by the widespread affection which she commanded. 'Among your splendid pronouncements', Eithne Kaiser told her, 'is not only that about failure not diminishing the worth of a cause fought for, but also one, some 13 years ago, . . . that strings were for pulling and axes for grinding. Like so much else about you, I have never forgotten it.'[10] It was difficult to forget her. Mrs Hamilton-Meikle writes: 'I met her first in Paris in about 1930, and she at once fascinated me, almost hypnotized me.'[11] Now, nearly forty years later, a Japanese student met her, and confessed: 'I did not know it would be so impressive . . . I felt, in your presence, as if I was in a dream.'[12] After her death, Nevill Coghill told me:

I have, of course, a host of memories and mental pictures of her, and I can hear the sharp, delightful, Dublin-distilled wit and energy of her talk (did anyone keep a tape of it?), but I have nothing in the way of episode or aphorism to offer you, that you could use to give the full effect of the tremendous person she was, so friendly, so courageous, so laughingly aggressive, so candid and yet so conspiratorial—and of course so *learned*, and *alive* with her learning! She certainly belongs to the Legion of Honour . . . I shall never forget the kingfisher blue of her eyes and the French matelot's cap and the blue and scarlet jacket and trousers with which she brightened Oxford. No wonder Maurice Bowra was inspired to say 'There goes Enid in all the colours of the Rimbaud!'[13]

She followed events, now, with growing excitement. On 18 October she wrote to me: 'Some people assume that, because Roy Fuller is in, I may withdraw, but I don't see that my votes would necessarily go to him! I think that anything might happen with six candidates. The elderly candidates . . . might divide up the "respectable" vote and let in MacSweeney. Or all the poets might divide up the poetic votes and let me in!'[14] Next day: 'I see that Yevtuschenko has been nominated . . . I also see in the *Observer* that there is now an eighth candidate, a seventh poet, Alan Bold, of Edinburgh . . . I'll have seriously to consider whether it wouldn't be more dignified to get out of that menagerie and withdraw, but I'd only do it on the last day, 11 November, when my full list was in.'[15]

On 21 October, Robert Graves wrote again. 'Any vote to you is a vote for *Oxford*, as opposed to *Elsewhere* . . . Remember, dearest Enid, that the *Custom* is for the candidate to keep silent and do no canvassing for herself or himself—or at least no *overt* canvassing . . . I do hope that I prove a *Queenmaker* as you have been a *Kingmaker*.'[16] Later that day he sent a second letter: 'Dearest Enid: . . . You are the only really decent candidate . . .: I mean you know your stuff, you are deep-blue Oxford, with a touch of vermilion, and are not trying to advertise your own poetry, or to add more weight to your name as a literary journalist; also you are one of the *undefeatables*.'[17] On 28 October, in a letter to the *Guardian*, he emphasized his points. 'Her election will decide whether Oxford intends to remain a serious University or to go all modern by the choice of a freak candidate . . . In fact Oxford needs Dr Starkie: for her courage, learning [and] wit . . . She is one of the Great Undefeatables and everyone loves her except the dull or mean-minded.' 'I've had two more letters of encouragement from Graves [this to me from Enid], and there is a letter in my favour by him in to-day's *Guardian*. I can't think it will be very useful to me!'[18] On 5 November she added: 'My own feeling is that it will be Roy Fuller as nearly everyone I've talked to has said that the Professor should be a poet. All I ask is to get a respectable number of votes and not to be the last of the "respectable" candidates. I can honestly say that I wouldn't mind at all not being elected, except a slight prick to my vanity.'[19] On 8 November she sent me a copy of the *Gazette*, with her formidable list of supporters. 'I can't count all the names here, but I think that there are 230, and that is only 38 less than Blunden got and his was phenomenal.'[20] On 15 November:

> I still think that Fuller will get it . . .
>
> I've decided, from today, not to answer the telephone during daylight, or rather office hours, as I'm being pestered by the Press. The *Telegraph* photographer waited outside my house and followed me into College. I said that I didn't want a photograph taken as I was ill. It was only when I threatened to call the porter that he left me, at the foot of the stairs in Somerville![21]

The Press were, for the moment, deterred; but television was not.

> At 8 o'clock this morning [this on 21 November] there was a ring at my bell and I thought it might be the post, . . . but it was the BBC. I was very angry and I shut the door in his face.
>
> It looks to me as if Fuller was coming up and gaining. Kathleen Raine seems to be out altogether . . .[22]

Voting took place on 21 and 23 November. On the evening of 23 November, the result was announced. Roy Fuller had received 385 votes, and Enid had polled 281.

> My first feeling was one of regret [she confessed to Eithne Kaiser], but this was quickly followed by a feeling of relief that I should no longer have to prepare all these lectures, nor write all the letters which the Chair seems to entail. But I was sorry all the same as I meant to do something different from what was generally done. It was generally treated as a Chair of English poetry, whereas . . . I would have lectured on large world movements in poetry during the last century, in the poetry of a great many countries—Symbolism, Dadaism, Surrealism, Existentialism, etc. etc. I think it could have been interesting. However it is all over now and it doesn't seriously matter.[23]

On 23 November, when the result had been announced, she and I had supper in her kitchen. She was philosophic. Next day I saw her again. She asked suddenly: 'Have you seen my portrait in College?' She knew that I had, but we looked at it once more.

Dear Professor Fuller [this on 25 November],
    May a defeated candidate for the Professorship congratulate you? I was certain all along that you would win and I think that it is a very good appointment, and anything might have happened this time as the electors seemed to go mad.
    It was I, in 1951, when I put up Cecil Day-Lewis, who altered the kind of Professor who used to be elected. Before that it was usually a resident university teacher, but, since 1951, it has always been a poet. If I myself had been voting this time, I would not have voted for myself, and I think you are very much more what Oxford needs . . .
    With warmest congratulations, yours sincerely,
                                        Enid Starkie.[24]

◇ 41 ◇

Most of Enid's adult life had been spent in Oxford, governed by terms and vacations, by college and university routine. After her resignation, she still attempted, sadly, sometimes desperately, to immerse herself in Oxford life. 'I'm trying, in term time, to cut down my engagements,' she told me early in 1969. 'The College and University engagements are things that I have to do, as part of my social duties.'[1] 'I have the French Ambassador's lecture on Wednesday,' she added on 23 February. 'On Tuesday I'm to hear Valéry's daughter lecture on her father, and meet her at a party afterwards. I've far too many engagements . . . I hope your work is going well. Mine is not going particularly well. I get weaker all the time . . . It is however getting on.'[2]
    Her driving interest remained the second volume of her life of Flaubert. On 1 April she went again to Paris to work on it. She used to go out from Paris to Chantilly to do her research in the Bibliothèque Spoelberch de Lovenjoul; as usual, she drove herself hard, and refused to indulge in meals. 'I'm writing this in a church

at Chantilly,' went her card to me, 'waiting for the lunch interval to end. It is bitterly cold in the church and also outside, . . . and I've not been warm since I've been here. There was a notice of your book in [the] *Evening Standard* of 1 April. I've kept it for you—it isn't v. valuable.'[3] The book was *Princess Mathilde*: my biography of the woman who had been a friend to Flaubert and, indeed, to most distinguished Frenchmen of her time. Enid had read the book in a day, and criticized it with vigour.

To her, the historical figures of nineteenth-century France remained as real as her Oxford colleagues; she still entered their lives with the warmth of a friend, and at times, it must be said, with the ardour of a partisan. I often thought it fortunate that Flaubert's selfish niece was not a member of the Senior Common Room at Somerville. Enid was still enthralled by the search for new material, for *l'inédit*. I happened to find a Flaubert letter mentioned in a catalogue, and told her about it on her return from France. She replied at once:

I'm much interested in that letter to Madame de Loynes—though she shouldn't be called that as she only married the Count in 1871. It isn't the letter in the *Supplément* in the *Correspondance* written when he was at Carthage. Suffel—whom I mentioned to you [on the phone] this evening—quotes a bit of it in his little book, and he says that it is unpublished . . . Suffel says, with a query, that it is December 1860. If he really wrote it in Carthage then it cannot be 1860 as he was only once there, in the spring of 1858. Of course he may mean that, in imagination, he was in Carthage as it was then that he was writing *Salammbô*. Is the letter for sale as I'd buy it if I could? . . .

I must go and unpack and then go to bed as I'm most terribly tired . . .

Saturday morning 12 April 1969
. . . I'm writing this in bed waiting for the papers and the post to come . . .

The post has just come and I've got your letter etc. I'll write to Blaizot about that letter [to Mme de Loynes], but you've not given any price for it—perhaps there wasn't any. I'd like to have it as there are so few letters to her . . .

Dr Fleury is wrong when he says that Flaubert toiled for ten years over one book. Five years seems to have been about his time . . . When one thinks that Flaubert was 58 when he died, he didn't leave so little after all—at least 13 volumes of correspondence and six novels— besides all the early works and one complete play and several attempts at plays with Bouilhet. He might have suffered from nicotine poisoning. His pipes were the size of thimbles—I've seen them at Croisset—and I don't think there is any evidence that he smoked as he worked. He describes himself as stopping to smoke.

Well, I must read the papers and get up.[4]

Enid lived, now, under growing physical disability. Her breathing was often hard, and she found it an effort to walk any distance, or go up a flight of stairs. She spent an increasing amount of time working in bed; she often complained of weakness. None the less, she had arranged to return to Paris on 20 August.

Her visit was disastrous. On 6 September, back in Oxford, she wrote to Dorothy Wadham:

I have just had a little over two weeks in Paris for work . . . Every day of the fortnight I longed for it to be over so that I could get back to my house where I could get warm, and make no effort. Every morning, when I woke up, I thought that there was another day which had to be got through. So poorly did I feel that I didn't tell all my friends that I was there—only those with cars!—and five days out of the fifteen days I went to bed after I got back from the Library, at six o'clock! It isn't worth being in Paris for that! I came to the conclusion that, unless I can get any stronger, this is my last trip abroad . . .

I got very far behind with the second volume of *Flaubert*. I have now done half of it and hope—if I don't get any worse—to finish the book by the end of the year . . . I don't suppose I'll ever write another book— I certainly couldn't without going to France—but I still hope to finish this one and perhaps to see it out.[5]

As a student, she had known poverty and illness and degradation in Paris; but she had always looked back on those years as a time in which she was unshackled by convention, a time when she had been free to be herself. She associated Paris with much of her emotional life; she associated it with her triumphant work on

Verhaeren. It was inescapably linked with Baudelaire, Rimbaud and Flaubert, with all the French literature she had read and taught. It was also, now, inseparable from the books she wanted to write.

I often urged her to write the two remaining volumes of her autobiography. She had made substantial notes for a book on her years in Paris; she had written a synopsis for her memories of Oxford. But she could not yet speak freely of Oxford, and the plan for her Oxford book was marked: 'To be written when very old.' She could not write about Paris until she had returned there and re-traced her past. She also needed to go there again if she was to write the life of Jules Laforgue. She had wanted to write it for more than twenty years.

Enid was worried, now, by her intense and growing interest in Laforgue; she felt that she might not be able to do research on him, or complete her book. I replied that I should be worried if she no longer wanted to write. I was, in fact, apprehensive about her future when she gave in her second volume of *Flaubert*. 'I don't think I could live without a little flame in my heart', she had written, years ago.[6] She needed, now, to work on Laforgue for the sake of her morale. He was rapidly becoming her *raison d'être*. She had developed an affection for his neglected wife, the young English governess, Leah Lee. She was anxious to discover her history.

On 21 October I dined with her at Somerville. She seemed tired and frail. On 27 November she wrote to me about my work on Verlaine. 'Are you going to Paris before Christmas to look up the Doucet Collection?' she added. 'If you are, I wonder whether you'd look to see whether there are any documents in connection with Laforgue . . . I don't suppose I'll ever use them but there would be no harm in knowing whether there were any.'[7] On 27 December she wrote to Dorothy Wadham: 'I've other books that I could do if I could get abroad. I don't know how I'll spend the rest of my life if I don't write. I've never been someone to sit about gossiping over cups of tea.'[8] On 3 January she told me: 'Weidenfeld came today and I handed over to him the typescript of my book . . . I'm not doing the Laforgue for a very long time, if ever

I do it at all.'[9] On 6 January, in a letter to Marianne Eyles and Frances Fowler, she wrote that the new *Flaubert* was 'probably my most learned book . . . I'd like this book to be good, as it may well be my last.'[10]

'I've written that book in weakness, and doubt of self, and I hope that it doesn't show too much.'[11] So she told the same correspondents. *Flaubert the Master* has clearly been written against the increasing pressure of ill-health; but its chief weakness lies in the lack of criticism of Flaubert's works. Enid discusses the process of composition, the condition of the notes and manuscripts, and the reception of the books by Flaubert's contemporaries. But she does not give a complete assessment of each text. As a critic observed, when the book appeared, she seemed less interested in the later novels than in the total phenomenon of Flaubert, man and writer. This seems a fair judgment. The mystery of genius must remain insoluble; but this biography is an honest and exhaustive examination of the man. 'With her *Baudelaire* and *Rimbaud*,' Cyril Connolly was to write, 'it forms a trilogy, a monument to her total devotion to the French nineteenth century.'[12]

'I haven't any news as this is my first day up, and I haven't seen anyone or talked to anyone.' This from Enid on 10 January 1970. She added: 'I've written 57 letters since last Sunday, and I still have 13 to write—unless any new ones come in on Monday.'[13] 'Who but Enid', asked Liselott Strauss, 'would have counted the number of letters she received and replied to over a given period? Like a child proud of its collection of sea shells or something and saying "oh bother those shells, they are just dust catchers around the place". Anyway she went on dusting her shells and answering her personal mail probably until the day she died . . . The ledger balanced, I feel sure she went to sleep peacefully.'[14]

Meanwhile, she continued to take a defiant interest in life. On 23 February, with a touch of irony, she sent a note to Francis Warner, the English tutor at St Peter's.

Dear Francis,

What is this gala evening you are holding in the Playhouse on Sunday

8 March? Is it going to be all gimmicks as I hate gimmicks and would not go under these circumstances? I see that the play lasts for 30 seconds with no actors, no dialogue, no scenery and no props. I also saw in one of the papers that the rest of the entertainment is planned for the enjoyment of the actors and not the public. I prefer the actors to be preoccupied with my enjoyment! . . .

I don't want to go to this gala evening if it is only going to be made up of gimmicks!

However if Sam Beckett is really coming I'd like to see him again.

I look forward to seeing you on Tuesday, 10 March, the last Tuesday of Term. I'll meet you at 7 o'clock in the entrance hall at Somerville, lounge suit and no gown.[15]

Francis Warner dined at Somerville, and Enid went to the gala. The correspondent of the *Guardian* saw her 'listening to Siobhan McKenna reading Samuel Beckett. She was perched on the edge of her seat like a girl at her first pantomime', he remembered, a few weeks later. 'It is moving but unsurprising to recall that she enjoyed herself so much so late.'[16] Bryan Kelly, the composer, adds: 'I wrote an orchestral work called *Divertissement* which I dedicated to her. The four movements are based on French folk songs. She knew that I was doing it but alas she died before the first performance.'[17] It was appropriate that Enid should have had her music; and the themes and title were peculiarly her own.

She was enjoying research, now, more than she had ever done. Her hesitations and doubts had been brushed aside, and she had returned to her first love, French poetry. On 15 March, she told Francis Warner: 'I have got mad about Laforgue and his works and I would like to get embarked on that. I think that I could do something good . . .'[18] She embarked on Laforgue, scribbled pages of notes and bibliography in her somewhat cramped yet dashing hand. 'There is nothing wrong with my spirit', she told a friend on 1 April. 'I am indeed working very hard in bed at my future book on Laforgue.'[19]

In the first days of April, her condition suddenly worsened. On 15 April, I was told that she had only months to live. Next day I went to Oxford to see her. She could not drink the champagne I had brought her, but we talked again about Laforgue. 'I want to write about him,' she said, 'if I get back my health.'

On Monday, 20 April, she walked into College for lunch; and that evening Janet Vaughan went to see her. Enid felt in excellent spirits, and she was planning to go to Paris in June. Even Janet Vaughan thought that Paris was possible. The doctors had been with her that day; they came again next evening. Dr Ridehalgh recorded that she was breathless when she moved, but when she sat down she soon 'became perfectly easy and both physically and mentally her normal self, discussing a book which she had recently completed and plans for a new book.' It was a book 'on a little-known French poet which she had just started and needed three years to complete.'[20] Her condition did not seem critical, but the doctors decided that she should enter the Acland Home next day, for a rest. Once the matter was settled, she opened a bottle of champagne.

It was the perfect end to her life. Next morning, Walter Starkie wrote, 'they found Enid on the stairs leading up from her study.'[21]

◈ 42 ◈

Enid's absorbing passion for the background and creators of French literature was her chief contribution to French studies. No-one knew her way more surely in nineteenth-century Paris. To her the literary figures of the time were real and absorbing; she understood and discussed them as living people. She knew the major and the minor writers, the conventional and the Bohemian; but she was drawn, instinctively, to the unorthodox and the rebellious: she watched them with fascination and sympathy in their spiritual distress and their human weakness. 'Enid always wants to be different from the rest', so her governess had said. Enid was always different. She went her way with brio and bravado, and she was drawn to those who had done the same. She understood the problems of sexual morality, and the burdens of religious doubt; she

was concerned with those who had known them, too. She spent
much of her adult life in oppressive loneliness, and she had many
moments of self-questioning. She sympathized with those who
had known similar unhappiness.

She herself was a dual character. She was a Victorian Lady's
Child and she was a Left Bank Bohemian. She was one of the
Establishment and she was a perpetual rebel. Her originality came
from the tension between these conflicting selves. But there remained a more profound and more disturbing conflict; Enid was a
respected Oxford don and a wildly passionate private person.
Throughout her career she needed to keep these two selves apart,
to hide her deep, unorthodox emotions from the conventional
world. Her struggle was reflected in the books she chose to write.
She had a secret self and a public persona. She looked beyond the
public persona of writers for the private selves which they sometimes tried to hide. She was concerned with the spiritual anguish
which lay behind the outrageous Bohemianism of Baudelaire; she
was concerned with the poetic purpose behind Rimbaud's calculated viciousness. She discovered and analysed the sexual problems
of Flaubert; and, turning to the twentieth century, she studied the
acute and unremitting problems, social, sexual, and moral, which
confronted Gide. In her work she explored not only her subject,
but herself. Ifor Evans wrote of her *Petrus Borel* that she had 'a most
unusual talent for anatomizing complex personalities'. She had a
gift for analysing those who had 'fathomed down into the darker
places, deep down beneath ordinary experience and made of life
some fantastic arabesque of emotion, indulgence and self-explora-
tion.'[1] That was a perceptive judgment on all her work; it was an
illuminating judgment on Enid Starkie.

One cannot claim that Enid was a scholar of the first order. Her
field was limited, her judgments were sometimes biased by personal and political sympathies; she lacked the breadth of knowledge, the lucid and dispassionate judgment which a scholar brings
to his work. She did not love literature for its own sake; she read it,
one suspects, not for aesthetic pleasure but for its bearing on her

books and lectures, and for its revelation of the men who wrote it. This may be why her purely literary criticism remains undistinguished. Her comments are often banal, and they are indifferently expressed. No-one with intuitive love of prose or of poetry could have discussed it in terms which are so lazily commonplace. Even when she wrote of the authors who were dearest to her, she discussed their work in laboured style. She was not, one feels, concerned with writing; and, though she was musical, she had no sense of the orchestration of language. Her appreciation of French literature is disappointing.

As a tutor, she sometimes failed to communicate with her less 'literary' pupils; as a supervisor, she could be lax and irresponsible. But her erudition, her perpetual thirst for *l'inédit*, her excitement, were exhilarating. If the task of a university teacher was, as she once said, to inspire, Enid fulfilled that task for any student with a taste for literature or an interest in research. Her supreme asset as a teacher was her personal fire.

Enid was tempestuous. Her moods were unpredictable. She was quickly moved to anger, she was instantaneously moved to tears; she was sentimental, ruthless and vulnerable. She also had an abundant capacity for pleasure: she delighted in food and drink, in social life, in gossip, in friendship, in the machinations of college and university politics.

She had a panache which was sometimes French (or Irish dramatic), sometimes almost vulgar. She cultivated an eccentric image. Perhaps such behaviour was merely designed to ensure attention; perhaps (one recalls Baudelaire's dandyism) it was also a means of self-protection. Enid was an amalgam of astonishing contradictions. She was flashy and fastidious, sophisticated and emotionally immature. She gave a sense of moral strength, yet she had allowed herself much weakness. She set herself no standards for her personal behaviour, yet many people felt that she was wise, and that she believed in high ideals.

What is certain is that she had amazing toughness and vitality, she radiated warmth and intelligence, energy and excitement. One always knew when Enid was present: she would draw a roomful of people into her orbit, and they would only ask to remain there. 'You are written into the fabric of our generation in Oxford', Janet Vaughan had told her.[2] For forty years, as a don, but still more as a personality, Enid was part of the Oxford experience.

Notes

Abbreviations: AG = Alyse Gregory
                   ES = Enid Starkie
                   SP = Starkie Papers
          SP (A) = Starkie Papers (Addenda)
       WJMS = William Joseph Myles Starkie (father of ES)

1. A Lady's Child 1897–1916 *pp. 7–26*

I

1 *The Times*, 19 August 1897.
2 Genealogical tree. SP
3 J. P. Rylands, *The Starkie Family of Pennington and Bedford, in the Parish of Leigh, Co. Lancaster*. Not published, but printed in Leigh, Lancashire, 1880, pp. 3–4.
4 WJMS: diary, 20 January 1919. SP
5 Ibid, 24 February 1919.
6 25 January 1967. SP
7 21 May 1937. SP
8 24 February 1957. SP
9 K. W. L. Starkie to ES, 28 November 1968. SP
10 31 October 1968. SP
11 *Boston Guardian*. Undated cutting. SP
12 ES: *A Lady's Child* (London, 1941); J. E. Auden (ed.), *Shrewsbury School Register, 1734–1908* (Oswestry. Woodall, Minshall, 1909); *Trinity College Record Volume* (Dublin, 1951); *Who Was Who, 1916–1928*, pp. 989–90. Undated obituary. SP
13 Undated obituary [July 1920]. SP
14 Sir H. Mack to the author, 26 April 1971. SP (A)
15 ES: speech at dinner for 90th anniversary of Alexandra College, 20 October 1956. SP
16 *Holiday in Kerry of May and John*. SP

17 Ms. notes. SP
18 *Irish Times.* Undated cutting [1967?]. SP

2

1 All comments by ES on her childhood and student days in Oxford are taken, unless otherwise stated, from her autobiography, *A Lady's Child.*
2 WJMS: diary, 1 November 1919. SP
3 To Alyse Gregory. Monday night, 11 October [1943?]. SP (A)
4 R. Tallard to the author, 2 February 1971. SP (A)
5 Walter Starkie to the author, 30 June 1970. SP (A)
6 'Nostalgie de Paris d'une Irlandaise', in *Aguedal* (May 1943).
7 Ibid.
8 *A personal view of France.* Lecture given at Roedean, 26 November 1950. SP
9 *Aguedal*, loc. cit.
10 *Fortnightly Review*, February 1942.

3

1 For details of Alexandra School and Alexandra College, I am indebted to the Principal of the College, Mrs S. A. Morgan. For Alexandra College, see also the *Irish Times*, 22 April 1964.
2 ES: speech at anniversary dinner of Alexandra College, loc. cit.
3 Ibid.
4 ES: speech at anniversary dinner, loc. cit.
5 *Aguedal*, loc. cit.
6 To AG. 'Monday night' [1943?]. SP (A)
7 To AG. 'Sunday' [Jan./Feb.? 1944]. SP (A)

2. Scholar of Somerville 1916–1920 *pp. 27–52*

4

1 A. M. A. H. Rogers, *Degrees by Degrees* (Oxford, 1938), pp. 10–11, 21.
2 Ibid, pp. 13–14.
3 Rogers, op. cit.
4 Somerville College report for the year ending Michaelmas 1920, pp. 48–9. For an account of the College in its early days, see Muriel St Clare Byrne and Catherine Hope Mansfield, *Somerville College, 1879–1921* (Oxford, 1922), and Vera Farnell, *A Somervillian Looks Back* (Oxford, privately printed, 1948).

Notes

5 Vera Brittain, *Testament of Youth* (London, 1933), pp. 507–8.

6 Against Vera Brittain's impression should be set Constance Savery's account of tea with Miss Penrose (quoted in a letter to the author, 20 March 1971):

> This afternoon Florence Duncan and I had the Pen to tea—it was simply awful! We provided her with bread, marg., jam, toasted scones, wee chocolate-iced cakes and a ginger sponge. She ate two pieces of scone, a slice of bread and jam (she never takes both jam and marg.), three cups of tea, a chocolate cake and a piece of dough cake—we had some College dough-cake as well. And she asked question after question —we discussed degrees for women, Gilbert and Sullivan (!), the abolishment of Greek in Smalls, a Government scheme of State scholarships, and about a dozen other things. She says that if the Government does not let us have Somerville in time for the October term, Oriel will turn us out, and we shall have to close—just think of that! It will take six months to get it papered and cleaned and repaired, so if they aren't quick, we shall be in a very sorry plight . . .

7 Constance Savery, loc. cit.

8 SP

9 Ibid.

10 Constance Savery, loc. cit.

11 Dorothy L. Sayers, *Gaudy Night* (London, 1935), pp. 20–1.

12 ES: appreciation for inclusion in Somerville College Council Report, 20 February 1957. SP

13 Constance Savery, loc. cit.

14 Ibid.

15 Ibid.

16 Ibid.

17 M. V. Clarke, *Fourteenth Century Studies*, ed. by L. S. Sutherland and M. McKisack, with a memoir of M. V. Clarke by E. L. Woodward (Oxford, 1937), p. xix.

18 Vera Brittain, *Testament of Friendship* (London, 1940), pp. 84–5.

19 Letter dated 'Monday' [1935]. SP

20 Dorothy Wadham to the author, 13 January 1971. SP (A)

21 Hilda Mellor to the author, 16 January 1971. SP (A)

22 Constance Savery, loc. cit.

23 Ibid.

24 Hilda Mellor, loc. cit.

25 Mrs Wedgwood Benn to the author, 21 June 1971. SP (A)

Notes

5

1   Letter to the author, 11 January 1971. SP (A)
2   Letter to the author, 13 January 1971. SP (A)
3   *Isis*, 23 October 1968.
4   *Cherwell*, 16 November 1966.
5   Letter to the author, 15 January 1971. SP (A)
6   SP
7   Constance Savery to the author, 15 January 1971. SP (A)
8   Letter to the author, 16 January, 1971. SP (A)
9   Letter to the author, 5 December 1971. SP (A)
10 Ibid. The programme, among the Starkie Papers, is dated Sunday, 24 June.
11 Quoted by Robin Carew in letter to ES, 3 February 1969. SP
12 Letter to the author, 13 January 1971. SP (A)
13 Vera Brittain, *Testament of Friendship*, p. 86.
14 SP
15 Dame Lucy Sutherland in conversation with the author, 20 January 1971.
16 WJMS: diary. SP
17 Ibid, 18 April 1919.
18 Quoted in letter to the author, 15 January 1971. SP (A)
19 Letter to the author, 15 January 1971. SP (A)
20 WJMS: diary, 25 April 1919. SP
21 Constance Savery, loc. cit.
22 WJMS: diary, 30 January 1920. SP
23 To Cecil King, 15 November 1936. (King)
24 *Sunday Times*, 12 December 1971.
25 10 July 1954. (King)
26 WJMS: diary, 3 July 1920. SP

6

1   *All Remedies Refusing*. SP
2   17 January 1942. SP
3   *Oxford Magazine*, 8 June 1950.
4   ES to Liselott Haynes (later Mrs Strauss), 28 June 1943. Quoted by Mrs Strauss to the author, 7 October 1970. SP (A)
5   WJMS: diary. SP
6   Sir Maurice Bowra: address at memorial service for ES, 28 May 1970.
7   Letter of 1920. SP
8   ES: after-lunch talk at Nottingham, 17 March 1959. SP
9   16 August 1920. SP

10 2 September 1920. SP
11 Letters to the author, 14 and 18 January 1971. SP (A)
12 7 October 1920. SP.
13 M. G. Beard: letter of 18 January 1921. SP

3. Sorbonne Student 1921–1924 *pp. 53–72*

7

1 ES: talk at Nottingham, loc. cit.
2 Ibid.
3 *Cherwell*, 16 November 1966.
4 Letter to the author, 13 January 1971. SP (A)
5 ES: Paris notes. SP
6 To William Hawksworth, 17 October 1949. (Ridehalgh)
7 Nottingham talk, loc. cit.
8 Ibid.
9 ES: *All Remedies Refusing*. SP
10 *Aguedal*, loc. cit.
11 ES: Paris notes. SP
12 Ibid.

8

1 Nottingham talk, loc. cit.; Hollins College Alumnae Bulletin (Autumn 1959).
2 N. de Praingy to Mrs Brooksbank, 24 November 1967 (Brooksbank); and ES, 'Nostalgie de Paris d'une Irlandaise', loc. cit.
3 ES: Paris notes. SP
4 To AG, 'Wednesday night' [1940s]. SP (A)
5 *Aguedal*, loc. cit.
6 ES: Paris notes. SP
7 Ibid.
8 To AG, 'Friday night' [1943?]. SP (A)
9 ES: appreciation of Émile Verhaeren, 1926. SP
10 ES: Paris notes. SP
11 *Isis*, 22 January 1969.
12 ES: Nottingham talk, loc. cit.
13 Alice Storms: appreciation of ES. SP
14 ES: Nottingham talk, loc. cit.

15 Ibid.
16 Ibid.

4. Assistant Lecturer, Exeter 1925–1928 *pp. 73–85*

9

1 Miss L. A. Baggs to the author, 29 July and 5 September 1971. SP (A); Mrs Russell in conversation with the author, 21 October 1971.
2 Sir Hector Hetherington, *The University College at Exeter, 1920–1925* (Exeter, 1963).
3 Letter to the author, 2 February 1971. SP (A)
4 ES: 'My job and why I chose it'. Radley, 5 December 1950. SP
5 Letter to the author, 13 January 1971. SP (A)
6 ES: Paris notes. SP
7 To Rosamond Lehmann, 'Friday night' [1945]. (Lehmann)
8 To AG, 'Wednesday' [early 1942]. SP (A)
9 To AG, 13 June 1950. SP (A)

10

1 To Rosamond Lehmann, loc. cit.
2 ES: Paris notes. SP
3 To Rosamond Lehmann, loc. cit.
4 ES: Paris notes. SP; letter to AG, 'Friday night' [1940s]. SP (A)
5 To Rosamond Lehmann, loc. cit.
6 Letter to the author, 14 April 1971. SP (A)
7 To AG, 21 January 1945. SP (A)
8 *Time and Tide*, 22 November 1947.

11

1 ES: *Les Sources du Lyrisme dans la poésie d'Émile Verhaeren.*
2 Ibid.
3 3 January 1928. SP
4 Professor Louis Bonnerot to the author, 30 October 1970. SP (A)
5 ES: Nottingham talk, loc. cit.
6 Quoted by ES in talk above.
7 Letter of 2 May 1928. SP

Notes

5. Sarah Smithson Lecturer, Somerville 1928–1934 *pp. 87–108*

12

1 For an appreciation of Miss Fry, see Enid Huws Jones, *Margery Fry. The Essential Amateur.* (Oxford, 1966).
2 Notes. SP
3 Letter of 5 October 1928. SP
4 Letter of 18 October 1928. SP
5 Rica Brown (*née* Jones) to the author, 23 March 1971. SP (A)
6 Letter postmarked 18 March 1929 SP
7 Review by Geraldine Hodgson [1928]. SP
8 *Revue bibliographique*, May 1928.
9 *Observer*, 15 July 1928.
10 Somerville College Association of Senior Members. Fourth annual supplement to the report of the College, 1928–29, p. 23. ES also comments on her awards in letters to Alyse Gregory, 1 December 1942, and to Hamish Hamilton, 12 August 1949. SP (A)
11 Liselott Strauss to the author, 9 September 1970. SP (A)
12 ES: personal notes. SP
13 Ibid.
14 Letter from Liselott Haynes (later Strauss), July 1942. SP
15 To AG, 'Friday night' [1940s]. SP (A)
16 ES: personal notes. SP
17 Professor Agnes Headlam-Morley to the author, 14 April 1971. SP (A)
18 Letter to the author, 15 March 1971. SP (A)
19 ES: Paris notes. SP

13

1 L. Martin-Chauffier, *Le Figaro littéraire*, 29 August 1959.
2 Ibid.
3 To [Dame] Lucy Sutherland, 24 August 1930. (Sutherland)
4 15 August 1935. SP
5 To Rica Brown (*née* Jones), 10 October 1932. (Brown)
6 To the same, 18 September 1933. (Brown)
7 Rica Brown to the author, 23 March 1971. SP (A)
8 Anne Kirkman to the author, 25 August 1971. SP (A)
9 5 September 1932. SP
10 Margaret Hooper: letter of 3 January 1967. SP

11 This, and the following quotations, are taken from 'The Golden Bed', the typescript of the article published in *Time and Tide* in 1944. SP

12 Liselott Strauss to the author, loc. cit.

14

1 Draft letter of 2 February 1933. SP

2 Letter dated 'Thursday' [1933]. SP

3 To AG, Saturday night [December 1941]; Sunday [January/February ? 1944]. SP (A)

4 *The Times Literary Supplement*, 15 June 1933.

5 18 July 1933. SP

6 2 April 1934. SP

7 12 April 1934. SP

8 18 April 1934. SP

9 23 May 1934. SP

10 Letter to [Dame] Lucy Sutherland, 19 September 1934. (Sutherland)

11 ES: speech at Rimbaud centenary, 17 October 1954. SP

6 Fellow and Tutor 1934–1946 *pp. 109–161*

15

1 Letter of 4 September 1934. SP

2 Letter of 16 July 1934. SP

3 To Rosamond Lehmann, loc. cit.

4 Letter to the author, 15 January 1971. SP (A)

5 Letter to the author, 15 March 1971. SP (A)

6 5 July 1935. SP

7 18 July 1935. SP

8 6 August 1935. SP

9 15 August 1935. SP

10 22 August 1935. SP

16

1 27 December 1936. SP

2 7 January 1937. SP

3 9 February 1937. SP

4 13 July 1937. SP

5 To AG, 17 August 1953; to Eithne Kaiser, 16 July 1959. SP (A)

6 11 February 1938. SP

7   5 May 1938. SP
8   21 May 1938. SP
9   15 May 1938. SP
10 1 June 1938. SP
11 6 July 1938. SP
12 9 July 1938. SP
13 22 July 1938. SP
14 25 July 1938. SP
15 7 August 1938. SP
16 27 September 1938. SP
17 18 January 1939. SP
18 18 February 1939. SP
19 *Materials for a Life of William Rothenstein*, by Robert Speaight. Notebook III, p. 82. (Library, Victoria & Albert Museum)
20 Undated note; like the following letters, it is among the Starkie Papers.
21 ES: notes for memoirs of Oxford. SP
22 10 August 1939. SP
23 30 August 1939. SP
24 16 September 1939. SP

17

1   'Joyce Cary, a Portrait', in *Essays by Divers Hands. Being the transactions of The Royal Society of Literature*. Volume XXXIII, ed. by Joanna Richardson (Oxford, 1963), p. 134.
2   To AG, 'Saturday afternoon' [1943]. SP (A)
3   To AG, 10 September 1940. SP (A)
4   16 September 1940. SP
5   To AG, 6 October 1940. SP (A)
6   25 November 1940. SP
7   To AG, 21 December 1940. SP (A)
8   28 September 1940. SP
9   2 November 1940. SP
10 Liselott Strauss to the author, 9 September 1970. SP (A)
11 *All Remedies Refusing*. SP
12 Ibid.
13 Letter dated 'Wednesday' [1930s ?]. SP
14 *All Remedies Refusing*. SP
15 Ibid.
16 Ibid.

Notes

18

1 Liselott Strauss to the author, 9 September 1970. SP (A)
2 To AG 'Saturday night' [December 1941]. SP (A)
3 To AG 'Friday, Banbury' [1940s] SP (A); notes for a novel. (SP)
4 SP
5 Ibid.
6 To AG, 'Saturday' [1940s]. SP (A)
7 *Tatler*, 26 November 1941.
8 To AG, 'Thursday night midnight' [June 1943?]. SP (A)
9 21 December 1941. SP
10 5 January 1942. SP

19

1 28 November 1941. SP
2 To AG, 3 December 1941. SP (A)
3 To AG, 9 February [1940s]. SP (A)
4 To AG, 11 December 1941. SP (A)
5 15 December 1941. SP
6 To AG, 22 December 1941. SP (A)
7 26 December [1941]. SP
8 To AG, 26 December 1941. SP (A)
9 1 January 1942. SP
10 Letter dated 'Monday' [January 1942]. SP
11 To AG, 13 January 1942. SP (A)
12 To AG, 11 February 1942. SP (A)
13 To AG, 15 April 1942. SP (A)
14 To AG, 'Tuesday night, 11.30' [December 1942]. SP (A)
15 To AG, 7 July 1942. SP (A)
16 To AG, 'Saturday' [1942 ?]. SP (A)
17 To AG, 11 November 1942. SP (A)
18 To AG, 4 October 1942. SP (A)
19 22 October 1944. SP
20 3 January 1943. SP
21 Unsigned report. SP
22 22 January 1943. SP (A)
23 To AG, 'Monday night' [1943?]. SP (A)
24 *The Times Literary Supplement*, 6 March 1943.
25 To Thomas Higham, 15–16 June 1947. SP (A)
26 To AG [1943]. SP (A)

27 *Aguedal*, loc. cit.
28 Ibid.
29 To AG, 8 September 1945. SP (A)
30 Mrs Hamilton-Meikle to the author, 28 March 1971. SP (A)
31 To Eithne Wilkins (later Kaiser), 21 January 1939. SP (A)

20

1   To AG, 9 April 1954. SP (A)
2   To AG, undated. SP (A)
3   18 June 1943. SP
4   To AG, 'Thursday night midnight' [June 1943]. SP (A)
5   To AG, 8 August 1943. SP (A)
6   To AG, 16 April 1946. SP (A)
7   To AG, 3 October 1943. SP (A)
8   AG: letter of 13 October 1943. SP
9   To AG, 19 December 1943. SP (A)
10 To AG, 3 October [1943]. SP (A)
11 To AG, 'Sunday afternoon' [1942-3]. SP (A)
12 22 November 1943. SP
13 To AG, 6 December 1943. SP (A)
14 To AG, 11 January 1944. SP (A)
15 13 January 1944. SP
16 To AG, 16 January 1944. SP (A)
17 Letter dated 'Sunday evening Jan.? 1944.' SP
18 To AG, letter dated 'Sunday' [January or February 1944]. SP (A)
19 Letter to the author, 18 January 1971. SP (A)
20 Letter to the author, 13 May 1971. SP (A)
21 ES: Paris notes. SP

21

1   19 October 1944. (Lehmann)
2   1 November 1944. (Lehmann)
3   15 November 1944. (Lehmann)
4   To AG, 'Saturday evening' [1943]. SP (A)
5   To Thérèse Lavauden, 20 January 1966. SP (A)
6   *Isis*, 22 January 1969.
7   *Oxford Magazine*, 4 March 1937; *Spectator*, 15 August 1947; *Cherwell*, 14 November 1956; *Nova*, January 1969.
8   Letter from J. Murray Brown, 9 September 1967. SP

9   *Nova,* January 1969.
10   To AG, 7 July 1945. SP (A)
11   Letter to the author, 5 April 1971. SP (A)
12   *Cherwell,* undated cutting [1962]. SP
13   WJMS: diary, 2 November 1919. SP
14   Dan Davin, *The Chinese Box.* Recollections of Enid Starkie, *The Cornhill* (Winter 1972–73), pp. 361 sqq.
15   Sir Isaiah Berlin in conversation with the author, 17 December 1971.
16   To Rosamond Lehmann, 'Friday night' [1945]. (Lehmann)
17   Ibid.
18   *Sunday Times,* 14 October 1956.
19   Molly — to ES [1935]. SP
20   Liselott Strauss to the author, 9 September 1970. SP (A)
21   To AG, 31 December 1945. SP (A)
22   To AG, 16 April 1946. SP (A)

7. University Reader 1946–1965   *pp. 163–234*

22

1   To Hamish Hamilton, 16 December 1945. SP (A)
2   To Hamish Hamilton, 13 January 1946. SP (A)
3   To Hamish Hamilton, 27 April 1946. SP (A)
4   To Hamish Hamilton, 16 May 1946. SP (A)
5   To Hamish Hamilton, 26 May 1946. SP (A)
6   To AG, 17 May 1948. SP (A)
7   To AG, 28 August 1946. SP (A)
8   ES: *Impressions of Paris* (1946). SP

23

1   6 February 1947. SP
2   Undated letter [February 1947]. SP
3   Letter to AG, 27 March 1947. SP (A)
4   17 February 1947. SP
5   To Hamish Hamilton, 'Friday night' [1947]. SP (A). The account, 'André Gide's visit to Oxford, 5–8 June 1947', remains among ES's papers, and it is given here.
6   ES: appreciation of André Gide. (Higham)

Notes

24

1   To William Hawksworth, 26 September 1949. (Ridehalgh)
2   To AG, 8 September 1947. SP (A)
3   To AG, 8 October 1947. SP (A)
4   11 October 1947. SP
5   Letter dated 'Friday' [October 1947]. SP
6   25 October 1947. SP
7   15 March 1948. (Lehmann)
8   To AG, 16 June 1948. SP (A)
9   28 June 1948. SP. 'Generations of undergraduates and townspeople remember her as a diminutive, frail woman . . . wearing a red Légion-d'honneur badge in her raincoat lapel.' (*Guardian*, 24 April 1970)
10 To AG, 11 July 1948. SP (A)
11 To AG, 4 October 1948. SP (A)
12 15 October 1948. (Lehmann)
13 11 October 1948. SP. In the spring of 1948, Enid met Gide in Paris, and he kissed her on both cheeks—'as an old friend of the family'. To Alyse Gregory, 17 April 1948. SP (A)
14 15 June 1947. SP (A)
15 To AG, 1 December 1942. SP (A)
16 To Thomas Higham, loc. cit.

25

1   28 March 1949. SP
2   AG: unpublished journal, 12 May 1949. (Manning)
3   16 May 1949. SP
4   28 May 1949. SP
5   ES: application for the Marshal Foch Chair of French Literature in the University of Oxford, 1949. SP
6   Professor Agnes Headlam-Morley to the author, 14 April 1971. SP (A)
7   To AG, 'Monday night' [1943?]. SP (A)
8   To AG, 'Sunday afternoon' [1942–3]. SP (A)
9   To Hamish Hamilton, 5 June 1949. SP (A)
10 To Hamish Hamilton, 10 August 1949. SP (A)
11 7 September 1949. SP
12 To William Hawksworth, 26 September 1949. (Ridehalgh)
13 23 October [1949]. SP
14 14 October 1949. SP
15 To William Hawksworth, 17 October 1949. (Ridehalgh)

16 Unsigned appreciation, sent by June Barraclough. (Wedgwood Benn)
17 Letter to the author, 21 June 1971. SP (A)

26

1 Gide's letter of acceptance, dated 11 October 1948, remains among the Starkie Papers.
2 To AG, 2 October 1950. SP (A)
3 Gide died on 19 February 1951. An unsigned appreciation, by ES, appeared in the *Manchester Guardian* on 20 February.
4 Unidentified press-cutting of 1966. SP
5 10 February 1951. SP
6 To AG, 30 May 1951. SP(A)
7 To AG, 1 June 1951. SP (A)
8 To Agnes Headlam-Morley, 25 June 1960. (Headlam-Morley)
9 To Hamish Hamilton, 26 June 1951. SP (A)
10 To AG, 5 August 1951. SP (A)
11 To AG, 20 April 1953. SP (A)
12 To Eithne Kaiser, 1 February 1967. SP (A)
13 P-E. Artur to the author, 13 April 1971. SP (A)
14 12 July 1952. SP
15 14 November 1952. SP
16 4 September 1951, 20 May 1952, 26 November 1953. SP. Among Joyce Cary's letters to ES is also the following note, sent from Freiburg on 5 June 1954:

> My dear Enid:
>
> I am having quite an exciting trip—at least up till now. This place seems so dead that it doesn't even smell—but I am glad of a fine day to rest and write my letters. Last night I went out after a local feast of calve's liver and pilsener and listened to a melancholy brass band in the little park. It gave me the most delightfully sad sensations.—nostalgia for the age when Turgenev characters made love and quarrelled in little German spas to the sound of such bands. I went to bed early full of tears for wasted things, and slept exceedingly well.
>
> I hope you will still be there when I get back. Have you started that Baudelaire yet? My love, my dear Enid.
>
> ever yours
>
> Joyce.

17 To Hamish Hamilton, 15 March 1953. SP (A)
18 Letter to the author, 21 March 1954. (Richardson)

Notes

19 *La Lanterne*, 4 September 1954.

20 *Le Figaro littéraire*, 23 October 1954.

21 *Discours prononcé par Miss Enid Starkie lors des manifestations du centenaire Rimbaud à Charleville, 17 octobre 1954.* SP

22 *New Statesman*, 16 October 1954; *Manchester Guardian*, 20 October 1954.

23 Professor Agnes Headlam-Morley to the author, 5 April 1971. SP (A)

24 To Cecil King, 6 January 1955. SP (A)

25 Professor L. J. Witts to Dr Herrin, 25 May 1955. (Herrin)

26 4 September 1955. SP

27 To AG. SP

27

1 This, and the following letters from W. H. Auden, are among the Starkie Papers.

2 *Oxford Mail*, 31 January 1956.

3 *Daily Express*, 6 February 1956.

4 *Evening News*, 9 February 1956; *Glasgow Herald*, undated press-cutting of 1966. SP

5 *Financial Times*, undated press-cutting of 1966. SP

6 *Oxford Mail*, 10 February 1956.

7 *Sunday Times*, 17 June 1956.

8 To Francis Steegmuller, 12 September 1966. (Steegmuller)

9 25 March 1956. SP

10 To Francis Steegmuller, loc. cit.

11 SP

12 Ibid.

13 To Francis Steegmuller, loc. cit.

14 SP

15 Ibid.

16 Ibid.

17 To Francis Steegmuller, loc. cit.

18 *Picture Post*, 1956.

28

1 ES: Russian diary. SP

29

1 Aline Lion. Letter of 27 June 1957. SP

2 To AG, 15 August 1956. SP (A)

3 Undated note. SP

4 To AG, 9 December 1957. SP (A)

Notes

5 Writing to Graham Greene on 27 October 1957, ES maintained: 'This was one of the most difficult things that I've ever done in my life'. (Greene)

30

1 Letter from Christian Fitzherbert, 23 July 1958. SP
2 12 November 1959. SP
3 12 February 1958. SP
4 *Spectator*, 17 February 1956.
5 Michael MacLiammoir, *An Oscar of No Importance* (London, 1968), p. 88. This refers to ES in 1960.
6 Letter to the author, 13 January 1971. SP (A)
7 Letter to the author, 15 January 1971. SP (A)
8 David Ball in conversation with the author, 18 August 1971.
9 To AG, 8 September 1955. SP (A)
10 Liselott Strauss to the author, 9 September 1970. SP (A)
11 To Eithne Kaiser, 15 November 1966. SP (A)
12 To AG, 12 August 1959, 16 November 1946. SP (A)

31

1 Telegram of 2 January 1959. SP
2 To Thérèse Lavauden, 5 October 1959. SP (A)
3 Speech at conferment of Hollins medal, 28 March 1967. SP
4 To Thérèse Lavauden, 5 October 1959. SP (A)
5 To Thérèse Lavauden, 6 November 1959. SP (A)
6 *Hollins Columns*, 3 December 1959.
7 To Thérèse Lavauden, 2 December 1959. SP (A)
8 Unidentified press-cutting. SP
9 To Thérèse Lavauden, 2 December 1959. SP (A)
10 To Robert Shackleton, 31 December 1959. (Shackleton)
11 ES: speech of 28 March 1967, loc. cit.
12 Letter from John R. Everett, 20 April 1960. SP
13 *Manchester Guardian*, 12 February 1960.
14 *Allocution de Dr Enid Starkie* [May 1960]. SP
15 *Daily Telegraph*, 13 June 1960.
16 *Irish Times*, 1 July 1960.

32

1 To AG, 28 December 1958. SP (A)
2 Letter to the author, 31 March 1971. SP (A)

Notes

3 Letter to the author, 15 June 1971. SP (A)

4 *Rand Daily Mail*, 16 September 1964; letter to AG, 16 September 1947, SP (A); letter to Eithne Kaiser, 16 July 1959. SP (A)

5 To Agnes Headlam-Morley, 25 June 1960. (Headlam-Morley)

6 22 July 1960. SP

7 To AG, 19 December 1960. SP (A)

8 22 December 1960. SP

9 *New York Times* Book Review, 29 January 1961.

10 *Daily Express*, 1 February 1961.

11 28 February 1961. SP

12 22 April 1961. (Roe)

13 To AG, 17 December 1961. SP (A)

14 To AG, 26 December 1961. SP (A)

33

1 To Hamish Hamilton, 5 August 1950. SP (A)

2 To AG, 3 September 1962. SP (A)

3 10 October 1962. SP

4 To Brian Hill, 10 November 1962. (Hill)

5 Letter to the author, 13 January 1971. SP (A)

6 To Brian Hill, 1 April 1948. (Hill)

7 Letter to the author, 15 January 1971. SP (A)

8 5 September 1966. SP

9 Professor Roy Fuller to the author, 13 April 1971. SP (A)

10 To Eithne Kaiser, 25 March 1963. SP (A)

34

1 To William Hawksworth, 26 September 1949 (Ridehalgh); to Mrs Wedgwood Benn, 21 April 1964. (Wedgwood Benn)

2 Eithne Kaiser to the author, 15 June 1971. SP (A)

3 SP

4 To AG, 26 June 1963. SP (A)

5 Patrick George to the author, 3 April 1971. SP (A)

6 22 September 1963. SP

7 To Patrick George, 29 September 1963. (George)

8 To Marianne Eyles, 19 October 1963. (Eyles)

9 2 May 1964. SP

35

1 Letter to the author, 5 February 1964. (Richardson)

2   Letter to the author, August 1964. (Richardson)
3   Letter to the author, 31 August 1964. (Richardson)
4   Letter to the author, 27 October 1964. (Richardson)
5   Dr Ridehalgh to Dr Herrin, 28 October 1964. (Ridehalgh)
6   Dame Janet Vaughan to Dr Ridehalgh, 2 November 1964. (Ridehalgh)

8. Reader Emeritus 1965–1970   *pp. 235–280*

36

1   To the author, 2 March 1965. (Richardson)
2   Dr Ridehalgh to Dr Herrin, 12 March 1965. (Ridehalgh)
3   To Dr Ridehalgh, 14 March 1965. (Ridehalgh)
4   Dr Ridehalgh to Dr Herrin, 16 March 1965. (Ridehalgh)
5   To AG, 15 March 1965. SP (A)
6   16 March 1965. SP
7   To the author, 19 March 1965. (Richardson)
8   To Dorothy Wadham, 20 March 1965. SP (A)
9   To AG, 21 March 1965. SP (A)
10   To Professor T. B. W. Reid, 22 March 1965. SP (A)
11   To Marianne Eyles and Frances Fowler, Easter Monday 1965. (Eyles and Fowler)
12   21 April 1965. SP
13   4 May 1965. SP
14   Dame Veronica Wedgwood to the author, 17 May 1970. SP (A)
15   28 April 1965. SP
16   To Marianne Eyles and Frances Fowler, 17 June 1965. (Eyles and Fowler)
17   ES: will. SP (A)
18   22 July 1966. SP
19   Letter to the author, 14 April 1971. SP (A)
20   To Dorothy Wadham, 24 July 1965. (Wadham)
21   Dorothy Wadham to the author, 13 January 1971. SP (A)
22   To Gordon Roe, 25 July 1965 (Roe); Gordon Roe, letter to the author, 15 January 1971. SP (A)
23   Letter to the author, 15 March 1971. SP (A)
24   Professor Agnes Headlam-Morley to the author, 14 April 1971. SP (A)
25   To AG, 6 August 1965. SP (A)
26   To AG, 24 October 1965. SP (A)

Notes

37

1   To the author, 13 December 1965. (Richardson)
2   Edmund Blunden to the author, 17 December 1965. (Richardson)
3   27 December 1965. SP
4   To the author, 4 January 1966. (Richardson)
5   To the author, 9 January 1966. (Richardson)
6   To the author, 14 January 1966. (Richardson)
7   To Graham Greene, 15 January 1966. (Greene)
8   To the author, 17 January 1966. (Richardson)
9   18 January 1966. SP
10   *Sunday Times*, 23 January 1966.
11   Edmund Blunden to the author, 24 January 1966. (Richardson)
12   To the author, 25 January 1966. (Richardson)
13   To the author, 26 January 1966. (Richardson)
14   Undated press-cutting. SP
15   *Daily Mail*, 27 January 1966.
16   Unidentified press-cutting. SP
17   *The Times*, 7 February 1966.
18   6 February 1966. SP

38

1   Letters from Isobel Henderson and Dame Janet Vaughan, 28 April and 13 October 1966. SP
2   Letter to the author, 29 March 1966. (Richardson)
3   27 April 1966. SP
4   To AG, 28 April 1966. SP (A)
5   Letter to the author, 5 May 1971. SP (A)
6   Letter to the author, 5 May 1971. SP (A)
7   Letter to the author, loc. cit.
7   Letter to the author, loc. cit.
8   Letter to the author, 13 March 1971. SP (A)
9   22 July 1966. SP
10   2 September 1966. SP
11   To the author, 2 September 1966. (Richardson)
12   *Cherwell*, 16 November 1966.
13   Letter from Sheila M. Rawcliffe, 1 January 1967. SP
14   26 January 1967. SP
15   To the author, 20 January 1967. (Richardson)
16   To the author, 7 March 1967. (Richardson)

17 To AG, 27 February 1967. SP (A)
18 Letter of 4 March 1967. SP
19 Letter to Philippa Foot, 30 September 1966. (Proudfoot)
20 WJMS: diary, 27 January. SP
21 To the author, 1 June 1967. (Richardson)

39

1 Undated letter [February 1967?]. SP
2 19 February 1967. SP
3 To authorities of Barnard College, Columbia University, 24 February 1967 (Breunig)
4 To the author, 17 July 1967. (Richardson)
5 To AG, 26 July 1967. SP (A)
6 28 July 1967. SP
7 To the author, 3 September 1967. (Richardson)
8 To the author, 8 November 1967. (Richardson)
9 To the author, 23 November 1967. (Richardson)
10 To Professor LeRoy C. Breunig, 5 January 1968. (Breunig)
11 Dr Ridehalgh to Dr Herrin, 24 January 1968. (Ridehalgh)
12 To Professor Breunig, 28 January 1968. (Breunig)
13 To the author, 10 February 1968. (Richardson)
14 To the author, 15 February 1968. (Richardson)
15 To Dorothy Wadham, 14 March 1968. (Wadham)
16 To the author, 12 April 1968. (Richardson)
17 To the author, 18 April 1968. (Richardson)
18 To Professor Breunig, 3 May 1968. (Breunig)
19 Professor Breunig to the author, 7 April 1971. SP (A)
20 Letter to the author, 5 May 1971. SP (A)
21 To the author, 11 May 1968. (Richardson)
22 To the author, 30 May 1968. (Richardson)
23 To Mrs Steegmuller, 6 June 1968. (Steegmuller)

40

1 To the author, 16 July 1968. (Richardson)
2 To Dorothy Wadham, 17 August 1968. (Wadham)
3 18 July 1968. SP
4 19 July 1968. SP
5 To the author, 14 August 1968. (Richardson)
6 25 August 1968. SP

Notes

7   28 September 1968. SP
8   Draft letter, undated. SP (A)
9   *Listener*, 5 December 1968.
10 11 June 1966. SP
11 Mrs Hamilton-Meikle to the author, 28 March 1971.
12 Letter from Kimiko Kanazawa, 11 July 1967. SP
13 To the author, 23 March 1971. SP (A)
14 To the author, 18 October 1968. (Richardson)
15 To the author, 19 October 1968. (Richardson)
16 21 October 1968. SP
17 21 October 1968. SP
18 To the author, 28 October 1968. (Richardson)
19 To the author, 5 November 1968. (Richardson)
20 To the author, 8 November 1968. (Richardson)
21 To the author, 15 November 1968. (Richardson)
22 To the author, 21 November 1968. (Richardson)
23 To Eithne Kaiser, 22 January 1969. SP (A)
24 To Professor Fuller, 25 November 1968. (Fuller)

41

1   To the author, 30 January 1969. (Richardson)
2   To the author, 23 February 1969. (Richardson)
3   To the author, 3 April 1969. (Richardson)
4   To the author, 11 and 12 April 1969. (Richardson)
5   To Dorothy Wadham, 6 September 1969. (Wadham)
6   To AG, 16 January [1944]. SP (A)
7   To the author, 27 November 1969. (Richardson)
8   To Dorothy Wadham, 27 December 1969. (Wadham)
9   To the author, 3 January 1970. (Richardson)
10 To Marianne Eyles and Frances Fowler, 6 January 1970. (Eyles and Fowler)
11 To the same correspondents, 15 December 1969. (Eyles and Fowler)
12 *Sunday Times*, 31 October 1971
13 To the author, 10 January 1970. (Richardson)
14 To the author, 26 September 1970. SP (A)
15 To Francis Warner, 23 February 1970. (Warner)
16 *Guardian*, 24 April 1970.
17 Letter to the author, 'Wednesday' [May 1971]. SP (A)
18 To Francis Warner, 15 March 1970. (Warner)
19 To Thyra Creyke-Clarke, 1 April 1970. SP (A)

20 Clinico-pathological conference, 2 December 1970. Notes. (Ridehalgh);
   Dr Ridehalgh: report on Enid Starkie. (Herrin)
21 Walter Starkie to the author, 30 June 1970. SP (A)

42

1 *Truth*, 7 May 1954
2 Dame Janet Vaughan to ES, 24 June 1967. SP

Index

ES = Enid Starkie

Index

Esposito, Michele, 25
Estève, Edmond, 66, 84
Exeter University, 218–9
Eyles, Marianne, 191, 214, 215, 227–8

Farnell, Vera, 32, 37–8
Flaubert, Gustave, 91
Flaubert: the Making of the Master, 226, 243, 249, 257–8
Flaubert the Master, 258, 271–3, 275
Fleurs du mal, Les, 144–5
Fowler, Frances, 191
Foyer International des Étudiantes, 63, 147, 166
From Gautier to Eliot, 219–20
Fry, Margery, 89, 97
Fuller, Professor Roy, 227, 269, 270–1

Gardner, (Professor Dame) Helen, 222–3
Garvin, Viola, 37
Gaudy Night, 32
George, Patrick, 228–30
Ghil, René, 67
Gide, André, ES discovers, 22–4; ES influenced by, 23–4; ES to write life of, 118; correspondence with ES, 118–21; ES obtains honorary degree for, 170–6; in Oxford, 173–6; ES writes monograph on, 170, 192; dies, 187
Gilchrist Studentship, 55, 57
Graves, Robert, 223, 266 sqq.
Greece, 226–7
Greene, Graham, 208, 226, 245
Green, Julien, 168
Gregory, Alyse (Mrs Llewellyn Powys), described, 125–6; ES writes to, 47, 65, 79, 93–4, 125–8, 136 and *passim*; ES stays with, 137–40; writes to ES, 126, 137 and *passim*; describes ES, 180; dies, 257
Gregory, Lady, 20
Gwynn, Stephen, 21

Hamilton, Hamish, 165, 182 and *passim*

Hansford Johnson, Pamela (Lady Snow), 211, 227
Hawksworth, William, 183–4, 185, 242
Haynes, Liselott (Mrs Strauss), 92, 129, 132, 252, 275
Hazard, Paul, 65
Headlam-Morley, Professor Agnes, 82, 156, 181
Henderson, Isobel, 115–16, 161
Hérold, Ferdinand, 67
Herrin, Dr Eleanor, 233, 237
Higham, Thomas, 144–5, 171, 174, 179–80
Hollins College, Virginia, 214–18, 262
Holtby, Winifred, 34–5
Hone, Joseph, 121, 135

Jones, Rica (Mrs Brown), 97–8

Kaiser, Eithne, 212, 228, 230
Kennedy, Margaret, 35
King, Cecil, 44–5, 195, 267
Kirkman, Anne, 98

Lady Margaret Hall, Oxford, 29
Laforgue, Jules, 135, 165, 274, 276–7
Langford Grove, Essex, 75
Larguier, Léo, 67
Lavauden, Thérèse, 155
Lefranc, Abel, 46, 65
Lehmann, Rosamond, 77–82, 154, 157–8
Leslie, Sir Shane, 135
Lewis, Norma (later Mrs Russell), 75
Lingholt School, Hindhead, 50–2
Lord, Annie, 25
Lorimer, Hilda, 32–3
Lowell, Robert, 245–7

Macaulay, Dame Rose, 35
MacLiammoir, Michael, 211–12
Mahaffy, John Pentland, 41
Mallarmé, Stéphane, 67
Martin-Chauffier, Louis, 95–6
Masefield, John, 34
Matarasso, Henri, 107, 193

Index

Mauriac, François, 68, 172
Mawdsley, Gwendolen, 51
Mellor, Hilda, 34–6
Mouquet, Jules, 104–5
Mulvaney, Dr, 21–2

Nerval, Gérard de, 2
Nicolson, Harold, 167–8
Nostalgie de Paris d'une Irlandaise, 17–20,
  23–4 and *passim*

O'Beirne, Lizzie, 16, 178
Olmsted, Evangeline, 211
Oxford, 29 sqq. and *passim*

Paris, 55–72, 60–2, 79, 96, 107, 122,
  146, 166–9 and *passim*
Penrose, (later Dame) Emily, 30, 31,
  34–5, 38, 42, 89
Petrus Borel, 178–9, 193–4
Peyre, Henri, 211
Ponchon, Raoul, 67
Pontigny, 95–6
Pope, (later Professor) Mildred, 31–2,
  107
Porquerolles, 96, 120, 123, 176
Proudfoot, Mary, 4, 253
Proust, Marcel, 47, 67
Pusey, Dr, 29

Queen's College, Galway, 11

Rackham, Arthur, 20
Raverat, Gwen, 75
Reid, Hilda, 35, 40
Reid, Prof. T. B. W., 239
Reynier, Prof. Gustave, 65, 84
Richardson, Joanna, 193, 230, 232–3,
  237, 239, 245–7, 250–2, 255–8,
  260–7, 269–75
Ridehalgh, Dr Frank, 233, 234, 237,
  238, 240, 256, 259, 277 and *passim*
Rimbaud en Abyssinie, 116
Rimbaud in Abyssinia, 116
Roe, Rev. Dr Gordon, 94, 112–13,
  242–3
Roedean School, 69–70

Rome, 116, 250–1
Rothenstein, Sir William, 104–5, 111,
  116–17, 121–3
Royal Institution, The, 180
Royal Society of Literature, The, 211,
  230
Rudler, Professor Gustave, 78, 98–9,
  193
Russell, George (AE), 20
Russia, 203–9

Saint Aldate's, Oxford, 89–90, 98
Sainte-Beuve, C.-A., 165 and *passim*
Saint Giles', Oxford, 99–100, 227–8
St Hilda's College, Oxford, 29
St Hugh's College, Oxford, 29
Savery, Constance, 31–2, 34, 36, 40–1
Sayers, Dorothy L., 30, 32
Schopp, Professor W., 76
Schumann, Clara, 25
Seattle, U.S.A., 189–90
Shackleton, Dr Robert, 4, 217
Shannon, Mr P., 225–6
Shrewsbury School, 11, 16
Simonetti, Achille, 25
Society of Home Students (later St
  Anne's College), Oxford, 29
Somerville College, described, 29,
  31 sqq.; ES at, 36–45, 89 sqq.; ES's
  affection for, 160–1, 241, 253; men-
  tioned, 26 and *passim*
Sorbonne, La, 46, 55 sqq.
*Sources du Lyrisme dans la poésie d'Émile
  Verhaeren, Les,* 65, 84, 90
Spain, 105–7
Starkie, Edyth (Mrs Arthur Rackham),
  20
Starkie, Enid Mary, birth, 9; child-
  hood, 14–26; character, 15–16, 42–3,
  52, 57–8; appearance, 36, 37, 211–4
  and *passim*; at Alexandra School,
  Dublin, 21–2; at Alexandra College,
  Dublin, 22, 25–6; at Somerville
  College, Oxford, 36–45, 85 sqq.; at
  Lingholt School, Hindhead, 50–2;
  in Paris, 55–72; at Langford Grove,
  Maldon, 75; at Exeter, 75–85, 218–9;